Dear Tara
     Than[ks]
and enterg[y]
and my flight!

Remember all of the
          BIRDS
in your life.
        Gerry Bradley
        July 26 - 2005

Birds From the Thicket

by

Gerry Bradley

authorHOUSE™

1663 LIBERTY DRIVE, SUITE 200
BLOOMINGTON, INDIANA 47403
(800) 839-8640
WWW.AUTHORHOUSE.COM

First published by AuthorHouse 02/04/05

ISBN: 1-4184-0363-6 (e)
ISBN: 1-4184-0364-4 (sc)

Printed in the United States of America
Bloomington, Indiana

This book is printed on acid-free paper.

Gerry Bradley sees things. More importantly, he sees things in people, things that other people would miss. I'm pleased to read his columns, and his magic will be here in this book, Birds From the Thicket.

James Geluso
Editor
Federal Way News

As a sophomore in high school Language Arts class, Gerry broke out of a shell and his path to maturity was lighted by a newfound awareness of his own potential.

In these days of superficiality and fluff, Gerry brings both an intense, caring interest in the human condition as well as a willing commitment to share his genuine insights.

-Birds From the Thicket could be a parable for many of us.

John Doty, Retired Teacher

The Lord has blessed Gerry Bradley with a talent for writing. I have always enjoyed his newspaper columns immensely. I love his "down home" style of writing and it is especially evident in his latest work soon to be published Birds From the Thicket.

Alvin D. George
Director of
The Pettinger-Gallery
Astronomical Observatory
Puyallup, Washington

I have known Gerry Bradley for most of thirty years. I have known him as personal friend, parishioner, hurting person, spiritual-mountain climber, and as one with a dogged-determination to take life head-on as more than just a survivor. He started life as a boy in Oklahoma, made it through college, served in the U.S. Air Force, was a policeman, school teacher, Boy Scout executive, salesmen…and now, in his 50's he burst like a sonic-boom as a "Norman Rockwell" kind of artist, only painting freshly in word-pictures rather than on canvas. He authors his own story, and he writes columns for local newspaper/weeklies. If you like words, descriptive, poetic, artistic, home-spun, down to earth Americana, you'll delight in Birds From the Thicket, his life journey in which you'll see something of your own I'm willing to wager.

Rev. Richard W. Denham, retired
Seattle, Washington

Gerry Bradley wrote a series of articles-childhood reminisces-for one of our newspapers, the Queen Anne & Magnolia News, several years ago.

In a deadline- oriented business, he was always on time.

Additionally, Gerry had interesting stories to tell about his youth in the Queen Anne neighborhood. They evoked a sense of what it was like to be there and to be alive and young in those years.

Gerry's stories a kids' eye view of the world that has changed much in the passing years and therefore had definite reader interest.

Mike Dillon
Publisher, Pacific Publishing Company

Foreword

A Greek writer, Nikos Kazantzakis, believed "when a man dies, a particular vision of life-which is his and his alone-dies with him. It therefore behooves every man to tell his story." That is exactly what Gerry Bradley has done in this book, *Birds From the Thicket.*

In it he evokes the depth of his connection with the "red earth of Oklahoma." Anyone who lived in those, precious mid-20th – century days in mid-America will recognize the joys and heartaches that come with growing up. More than that, readers will find the ease of recollecting their own early years, no matter where they lived.

Among his heartaches was the author's battle with a bipolar mood swing disorder that interrupted a teaching career and forced him to seek ways to control it. The miracle he recognizes in maintaining that control has also provided the impetus to express his self through words on paper. He wanted to *show* others his story-in a book on the shelf. And that he has done.

But Gerry doesn't stop at writing *his* story. He shares the stories of those around him, beloved family and everlasting friends. He looks to them to join in the tumultuous birdsong of memory, enriching their lives as well as the story.

Birds has become an entwining of lives, from today and from yesterday, lives that grew from Gerry's original story of self into an interlacing of friendships, happiness, sorrow, and all the exhilaration of growing up with expectations of tomorrow, And all the time he expresses his gratitude for these friends and his ultimate joy of life.

Val Dumond – Editor – Writer and Mentor

vii

Dedication

Foremost is the way my *"Strawberry Girl"* has purposefully assured me time and space to think, layout the facts, plan, write and rewrite, aiding in the print cycle. I won't be able to show near enough gratitude to her for this huge gift revealing all of her love to me. She is the love of my life now some twenty years.

To my aunt Adeline Lizar who said from the beginning she would be proud to be the editor of the book. She was as present as a lighthouse on shore guiding us to an ever-clear kind of safety. Her willingness to help by critiques, polishing of the entirety of the story to its end could not have been more perfect. How fortunate my wife and I were to have such a quality visit with her before her passing in December 2001. I won't forget her being a perfect "cheerleader" through and through.

I want to thank my illustrator and dear friend throughout the entire project. I can still remember asking whether she would consider being the illustrator and to hear her say, "I would be honored." All it took was for her to hear what the title was, as she dearly loves drawing any and all birds. She was able to see how we could combine our talent for the presentation of *Birds from the Thicket*. Her soaring talent will be the lift so needed in completing the entire story. Having her accept and share as she did was far beyond anything anticipated.

I equally want to express my appreciation to my photographer and her entire artful offering, to enhance the overall contents, to be lifted from the pages by the inclusive photographs decidedly, a part of the story, to lend more clearly to an understanding of the characters and their timeframe throughout the storyline.

The question I have heard over and over has been, "what have you used for research as you wrote the book." My reply has been what proved best was the book held over the years, my baby book, prepared by my mother, and all of my yearbooks from every school I attended down all the tracks in my life. And to have the gift given to me by God, that of which could only be called, photographic memory or the closest possible, of which I could draw from throughout.

Before finishing came four who were so much more than the finishing touch. The first was, being interviewed by John Larson of The Tacoma Weekly, who wrote a more than perfect piece that caught the attention of Janet Hansen, who became my publicist. Each helped bring the final staging for the complete story to soon be shared with readers at large.

There remained two strokes needed. They came by, the work that Rachael Ray who did the final editing, which was accomplished through all of her pains incurred before our meeting each other. And final reading was, accomplished by, Cathy Baron, and all of their efforts more than confirmed the book was truly ready for the publishing and availing for each of you as you read and realize "There is Light At The End of Tunnel".

And let me say a hearty thanks to every Bird, every key character throughout the story, but to all of the Birds that were so supportive and always there through each stage of writing the book. Had it not been for you, in all probability the story would never have been. I hope all of you will accept this expression of love and respect for your presence throughout my life. You have always been present each and every day. I have been able to count on you where not even thought of on your behalf. The reason being, you do all of the wonderful acts everyday for so many in your midst, as you have done for me. Thanks to each and every one of you.

Lastly, this is directed to all who are dealing with Bi-Polar, (Manic Depression) or family members, friends that have a direct relationship to that shared. The mainstay has been, for each and every one of you, so you may see in your own lives and circumstances there can be hope and "light at the end of the tunnel" in your lives as well. My greatest hope is this will be discovered by you as you become familiar with the story.

Gerry Bradley

Preface

I found while attending Seattle Pacific College in the pursuit of my Degree, what was needed most in therapy was the diagnosis, which came years later. I will bring to light all that happened prior to this miraculous finding.

After all of those years, the end result was clarified in literally minutes, where the course of action was equally clear. A branch of hope was held out to me, to finally know I could do something about it to gain a level behavioral pattern. All that was needed was my description then for all of my life. The very thought that the doctor could determine what the trouble was; it could be treated and it was a perfect platform to start from. Along with taking the prescribed medication and having regular level checks so to attain the correct bloods level, the out patient program would be the only other step necessary. Emergency walk in was available if I needed any additional help along the way. That constant check has continued for twenty-nine years and will continue into the future. Following this path enabled me to walk away free!

What has been needed has been a specialist with psychopharmacology background, for they have the expertise one such as myself need most. I have been left with a constant tremor in my hands. Certainly this has posed a problem throughout, but never such a stigma to alter my professional growth. Along the way it was suggested to try various medication to alleviate the tremor, but each time the affectation was too severe, hitting my heart or pulse rate.

I have always known the end result could damage my kidneys. Regular checks counter or at least make me aware of any breakdown. All of the aforementioned passes the results of the Bi-Polar syndrome of high-low behavior. In my case suicidal thoughts came into play. I finally turned for help and was determined to follow precisely that prescribed. These findings were far from what others have dealt with such as: Patty Duke and Josh Logan, to mention only two prominent names as to their accounts in their books.

I agree with Patty Duke, when she wrote that it was "A Disease Thank God". She was involved in constant hospitalization and therapy for years, and Josh Logan would literally walk off the street and disappear to be found by loved ones ambling the streets in his hometown in Georgia. After his return, he would once again take up the banner of Director, by bringing us performances as "South Pacific". In my case I found in between the depression came manias. I had my fill of elation, where I felt good, and didn't want to waste time sleeping. This was as though having a "creative burst in my brain and there would be so much going on." Such times would be when I was "sure of myself" and when "I was very productive." Dr. Akiskalm summed it up saying, "They can accomplish a lot, and even though they take risks and sometimes act impulsively, they are charming and intense. They generate a sense of excitement; people catch their highs and tend to like them."

Further, "hypomanic (or manic) periods often come at the end of a long depression during which the person has vegetated and accumulated a long list of obligations." This turns in the favor of such an individual for the "energy allows him to discharge duties quickly and effectively, and efficiently, so that people are enormously impressed." For example a salesman might sell twenty-five cars when others are selling only two or three.

Can you imagine that those suffering such would want to bottle their mania?

After all when you feel "up" that means "you feel fantastic, beautiful, and super competent." That's when you can get along on little or no sleep and "feel as though there is nothing you can't do." All of this seems to be seasonal as well, with depression coming in the autumn and winter months. The ties to this are definitely hereditary. In my case, all seems to link to the feminine side of the family being passed from my great grandmother, down to my grandmother, then to my mother, and finally I have become the recipient.

It's the "unpredictable mood swings that have left a trail of debris and devastation behind, and have taken an incredible toll on relationships, families, careers, and self esteem."

There is a sense of safety that I can vouch for, and years of having "the control of lithium, which lets me focus my energy on my performance."

All or a portion of the aforementioned have direct relationship to that incurred by me throughout my life, or specifically from the moment such became evident in daily life.

Patty Duke said, "I often think of us who have this illness…to have…our own 'creative' ways of surviving." Ways to identify one with this illness might be to see them "going on outlandish spending sprees." Fortunately, I have been freed from this. But those about us may find us, "well-liked, man-about-town types, charming, attractive to people, but all of this can be quite the opposite for those "living in the same house with the manic depressive traits."

You will see this uncovered later in the story.

I literally allowed this to carry over through the years; however, when I made up my mind to finally tell my story, all of those foibles fell.

When I began taking the medication and following all prescribed, it was as though all was harnessed which is much more than being balanced. In truth the illness will always be with me. Now it is controlled enabling me to be productive regarding the charges that are a part of my life.

Let me take it a final step or viewing, which is incorporated in the story line, always remembering in Dr. Jamison's words, "Mental illness is just not that simple. While many of the manic depression's victims have lived tenuous lives that ended in suicide or confinement in mental institutions."

From this high point, I know each day how vital it is to take my dose of lithium so to remain on course, for all of the morrow.

Patty Duke and Gloria Hochman, INTRODUCTION
"A Brilliant Madness "A Disease Thank God"
xvii-xxviii

ETHIOPIAN PROVERB

He who conceals his disease cannot expect to be cured.

Table of Contents

Chapter 1

My Red Dirt Heritage

It was on a Saturday in May of 1998 that we arranged to take a ride aboard a thirty-five foot craft beyond the inlet of Gig Harbor. The conditions were rough seas as we closed on the Narrows Bridge. I questioned why we were out on such rough waters. We remained steady to retain the special cargo we had aboard. All would be finally taken care of on this beautiful blue-sky day. Before launching, I asked, "Where are the packages?" What I was about to do would be the hardest duty I had ever carried out in my life. I was there to fulfill the final request of both of my parents. They had always made it known they wanted to be cast into the sea. Jesse died on March 12, 1998 and my mother followed her Merchant Mariner dying on March 26, 1998. This was the most fitting place for them, as we had grown up on the ports, while following Jesse's career to its end. Even though the sky was so magnificent, within I was weighted down with heavy clouds encompassing my heart and soul. Then I heard, "Here's Jesse, as they handed me a plastic sack, held in a single gray box, which I selected because it resembled all of the vessels he had been aboard while serving as a Refrigeration Engineer before his retirement. I squatted down and gingerly released the contents into the swirling waves to hear, "Here's your mother." I took the bag and hesitated before releasing both of them. All was well for me until those on board began to throw flowers over my back out on the water, which proved far too much, yet brought me to drift, just as the petals of the strewn flowers, back to the beginning of the story that I knew had to be told.

Even though the blowing dust off the Oklahoma plains just didn't seem to let up from morning to night in those days, later written about by John Steinbeck depicting the conditions in *The Grapes of Wrath*, there remained towns, such as Skeedee, which is the setting for the introduction of this story.

The little town of Skeedee was nine miles northeast of Pawnee, Oklahoma. It was established to care for the surrounding farmers and their families. The population was two hundred and fifty to three hundred. Looking up and down the streets you would see a grocery store; drug store minus a pharmacist; two filling stations; a telephone office; a post office; two churches, one being The Church of Christ; and a Railroad depot. There was a statue that stood in the center of town of Colonel Walters and Chief Baconrind with their hands clasped stressing friendship. This symbol was a center of attention and the town fathers would frequently bring movies to be projected on a screen, which hung on one side of the statue for all to view. This was quite the event! People gathered and sat on the ground, or brought chairs from their homes, to be entertained and lifted from the straits they all faced during those years leading up to 1935. Very few owned their own cars so there were none sitting in cars for the movies.

I want you to take a brief walk back in time with me where all will become clear to you. It's two, certainly not more than three, blocks to one of the homes in town.

Accept my apology for asking you to go out in this bone chilling, winter weather. We're nearly there. It's the last little white house at the end of the block. Now you can see the little house overlooking the valley below leading you to the top of the hill overlooking the Railroad depot. This is where you'll be able to purchase your tickets for your departure, after you hear the whole story about to unfold before your eyes. We had better be quiet so as not to disturb anyone. Watch out for ice on the ground lest you fall!

I know you can remember hearing when we were children, not to write on the windows all steamed over, covering the thin glaze of the icy panes of glass. That will be vital, as our view into the little white house, will be through these panes of glass. If you look closely, you'll see all in that little town, just as Clarence the Angel did, when having to gain a full view of George and his playmates in *It's A Wonderful Life.*

Undoubtedly, your eyes are drawn to that little babe in the center of the room. Keep your attention focused on her, as we will be following her in that hand-sewn dressing gown. She is readying for nightfall to get a good nights sleep, so she will remain in good health and full of energy for another day of playing and helping out where she can.

I want you to concentrate on her hazel eyes and her evident spirit. There is a reason for us to peer into those eyes, for doing so will enable her to actively look out, and we'll be able to understand her and other key members within that house. To help our perspective as we look further, it's important that we know she has recently been dropped off by her mother, after first asking the parents to take her little daughter into their home and to take care of her.

This was due to her mother living and working in Enid, Oklahoma where she was unable to keep her child. More of this will be clarified as we continue looking and allowing the little girl, who happens to be Helen Louise Arnold, my mother, to reveal all about her as she looks out through her own eyes.

Those we're seeing coming into the living room is her grandfather, Poppa, and her grandmother, Jenny Lizar, entering from the kitchen to check on the little girl.

It will be evident to you that her mother, Joyce, one of nine brothers and sisters, will be seen throughout the story line coming and going in this little girl's life throughout her growing up years. Her favorite, due to his age, was Boyd. It is more than understandable to see this with so many family members, to see this little girl turning her head every way but up in order to cope with all of the activity in that house.

We better button our overcoats; with the temperature dropping, we're going to have to bundle up from our heads to our feet, while following all beyond the fragile panes of glass.

As is true in all homes and families, Poppa and Jenny would take turns holding and rocking little Helen Louise through bouts of sickness, or let her drop off for a nap, or lose attention when the grandparents were telling her of their younger years.

Little Helen Louise grew up hearing how Poppa stood beside his loving bride Jenny outside of a little sod hut on the plains of Oklahoma.

Early on, the entire family decided to refer to her as Louise, since one of the aunts was named Helen. This eliminated the confusion when calling her for whatever purpose.

Louise learned to listen closely to one and all, and heard that the sod-hut, of which Poppa and her grandmother shared comments, had a front door and only one room. The walls and the roof were held together with mud and straw. What made this part of the story real was seeing the early photograph they had kept all of those years.

Her grandmother told her and others in the family that she and Poppa had high hopes that all ahead for them would be a great improvement indeed.

Brr! You're right, we're going to be frozen to the bone standing here, but the story is becoming clearer and our departure lies ahead down those Southern Pacific Railroad tracks. Lets take turns crooking our elbow and wiping the windowpanes to have clarity of all happenings inside.

A bit later, Louise heard how her grandparents were among the original Sooner's running for their own land, which wasn't much, rather a meager beginning for their hailing from Missouri. They did as so many across the plains did and turned the rich soil that became, "the food basket for the country".

Little Louise came to realize her grandmother did the very best she could during the years of her upbringing. One thing was a certainty. Jenny was a wonderful seamstress. She had real skill when it came to using her hands, sewing a vast wardrobe for Louise.

And now that you have kept an eye through the icy panes of glass, I know you have been able to see that Louise had a different dress to wear every day.

Long before her school days began, she learned some crucial lessons that followed her into her latter years. I know you heard that loud thump during the night. You had to be as appalled as I seeing this transplanted little girl beneath all of those covers, caught up in the constant tugging and pulling of those covers off of her, to be kicked from the bed by one of those hateful aunts. As she fell to the floor below she heard, "We didn't want you here in the first place."

Isn't it wonderful after such nights that she would rise to the constant strength of Poppa and her grandmother?

Now we're beginning to see how she is growing older and experiencing how she and Boyd would see Poppa in the distance, making his way down from a long day of working at the railroad yard. Both of the children looked and saw how dirty he was in his soiled bib overalls, hat and heavy work coat, as he took stretching strides across those tracks, continuing down the hill into the valley where he greeted the hobos.

They were always friendly toward him because they knew when they were in the worst straits, they could come and knock on the back door of the Lizar home for food. They found, like members of the household, that Poppa would say, "There is always enough for one more to eat."

Such a stance before every member in their family, conveyed how he practiced what was taught in the Church of Christ, their place of worship.

Notice how the children were there, waiting to ask if there was anything they could help Poppa carry from his day of work. Even after greeting Poppa as Louise did, she watched him enter the back screen door, sit down, and take off his work clothes and boots. All the time he would be talking to his Jenny, who was scurrying about making dinner for the family. She would ask him about his day at work and he would soon find out Louise had gotten into some kind of trouble. Afterwards, he would just sit there and look at Louise, never touching her, but she said, "He didn't need to, as the look was severe enough."

I know you have come to realize through our vantage point that those days were much the same during such ghastly times of The Great Depression. I can recall hearing my mother, tell me about those devastating times for millions in the cities. However, those in Skeedee and similar places faired much better because they grew their own vegetables, crops and had stock, so the need wasn't as crucial for them. At the same time, she would say that to receive an orange for Christmas was so wonderful. Such fruits weren't that plentiful and were so appreciated.

As we peer through the panes of glass, we can't be struck more than when seeing Louise, and other members of the family receive this fruit as their gifts with such grateful spirits. Those holiday periods would pass all too quickly, bringing Poppa and all in their family to see those trains, which Poppa worked on, coming and going, as members of their family did as they progressed through their schooling.

Poppa was known by all within that house and throughout the town as a generous, loving husband and father to his family.

I would be Poppa's great grandson who he would never meet. I had significant time with my great grandmother Lizar, who raised Louise, my mother, all the years before. Such times, including visiting her at that little white house we have been standing outside getting a full view all this time, became mine. One visit I never forgot, because mother sewed my very first long pants suit for the trip to see my great grandmother Lizar. I even have photographs that I have kept all of these years.

I know you'll not forget the constant swinging and slamming of that back screen door, which better described that household during those years than anything else.

It probably didn't take you that long to see how her grandma was anything but patient with her as a child under her roof. There was real strife during those years.

Later, the picture will make more sense, when thinking back to those days, forming Louise, as it did. At the same time, all who came and went through that screen door into the throngs of their family, still had to make trips out to the memorable site that could never be forgotten, the out house. One of the boys would periodically drop a silting of lye for cleansing. Those experiencing that lye and the odors were permeated for the rest of their days, with an odoriferous result. As to there being any privacy that was a joke, as every time the swinging door opened or closed, the spring hinge squeaked becoming even over the years.

This next scene requires some sensitivity on our behalves. You might have known they took their baths in old square metal wash tub filled with hot water off of the stove, but not too steaming, for their moment of scrubbing that red dirt from their bodies. They followed this with toweling and a powdering down and jumped into their nightshirts before hopping into bed.

So you can have a thorough picture of the scene, it is important that you realize Jenny Lizar was anything but easy to live with, which had lots to do with raising a nine-member family. When my grandmother, Joyce, approached her parents with the request of taking her daughter into their home it brought considerable disagreement. Neither she nor Poppa would have ever imagined doing anything such as this.

Jenny Lizar was a hell bent woman! That is anything but hard to understand having lived as she had. She didn't just raise those nine children plus Louise. She kept all going on the home front at the same time.

Think back to our seeing her slight form, wearing house dresses, with her wire framed round glasses and her graying white hair in a bun on the center of the back of her head. She wasn't a very tall woman even in her earlier years. I know you have been able to see she was very demanding, lacking patience, and would flare much the same as a rocket on the fourth of July at the slightest provocation.

It was many decades afterwards that I realized she had the varying, changing kind of behavior that wasn't always understood by the members of her family. But all of the findings wouldn't become evident until much later within my life, as to the meaning of such severe behavior that she exhibited to all within her family.

To think how the findings would have helped my grandmother, and mostly my mother, which would have eased all within my life to be sure. The more I heard of my great grandmother, and was able to compare our similar behaviors together with my mother's, I was certainly left believing my questionable behavior had to be linked to heredity through the women folk in my life.

Continuing with the viewing you're in the midst of, I know you can see how abrupt her behavior was toward individuals and members of the family. These traits were particularly evident when caring for Helen Louise.

As time passed, the members of the family made their way, down, the roads of their choice, taking them further away from that tiny berg of a town.

Before the scene that you looked in on originally, Louise's mother, Joyce, married Robert Arnold, a farmer across the fields away from town. They gave birth to Helen Louise, on January 22, 1923. Helen Louise's mother took her away with her when she and Robert were divorced.

All of this led Joyce to Enid, Oklahoma where she was able to locate a job as a waitress. That was when she turned to her parents for their help with her child, Helen Louise.

Even though we have seen the division occurring, Louise was in a setting where she was the very youngest member of the household that included her grandparents, aunts and uncles. Consequently, she had the equivalent of many brothers and sisters to take care of her and to look out for her.

I know you could see from the start she was loved by her uncle Boyd. This was due to their being so close in age. Boyd, kept a vigilant eye out for Louise all the way through their years of schooling. They played with each other as children and shared wonderful moments attending school in Skeedee through graduating at Skeedee High School. Helen Louise graduated with her class in May of 1940.

Now trust me, your view isn't because of hoary glass, rather you just need to rub the surface more thoroughly, for the toasty air inside and the bitter cold air outside will cause contention as you continue to look at the whole story being portrayed.

When thinking back to the overall view, I know you saw immediately that her uncles and aunts didn't want to take an infant into their home. She turned out to be a pain for one and all. That was somewhat understandable, as all of them were well on their way to being grown, readying for their own futures. This decision brought real upheaval for the entire family. Even so, she remained all of those years.

There she is attending Junior High School, where shortly afterwards their school and town received a brand new teacher by the name of Miss Ray. The new, teacher, was invited by Poppa, Jenny, and other members of their family for weekends and holidays. She observed how Louise was well liked by the faculty and her fellow students and watched Louise, develop into a good student. Louise revealed this by the way she opened up and shared how her mother came for short visits with her classmates.

Miss Ray and Boyd became smitten with each other and in the end became husband and wife.

Not only did we see Louise so pleased over these visits, we shuddered to see how my grandmother awaited her arrival on the bus, as she came to visit at the tender age of five years old.

Imagine any child doing such in this day and time.

As those visits continued during the years, Louise was introduced to Rummage, and neither Louise nor Rummage ever took to each other from the start.

Yet, I found years later he was listed in my Baby Book as granddad. He was a well-known bootlegger in the Enid area and the surrounding Garfield County.

We have seen this little girl grow up before our eyes. You will see sights afar just as I heard her tell me how Rummage always wore his Stetson hat, cowboy boots, and leather sports jackets signifying he was doing rather well. While my mother was visiting, for a time she was making the runs at night to his key customers. You can imagine the stigma attached to this when she was off to attend classes at Enid High School the next morning, after her deliveries the previous evening. The strife she took upon arrival by her so called fellow students, who knew who she was the one delivering the booze for their old man the night before, became another confrontation she had to deal with afterwards.

Think back to the little girl that bounced off the floor all those years before with a kick in the butt to bring her to fall below.

Here she was all those years later receiving this guff, which she didn't take. Instead, she would raise upon her feet and reply, "That may be, but your old man got his booze didn't he." That would quell the subject with a certainty. She exhibited how strong her spirit and fiber was and remained so throughout her life, literally to its end.

Keep looking and more of the true story will be pronounced. The friction intensified between Helen Louise and Rummage, up to her asking him to help by sending her to attend Nursing School. He adamantly denied her this opportunity.

Nevertheless, we are watching her graduate with her class of May 1940, from Skeedee, even though she traversed back and forth during the years to spend time with her mother in Enid, while growing up in this little white house. We have stood outside all of this time to see her life and those about her grow in their ways during the years.

I agree with you that Poppa's always taking time as he did for one and all after returning from work was so important. We have been able to see him listen to each of their needs, take time to play with the boys and the girls and to laugh with them as they all grew up. As you have seen, Louise grew up having such love for her grandfather and her grandmother.

Her accounts of her growing up days with Poppa and her grandmother were so memorable and the most loving times of all.

Before each of these views you've seen, Poppa and Jenny were more and more alone, as in their first years, standing next to the entrance of their sod hut they began in together. Here, in this little white house on top of the hill overlooking where Poppa had carried his lunch pail back and forth to work on the track, they were hearing a more hollow whistle, of the regular trains chugging and spewing their smoke into the valley below and less and less of the sounds of their growing family.

I've shared so much more than that of my heritage. I've introduced what has to be the forerunner of *Birds From the Thicket*, heralding the complete line of the story which lies ahead, whether in flight, or on the turns on the track itself. Come on y'all and take the journey with me in terms of miles and time and don't lose sight of any of the birds that are featured throughout the story.

They have always been there to stop, and I know you have heard the sweet song, only to be found in a glance on a branch above.

How many times I have been stopped in time, even for a moment, to hear and see their magnificent plumage and to realize how each of them brought me to softly stand and thank them for their presence, their song to uplift my spirit, and to either see them disappear from view or to turn and know I have a spirited gait in my step carrying me to the next flying friend ahead.

Let's not be remiss as the train schedule is in your favor. We'll hurry and get you to the railroad depot just in time for you to purchase your tickets for your next destination down the tracks.

How fortunate I've been to have you beside me in all of our viewings. I wish y'll God's speed in each of your journeys. I do hope you'll remember all of them here in Skeedee, a little town that meant so much for all who lived here then.

All of you on board are heading for Enid, Oklahoma where the rest of the story unfolds.

Childhood Stories

I was a happy boy and enjoyed all of my friends. I believe I was well behaved for the most part; I wasn't a demanding child. I was sure my parents loved me. All of my relatives revealed how they loved me. At eleven months, I recognized my daddy's Pepsi Cola truck.

My first word spoken was "Hi". When shopping with my mother and walking down the broad walks of the City Square, I would bid one and all with a big, "Hi Boy". Such moments as these are like a photographer completing one more record of a given sight or moment in time.

One moment was seeing my dad and Uncle Henry have more fun than they had in years. It was the Fourth of July and they had made plans to shoot off firecrackers. All of us sat and watched "grown boys" before us hop, dance, laugh, and giggle over each of their fanfares planned for our celebration. The sight of them and the sheer joy was very memorable. At times it seems like it all happened yesterday.

My dad was quite a baseball fan. Not only did we as a family attend the neighborhood games, we followed the Minor League games. On one warm, Oklahoma evening, he asked me to go with him to see the City baseball game. He was so excited, totally enthralled throughout the game. The stadium was full of the same frantic baseball fans. It was typical for me to watch much more than the game.

Dad was dressed casually in his beige cotton pants and a short sleeved sear sucker shirt. His gestures and tone and fever for the game, were noticeable. I found he was quite aware of the specifics of the game;

it seemed as though he knew everyone in the stadium. This was a heated game!

I caught a glimpse of my dad who wore his felt hat with the bill turned up. He was sitting there antsy throughout the game, but that hat was way back to one side of his head, never to fall off. What struck me was he seemed more like a boy, thoroughly enjoying every moment of the game, stadium lights, the maze of waving arms, and spilled pop, popcorn and peanuts, as all rooted for our team to win. That was such fun seeing him so unlike his usual behavior. From then on he and I talked baseball!

Traveling became embedded in me from my earliest years. This was evident from the start. My younger brother and I were always in our coats and hats carrying our cases bound for new places.

Years ago, we met this new family in our neighborhood who became our friends. They were Technical Sergeant Chuck and his wife Betty. The other member of their family was grandpa Ken, who had all of his medals, holsters, pistols, rifles and his bayonet he carried in the Spanish-American War. He was so proud of having served our country in this way.

Chuck and Betty came to love me so much and said more than once, "If we could, we would adopt Gerald Kent." Mother just smiled, as she knew how they felt all the time. They had never had children of their own.

Chuck was stationed at Vance A.F.B. in Enid. I remember he owned this motorcycle called a Harley; that he rode back and forth to the base. It was painted lime green. You could hear him coming down the street and you couldn't miss it due to that awful shade of green.

I've never forgotten how they would invite us over to their home on Saturday evenings. Betty would always bake a special dessert and serve coffee. They would have Nehi and RC Cola and homemade ice cream as a special treat. Chuck and Betty were from Louisiana and wouldn't miss hearing the Grande Ole' Opry on the radio Saturday nights. We all curled up in a circle and listened to all of their country favorites; chit-chat" continued as we listened. These were warm, loving nights with dear friends. Grandpa Ken would pull out his sword and he would share another story about marching up San Juan Hill. Chuck would go into the kitchen and when he returned he would be carrying a wire basket and a bag of peanuts. He roasted peanuts in a basket over the fireplace with its perfect embers. He never roasted them too long as he had been roasting peanuts since he was a boy. Then he would say afterwards, "Be careful, they're real hot!" All hands reached in and you would hear one big "crunch" as we bit into them.

One evening Chuck and Betty began telling us of a trip they had been planning. The three of them were going to Albuquerque, New Mexico for their vacation. They said, "We've talked this over and decided to ask if it would be all right to take Gerald Kent with us." My folks didn't seem surprised. All they did was ask me if I would like to go! I replied, "I'd love to go!"

The morning came and I was so excited to be going on such a trip. Mother had everything packed and had reminded me to mind them while we were gone and to have a good time. Thinking back this had to be hard on mother, yet she didn't show it. I gave her a big hug and kiss as we left. She stood there and waved as we started to roll away. I looked out the car window and was sure I saw her standing with the screen door opened, stating to cry.

All three of them had planned our trip meticulously. Chuck drove the car, grandpa Ken sat in the passenger right front seat and Betty sat in the back seat. They had prepared a place for me in the center of the front seat so I could see where we were going. I didn't miss any sights along the way.

They pointed out the rattlesnakes swiveling across the highway. Some had already been hit and were lying across the road. They would say, "See that coyote and look at those Jack rabbits." Chuck hit a rabbit once because there wasn't time to swerve and miss it.

They got their maps out and taught me how to read maps. Then they helped me understand the road signs we passed.

Betty had prepared a cooler of good food; we munched on our sandwiches, potato chips, fresh peaches, with the juice trickling down our chins and homemade cup cakes. We had cold Pepsi's to drink with that delicious lunch. She had prepared a large thermos of hot coffee for them and they all commended about the fine coffee along with our lunch we had shared. We listened to Country music on the radio. Then we sang right along with a twangy blend. I had never seen the three of them so happy.

Chuck and grandpa Ken showed me how they planned our route. There was so much going on I stayed awake the whole way. They stopped at all of the sights and vistas so I could see them. Betty said to Chuck, "Be sure we stop so Gerald can see Billy the Kid's burial site." Chuck told her, "I'm planning to shortly." It looked as though it was directly ahead, so we pulled over to the marker off the highway. Chuck stopped and said, "We knew you would want to see *'Billy Bonney the Kid's grave- site"*. The marker had posted this information which Betty helped me read, *"Here lies the Most Notorious Outlaw Of the West, Shot and Killed by Sheriff Pat Garrett in Indian County New Mexico, at Fort Sumner New Mexico"*. Chuck and grandpa Ken told me he was a young boy who became known as a ruthless killer.

All four of us were starting to feel that desert heat, so we walked back to the car and continued west.

Betty said to Chuck, "Let's stop farther up the road and have a nice dinner." Chuck replied, "Hon, that 's a good idea."

I was all eyes and ears the whole trip! After all this was the longest trip I had taken up to now. All sights were new to me. Grandpa Ken told more stories of his conquests than ever before. He was proud and pleased at how I said, "That road sign means and that marker means," related to the maps needed for the journey. I realized how well Chuck and Betty treated me as if I was their son. I sure felt that more, mile by mile.

When we went into the Road –Side-Diner, I really felt their love and pride in having me with them. Before we sat down, all of us needed to go to the bathroom. This gave us a chance to wash up and begin to feel clean from our day of traveling. We joined each other at one big booth. I noticed the diner had a lighted neon sign. I was sure they left it on to help the truck drivers find their way at night.

There were quite a few big trucks and trailers parked on their lot. When we entered the truck drivers all looked up to see whom were the newcomers arriving. They had friendly faces and sure looked like they liked their food as several had cleaned up their plates. Some were ordering and finishing their pie alamode and coffee. They sat and talked with other drivers.

We were deciding what we were going to eat. The waitress came and said, "How are you folks, you sure came at a good time because we've got," and she told us what the specials were. Chuck and Betty ordered two specials and Betty knew what I wanted. She asked me, though. I don't know how she knew, she told the waitress, "He, wants a big cheeseburger, with everything on it, fries and a large milkshake." "What flavor?" I told her, "I'll have chocolate." Grandpa Ken decided on their meatloaf plate with mashed potatoes and gravy. We sat and talked about our trip. I learned a lot about Chuck's work as an Aircraft Mechanic. We finished our meals and our waitress came back over and asked if we would like homemade pie. "Sure", said Chuck, "Make mine Apple". After we decided and had our pie, we were really full. We thanked our waitress and Betty left her a nice tip, while Chuck paid the bill. We heard our waitress say, "Come again and have a safe journey."

All four of us joked and kept saying how full we were. Grandpa Ken said, "Wasn't that fine food and service?" He kidded me as he always did by saying, "Gerald Kent, are you sure you had enough to eat?"

The sun was going down before us as we were closing in on our destination of Albuquerque, New Mexico. We were approaching the city while Chuck and Betty were doing their best to show me the main spots as we drove into town: the Baseball Park, City Hall, the Fire and Police Departments, the very best place to eat, and the Movie Theatre.

I remember we stayed with relatives and saw friends of theirs. Our stay was active as we were going here and there the whole time. They really were showing me off as though I was their son to all of those people. Everywhere we went they were feeding us all the time.

Gerry Bradley

One night before we left we went downtown to a movie. Afterwards, we walked outside the theatre and sat on a long bench and talked and looked up into the dark sky. This view of the stars far surpassed any movie we had seen. We walked back to where we were staying while in that southwestern city. They marveled at how I never showed one sign of being homesick. I am sure their vacation was mainly having me with them. They said that it would soon be time to return.

Morning came sooner than any of us could imagine. We loaded the car and I felt air-borne, because those I met while there were lifting me and hugging me. Some of the women kissed me on the cheek and said, "You all come again anytime."

We loaded the car and Grandpa Ken got in the back seat with Betty. I reached in the glove box and got the maps. Chuck checked one more time to be sure we had everything loaded. He made sure we were comfortable. Chuck got in behind the steering wheel and turned to Betty and me, winked and said, "That's like our Air Force pilots do with their checklist before taxiing for take-off." Then he placed his hands securely on the steering wheel, placed his right foot on the pedal, then lifted his foot over to the brake pedal. He turned his neck and stuck his head out to check for any traffic and said, "Bye Now," and we were rolling away.

Before we left, the lady fed us a fine breakfast. Betty packed our cooler with food and cold drinks as before. I had enjoyed special times with Betty while we were there. She and I had some fine visits, especially in the backyard sitting in the big lawn swing, all shaded from the heat of the day.

We were back on the highway and on the way home. Now we enjoyed all sights, but on the other side of the highway. Later that morning we stopped at a rest stop and had a bite of good food Betty had prepared for us. Betty came and sat up front with Chuck and me. We were driving along and I said, "Look there's a lake up ahead right across the highway," Chuck and Betty said, "Let's see," and we drove to where I had seen that lake! You know what? There was no lake! All three of them laughed, then they explained to me what I had seen was called a mirage. Chuck and Betty shared the mirage was formed by the heat collected on the ground of the highway. Betty said, "It sure looks real doesn't it?"

I knew and felt I had come to love them and I knew they felt the same for me. I had such a fine time telling them what sign was what along our route home. We kept count of the snakes and dead animals all the way home. When we arrived back home, we were true traveling companions.

Chuck drove right to my house. He got out with Betty and helped me with my things and they told mother the biggest thanks for letting them take me. All three of them were talking at once, but they mainly wanted mother to know I hadn't been home sick once and I wasn't one bit of trouble. They told her that I was a perfect little gentleman the whole way. Mother reached out and placed her hand over my shoulder with such pride. And she thanked them for taking me and bringing me home as they had discussed. Then Betty and Chuck came up to me and gave me a big hug. As they walked to the car they reached out and held hands. Chuck opened the door for Betty and turned back to say, "Bye for now," I stood there and waved goodbye to all three of them and yelled "Thank you for taking me!"

My mother and brother were glad to have me back. That night I told them about the trip, every detail. Later that night my brother and I were laying in our beds and I kept telling him things like how I saw Billy the Kid's burial ground. Mother said, "Now it's time for you boys to get to sleep." Before I went to sleep, I knew all that happened was no mirage.

Chapter 2

Fondest Memories of the Early Years

I have never forgotten when mother pointed out all of the flowers around our home. She would show me the clinging flowers along our picket fence line, the Morning Glories. From there we would prune and weed around the Pansies, Nasturtiums, Gladioluses, Marigolds, and always Petunias of every color and variety. Somehow, in the heat of the day, we would check and make sure of the heartiest of all, the Zinnias.

When mother died, my mind was like a kaleidoscope with images of an array of memories, sights, smells, places and special moments my mother and shared with each other, treasures in my memory then and long afterwards.

In my moment of grieving, I could see those Zinnias and always look for Zinnias which became my mother, always he heartiest of women to be sure.

Everyone said those memories will mean so much in the years to come.

Such a memory was when we delved into a venture where we decided we were going to raise chickens. My Uncle Jasper did all he could to help us get started, guiding our efforts along the way. We made sure our heat lamps were effective during incubation and, before we knew it, we had baby chicks everywhere! Our chicken hut was primitive, yet ample, holding in the heat, keeping the varmints out and keeping the chicks safe. This became our venture. As the chicks began to grow, eat, sleep and peck at each other, we became very proud of our efforts. It seemed as though all we did then was care for those chickens day and night. They were Plymouth Rock chickens, not just any chicken. About the time we started to see promise in their growth, we began to "count our chickens before…" even to the details of marketing our fryers.

One morning, I heard mother holler and I ran to see what was the matter. She said, "They're dying on us!" We scurried and started feeding them, one after another with eyedroppers to save some, but the moment was against us in the end. We knew we were licked.

Finally, every one of those chickens died and there wasn't a thing we could do to save them. I can assure you we never forgot that joint venture. Doing this together was what was most meaningful.

Another memory included the ponds, creeks, lakes, and reservoirs above the dam, where I learned to fish with my mother. She taught me how to fish, down to baiting my hook, tying my leader, placing the weights just right and selecting the right bobbin.

Now, there was a real art in finding the right fish'n spot. We would be off bright and early and sometimes our drive would be a piece. Mother would say, "There she is," and we would pull up, stop, unload our gear and lay out our plan. She would take the lead down the trail along the bank of the creek to the very precise spot where she was sure we would catch the most fish. We wore long sleeve shirts with hats on to protect us from the whip of the branches, whistle weeds and the scorching heat of the day. When we found our exact spot, we would light along the side of the creek bank. Each of us readied to cast out our lines, not only to a perfect spot, but the precise depth and distance from shore.

To get me started, she helped me select my little rod, which was only two to three feet long, a perfectly matched reel and all of my gear. I remember how we bought all of this at the Sears and Roebuck store in the sports department. That was a special day and time.

Smack! We'd still have to slap at those mosquitoes not to lose attention as to our bobbins bouncing. When those fish would bite, we'd be busy reeling them in not too fast or frantic. She'd help me to know when to let them run a bit, then to slowly and steadily reel them into shore.

Part of the mystery was in not knowing if we had a Channel Cat, or Mud-Catfish, Crappie, Perch, or a Sunfish, all caught in a day. She helped me take the hook out of their mouths. This was tricky especially with the Catfish. They had those stingers to watch out for every time. You know what? We would fish like that all summer.

One evening, we went to the city park lake. We crawled under the falling weeping willow branches along the shore and sat down and had the time of our lives. She and I fished until before dark. We had such fun because every time we threw in our lines, we would pull in another fish.

Everyone in the neighborhood froze all of the fish caught though the summer. Then came our neighborhood fish fry. All of us contributed to this affair. I learned how to bake, so I baked all of the cakes. These were grand times where we could "chit-chat" into the night and brag about our best fish'n holes. How I loved my fishing teacher and partner, and appreciated all she taught me throughout my life.

While sharing about all of these fish'n trips, I have to tell you of one of our trips to test out a new site for future fish'n.

We all jumped into our old black 38 Chevy with a ragtop that was tattered, but this was our first car and we were really pleased to have it. Of course mother wasn't, as it wasn't to her liking. In fact, she was embarrassed to ride in it because it wasn't a newer model. The two of us boys and dad didn't care, for now we could get out and take rides once in awhile.

This particular evening before dusk we took a short drive out of town and found this small lake setting. While mother and I readied our gear and were about to walk down the beach, dad decided he would stay in the car and take a nap. I walked ahead of mother, and she stopped to throw her line out and I sat down on the dry rocky ground. Before I knew it, I heard mother shriek and yell, "Don't move, don't move son, stay completely still!" I froze right there and looked to see this long snake swivel past me headed for the water. By now, dad was alarmed and was running down the beach with a heavy piece of driftwood. Both of them kept screaming for me to not move and dad arrived in time for both he and I to see another long dark snake come out from the bog like swamp to my rear and swivel beside me as it was trying to get into the lake as the previous snake had done. Dad started to beat that snake over and over, stopping it from entering as the other snake did before. Sure enough, he killed the second snake. Both he and mother yelled for me to gather my pole and equipment and get off that embankment immediately.

I later found those snakes were Water Moccasins, extremely poisonous. And that was the last time we went to that fish'n hole!

More Happenings During Those Earlier Years

My memories of teachers and children with whom I attended school were very positive. We had good schools in Enid, Oklahoma. There I found wonderful friends and a positive place to grow up.

I remember Mrs. Lime, my second grade teacher at Garfield Elementary School in Enid.

When thinking about her, I vividly remember how I thought her name was perfect to match her wrinkled "lime like face". Another fact was how dark-brown, almost black, were her eyes that blended with her tanned skin. She was a disciplinarian, but fair and equally loving toward us kids. I know she helped me where needed in learning necessary skills of writing, mathematics, penmanship, but foremost in uniting with my fellow students in the classroom and on the playground. Literally out of nowhere, I would be seen breaking down over the smallest of happenings while out on the playground, which brought my fellow students to wonder as to what was the matter. When looking back to such, I can only be brought to think that the behavioral patterns were within me, but no one had any idea as to the reason for any of this surfacing. At times, the teacher would call my mother, to come over to calm me, and by that time I would be all right, ready to play, or join the other students in our studies.

May the spirit of Mrs. Lime know how much she set the tone for me to pursue the path that would lead me to teach and write in my future.

I find it difficult to respond as to the person my father was, as my thoughts are of two men and two differing plateaus of thought. The first was with me until 1951 at age ten. I had to be like so many sons who worshipped the ground he stood upon. He could do no wrong.

I was aware of the ongoing strife between my parents. He was shiftless always moving from job to job! My mother couldn't rely on him. When we needed shoes he would buy brand new sets of cowboy holsters and guns and be so pleased to bring them home for us.

As a boy, I realized so much of which I later confirmed was true. He had always been babied clear back to his grandmother, who offered to send him to college. He would hear none of it.

How does a young boy growing up realize things are not right? When he married my mother, he was twenty years older than her. Needless to say, that fit wasn't right for them or us as the years continued.

He had one job of which I was very proud of him, that was being the Pepsi-Cola driver distributor.

At four to six years old, he took me with him on his route for the day. I knew he loved me, as he would proudly show me off to one and all. He made sure I saw all the points of interest along the way. As you would imagine, he would spoil me.

Those formative years up and through my being five proved to do more than imagined. I didn't realize until years later that this experience of Red-White-and Blue, better known as Pepsi-Cola, marked me with that logo, logo's and all inclusive with advertising.

My life has been marked by having a route to care for, as perhaps his had not been. You see, he left Pepsi and moved to Nesbitt Orange, then to R.C. Cola, and on and on. I had ridden with him over those early years, up and through my being in the second grade and been to the bottling plant, and watched the bottles slide along on the rubber mat and be filled and see the bottle caps pressed on the top of each bottle, seemingly never to forget.

He was offered the management position of the Pepsi plant in Enid and he turned it down. Sadly, we wandered from pillar to post while we were still together.

During my first grade, he left with a friend and went out to Washington to work in the apple orchards. Later, he called for us, so we traveled by train to Wenatchee, to meet him and continue to Okanogan. While there, he worked picking apples and served as a Security Guard in the storage warehouses at night. Mother worked in the Dining Hall feeding the crew every day. We lived in a one-room cinder block cabin.

I attended the first grade at the Virginia Graham Elementary School, where I rode the bus to and from Okanogan. I remember how, at the end of the season, he borrowed a friend's truck so we could return home to Oklahoma.

It wasn't until I was thirty-five years old, while on a summer vacation that I found myself standing awe struck at what was left of that cabin. The real wonder was in entering Okanogan, after all of those years, and meeting an elderly couple of whom I inquired as to the direction to the Wade Ranch. They chuckled and said, "You will find the ranch up to the corner and take the first left and continue down the slope into the main entrance." I was hit with a shock upon seeing where it had been. Only one month before the cabin had burned down. I stood and peered through my tears and memories, and realized I had come from a migrant farm-worker's environment.

Keep in mind, this was still before the realization of the excess baggage I had been carrying all of those years; to find the cause and so many times the effects such as at this moment. One profound factor that always rose to the top, were those same tears that many times went out of control, as did the ability of being able to retain and keep all in proper perspective. This experience revealed all of the end results, including the sorrow and the lack of being able to understand their non-caring spirit for the moment, which had its effect on that vacation trip and thereon.

Even as I write, I can still smell those orchards, their spray, hear trickling irrigation ditches and see the barn like building where the dining hall remained.

Before coinciding with what would be the biggest journey in my life, he earned our livelihood by delivering cleaning and laundry throughout Enid.

He was a very sick man. I have never forgotten seeing him standing in shredded pajamas as he gasped for breath during the night. He had severe asthma, which later was diagnosed as tuberculosis. I know he had to be near dying, for he spent four years in the state sanitarium.

Later, he arranged to leave with a friend of ours to pick up his load of produce in Salt Lake City, Utah. The intent was to get where the altitude and clear air would prove healthy for him. What came of this was the realization he had abandoned us; letters were few and far between and no support was sent. While this continued, my mother was working as a waitress at what came to be my very favorite spot then and throughout my life. The spot was the "Chit-Chat Café".

The outside was painted clean white; all of the trim was in red, including the painted on sign on the outside siding, to welcome one and all to the "Chit-Chat Café". There were other signs, such as the one hung in the window of the door that signified this spot was open. Two of those Neon signs were hanging in the front window up high, so to not take the view from those inside, saying they carried Pepsi, "More Bounce to the Ounce", and you could be sure they had ice-cream delights just waiting for you to select exactly what you wanted on every occasion. When you walked in, the layout was shaped like an L. The counter was directly in front of you, where you stopped on your way out to pay for the marvelous meal you just enjoyed.

That fact wasn't hard to believe when you either saw people licking their lips as they were walking outside or heard them rave about their hamburger, fries and milk shake.

Behind the counter, you could look in the kitchen and hear and see all those sizzling meals about to be served. The waitresses were so special and you knew they were friends by the way they kept up such a friendly chat with all. One or more greeted everyone as they entered. The waitresses were immaculate in their frock like dresses and aprons. Each kept their pencil stuck in their hair or in the pocket of their aprons to take down every order. Even as you sat you would hear this constant "Chit-Chat" coming from the kitchen with, "Orders Up" and, whether it was my mother or one of the other waitresses, they would pick up those platters with the ease of a juggler of hot plates. The meals were carried and delivered to each of the tables. Then they would ask if there was anything else you needed, maybe coffee or cream.

If you had been looking at those in the booths or the whole place, you would have sworn that famous painter, Norman Rockwell, had been there.

The "Chit-Chat", was like an extended family for me. I wanted to spend as much time there with mother as possible. She was doing all to keep us together as a family. This was my way of saying my deep heartfelt thanks to her. Everything was warm and welcome there, besides, it was always good for a tune on the jukebox. One tune was a favorite and always reminded me of mother and all of her regulars, *"The Tennessee Waltz"*.

All that was needed was sawdust sprinkled on the floor so everyone could join in a waltz.

Where you got the very best view was at the front counter, which overlooked all of the booths and tables. Why, there's the Enid Chief of Police, who became our friend, even to the extent of seeing that I had an old Smith and Wesson 38 revolver with the firing pin severed off to be safe. He was a tall man who wore a moustache and you could sure tell he had plenty of experience over the years, as the roadmap was all over his face, and even showed in his hands stirring his coffee. He would no more sit down and be visiting my mother in a friendly conversation, and in would come the Fire Chief. You always knew they were there together, for they seemed to enjoy joshing each other. Each greeted the other as "Chief, good morning, Chief", grinning all the time. Then one or both would kid mother and say "What's the special this morning for breakfast?" She would tell them and they would order.

By now the clothier and a couple of his staff would join the Chiefs, although they usually took their own booth up by the window looking out on the City Square. Mother shared with us how they always stood out, because they always wore the best in new fashion. The owner of their store seemed to like his pancakes, as that is what he always had.

Other business people came in and sat at the counter, greeting all within and ordered their morning coffee. A typical sound that seemed to come from the "Chit-Chat" was "Ah" after sipping their coffee.

The Police Chief would get up and go over to the counter and be paying his bill, all the time continuing his conversation with the Fire Chief, as he was on his way back to the Police Department.

You know what, both of those Chiefs were in the auditorium when I played my solo in the Spring Concert.

Regulars would come and go, as the owner of the Music store did, where the instruments were in the window. I wouldn't ever have imagined that the day would come in the future that I would be playing one of those sousaphones.

Other ladies about town came and went, but while there, they not only had their drinks, breakfast, or lunch, they would get their mirrors out and make sure their lipstick was just right and their hair in place before going back to their offices on the City Square. They clicked out in their pretty dresses and high heel shoes with that definite line showing on the back of their legs as they walked away.

The owner and his wife always came out of the kitchen to greet those already there for the morning, now that they were a bit caught up due to the rush. That was how every day went. The door kept swinging all day until they closed at night, with all of those fine people there to "Chit-Chat" with each other

I made my last trip home after all of those years away. The first place I asked to see was the "Chit-Chat Café", and immediately found it wasn't there. Instead a new Bank was at that location. That place and those people have been present in my memories ever since.

I was ten and it was 1951, after dad's departure, and our family had to reckon with the real picture. Mother was doing her utmost, but she couldn't do it alone. There wasn't enough to care for our family. She had corresponded with my grandmother out in Seattle, Washington and they had arrived at a plan for us to leave Enid and join each other in Seattle.

There was more assurance to raise two young boys there than chance it where we were.

My mother asked me to sit down, so she could explain everything to me. She said, "You're old enough to understand what I have to share with you." She explained that due to there not being any contact or support from my dad, we had been invited to join my grandmother in Seattle. She went on and told me we would be moving from our home in the near future. All of this news and preparatory steps before departure was like the shock of two trains traveling on parallel tracks, passing each other bound for differing destinations. And those shock waves intermittently had a deep seeded affect on me from thereon.

My memories of those teachers, boys and girls I went to school with, and vividly recall subjects studied, such as penmanship, geography, the details included in the New England states, were such good memories. There was carry through to my home. I had the worst time learning my multiplication tables. My mother sat with me night after night with flash cards. The end result was I learned them backwards and forwards.

Opportunities came from the first grade and beyond. I was asked to play the xylophone solo in the Annual Spring Concert. I took piano lessons and participated in recitals. The church organist began to teach me how to play the organ. I was active in Cub Scouts and thoroughly enjoyed all in our den and pack. My mother was our Den Leader, and she gave it all she could, to insure the program was the best for all of us. Before departing, I turned out for track events sponsored by the Kiwanis Club in Enid.

What stands out is that I have and continue to remember wonderful events such as the May Pole Day and other festivities during each school year.

You might wonder why the May Pole was so bright in my mind. It was due to the preparation by our teachers, who helped us make long streamers. All of those strands were somehow connected to the top of our flagpole in front of our school. We children gathered out front and took our turn taking one colored streamer around the pole, then we gave the strand to another student. Before we were dismissed we were able to see the pole striped from its top to its bottom.

During the week, each class had been making paper May baskets. A big part of the event was to gather spring flowers and place them in our baskets. We were to take them home and deliver them to our families.

I still remember how excited I was, for I had delivered a special basket to my loving aunt. School was out and I walked to my aunt and uncle's home and left the special gift for them to find when they opened their front door.

I enjoyed doing all in the spirit of a surprise. Such moments became permanent, never to leave me.

There were other memories, such as walking to the movie downtown at the Chief Theatre, especially on Saturday afternoons with my brother. That always seemed to be a special time we had with each other. As you have guessed, the movies we saw were Westerns and Adventure films. After seeing our favorites, to including heroes such as Gene Autry and his horse Champion, Roy Rogers and Trigger and his dog Bullet, who always solved every problem on the ranch and in the town, we were well satisfied and clapped long and loud at the end of every movie. We left the movie theatre just in time to squint as we adjusted from the dark inside to the glare of the afternoon sun greeting us. We always knew what came next.

It was just as exciting to meet mother while she worked at the "Chit-Chat Café". Sure enough, there would always be quite a crowd of tired shoppers having their cold drinks and mother's regulars that she would tell us about from time to time.

When we walked in there would always be one or more greeting us and asking us about the film. Mother would stop for a moment, stand proudly and listen to the complements about her two boys. It was always good to see her in that calico like dress and apron, taking time to comment to her customers about their weekend plans ahead, yet sneak a big smile across at us where we sat. We would mount those stools just like our heroes had that afternoon leaving a cloud of dust on the trail. Mother would ask us what was our pleasure today? We knew she knew, as she had started our milkshakes and served them in those King sized malt glasses.

My brother seemed to always have Chocolate and I would have a Strawberry flavored shake. Mother poured them just half full and made sure to give us long straws, then set the tin down she had mixed our drinks in, had others heard our thoughts, they would have heard, "Oh Boy," to the very last loud slurp. Sometimes, we would have one of those fat hamburgers with that buttered top on the bun as well. All that was left was to smack our lips, have a long sip of ice water, give mother a big hug and a kiss, and tell everyone as we left, "See y'all next time."

She knew exactly the route we always took to get home. There was one spot we always stopped at before making tracks for home. It was a must to stop at the Sears and Roebuck Store, especially to take in the saddle section of the store. We walked through smelling that fine leather from those saddles up on sawhorses to touch, rub and smell. The man knew us, as we were going to be his future customers. He had let us look and take it all in for years. Finally, we knew we had to get home, as that was a big part of the agreement made with mother to have those fine days.

After we had dreamed and thought about every plot on the range, and heard the locomotives chugging up and down the track, we arrived at home frazzled. Mother arrived afterwards and asked us about the movie and told us some stories from her day at the "Chit-Chat". The evening came on us so fast and we sat down and had our supper. Mother always cooked us the best meal, even if it was beans and cornbread. We didn't have a television, but we sure enjoyed listening to the radio stories. Before you could imagine it, mother would say, "You boys get your baths and get ready for bed." It was always good to feel squeaky clean afterwards. We would all kiss and say goodnight, but if you happened to listen quietly, you would hear us talking about the highlights of the films we had seen that afternoon. We had the finest for we loved each other so much.

I did well with my subjects. All of the neighborhood kids got along well, for the most part. We played and went roller- skating outside of town at a favorite old red barn like building turned into the skating arena, where families gathered every week for holding their partners hands around the rink.

Those nights of being with our best friends were the best! What stood out was, being taken by Mr. Pete Nelson, one of our favorite neighbors, who owned a four door Packard. There was plenty of room, even as he patiently, made the stops and picked the kids up in the neighborhood. We were a little cramped, but we kids had such a good time; Pete would laugh right along with us the whole way. He took us right up to the rink and came in and watched us skate, then took us home. That night was the off week, because the very next week he did the same thing for us, except this time it was Square Dancing, held in town at the church. This loving man and father saw that all of these opportunities were ours every week. He didn't know it then, but he became a Bird for all of us.

Even earlier, more impressionable was the horrific fight between my daddy and mother. Who can remember as to the reason for warfare behind our closed door? Mother, became like a wild animal, clawing at every object she touched. All was thrown on the floor, items on the walls, dishes from the cupboards and then food from inside of the refrigerator. What marked me forever was when the catsup was thrown throughout the entire room, as though blood had been spread everywhere. All of us were screaming for it to stop. All the time, there was this sensitive little boy that hoped that the result would bring quiet and order and that such times would not happen again. I saw such behavior all too many times in the future years.

My dad disciplined me sometimes severely. Mother wasn't able to change his mind. One time, mother came after me with her high-heeled shoes to be stopped by my dad.

While in the second grade, my brother and I walked down to the neighborhood grocery store. I don't know why I took a penny piece of candy. After returning home, my brother tattled on me. Mother went out in the yard and cut a willow branch off, then she came in and yelled and screamed at me at the top of her lungs. "You're going to return that candy, pay for it, and apologize." If that wasn't enough, she thrashed me with that branch all the way to the store and all the way home. All the time, I was being called and heard language I had never heard her say before.

I learned years later about something called negative tapes and how they influence us as human beings.

That hurt lasted beyond the apology. From that time on, a lack of trust or brotherly bond was severed. My place was as "the man of the house" and later, the dichotomy became evident, as to there being room for another who became my step dad.

Backtrack with me to where we lived in Enid, Oklahoma. If you were driving up the street, happening to take the turn and look out your window, you would see me staring at your car and you would swear you saw me say hat your car was, the model and its year. Had you been able, you would have seen the proud look on my face, for I knew every model and year and enjoyed sitting out below that big, towering Cottonwood tree, which was like a friend with such deep roots.

One time, while I stayed home from school because, I had mumps on one side of one jaw, pronounced, but only on one side, I was sitting out on the porch getting some fresh air. My brother abruptly came out on the porch, slamming the screen door behind him. He didn't say a thing, just took a firm stance, with a really nasty look on his face and before I could either dodge or step aside, he socked me in that one inflated jaw. I let out a scream that could be heard at the end of the block and mother came running and found what he done. That was one time he really got it, which wasn't that often. All of this left me with deep hurting feelings. As incidents took place, I knew the gap was wider between us as brothers.

That house we lived in was a duplex, where two families lived side by side. We were proud to live by the owner, Grammer Nels, who became my first piano teacher.

She was a wonderful woman and was the mother of her daughter Sue's husband Pete Nelson, who lived down the street along with their two daughters Emile and Natalie.

All within that neighborhood were like family that shared fishing, neighborhood fish fries and emergencies when they arose.

We kids played and rode our bikes and pulled pranks on each other. Our play went from early morning throughout the day during those summer months. Every one of us attended the same school, so our being as close as we were was quite natural. Our games included: kick-the-can, hide-and-seek, ally-ally, or free throwing the ball over the roofs, yelling to the opposing team that the ball was on the way. All of these were ways we spent our days and years with each other growing up, in the town of Enid, Oklahoma which had always been home all of those years.

Part of our spare time was spent sliding on the sheet of cardboard down the slope next to those Rock Island tracks. It was great fun and was completely safe, as the upward slope would stop us in time, so not to collide with the tracks.

To retreat from the heat of the summer days, I would lay back out on that old porch, with the single laid boards that needed repairing, with dark gray paint, to match the rest of the house. What was best was to sit out there and take in the thunder and lightening storms with the pouring down rain. I have always remembered the crashing lightning, followed by the boisterous thunder. The sky would become as dark as the bilge coming from the locomotives steaming down the track with the billowing, rolling clouds the rain pelting down so hard, the drops spattering and finally forcing me off the deck of the ship.

Where I saw the entire panorama of the neighborhood was the summer dad and I crawled up and down the ladder we were roofing. That venture became his and mine, and we seemed to be up there forever, shingling the entire roof of the house. This, undoubtedly, was cost efficient to do the work or, who knows, it may have helped our family by not having to pay rent in return for our labor. All I knew was we worked long hours up there in that heat. Both of us were constantly wiping our brow and having mother make us pitchers of lemonade to keep us cool. While we worked and growled at hitting the hammer right on our thumb, which smarted, we talked with each other the whole day. Dad was a good teacher, explaining each step we were doing and how. He needed my helping hand the entire way. I remember how days later, the work was coming to an end; we were able to sit and smile, with that satisfied look of having completed such a job all by ourselves.

Before we made our final trip down the ladder, I took one full look all the way around. As I looked at everything at a different view, I saw that old Elm tree out back where I had climbed earlier, so high that I found myself unable to get back down. I knew I was in a fix and panicked, as I couldn't remember or figure out a way to get down. This state brought me to have more than tears falling down my cheeks. While sitting on that limb, higher than I had been before, I knew I was in real trouble. No one was home; I felt how I was shut-in and nearly closed off by fear not felt before. As the wind was blowing through the limbs and branches, I was teetering on new emotions never experienced before. I know I cried to that Jesus our family worshipped, and this seemed to steady me, including my reasoning powers. Moments later I stepped down on the ground below. From then on, I didn't seem to have near the trouble when climbing the old Elm tree.

I looked on the roof of our chicken hut where mother and I had worked so hard together. Next to it was the old garage where we kept our storage, where I discovered the gift for Christmas I wasn't supposed to see.

I looked across the street at the pear trees where we remained away from the bee's nests.

The pond where I was told my brother had fished me out was just down the street. One of the kids had pushed me in only to meet the fists of my brother afterwards.

A bit further down was the big old tree where my brother tied the girls and kissed them boldly in front of everyone watching. Due to this, he became the talk of all throughout our neighborhood, for he was more than impish. Every act left me so embarrassed and brought me to feel as though I had been turned inside out. He rightfully gained before its time, the title of "Dennis the Menace"; the families would gather their kids from outside and take them inside their homes until the terror had passed.

A final look was clear to the end of the block and brought me to see and recall that old tree, with the knobby, spiny bark, that I collided into with my bicycle. That bike was the most important gift, even though I knew it was used and gray colored, but I realized how hard it had to be for my folks to get it for me that year. And to think the girls down the street laughed at me at first because it wasn't brand new like theirs.

Dad said, "You've done a fine job, go on down and tell your mother we'll be there directly, after we wash up, to have supper."

There was a time and a place for my thoroughly enjoying being a boy, and never in a thousand summer days or years, would I have imagined all that lay ahead for our family. I wouldn't have even thought, much less believed, as I grew older, this unknown behavior would surface and have such an effect on me in daily life. Those emotional and sorrowful moments that made my parents and relatives begin to wonder what and why, came and passed.

Chapter 3

From Home to the Northwest

Sleep was impossible the last night, as we had to be at the railway station at two a.m. The lack of sleep was due to much more than the time frame of boarding the "Carrier of People". Mother had met this gent who kept calling, trying to convince her not to leave. Both of them remained, talking louder as the night passed.

How do we as children know such is foreign to us? Is it because we can hear new tones, beer bottles being opened and smell the smoke from their cigarettes and cigars? The clamor kept me awake and left me feeling angry at this going on. Our home never had this kind of behavior present before!

I can remember seeing all of the empty beer, bourbon bottles and clutter from their smoking when I awoke and dressed.

As we walked out of what had been home, I stopped and took another mental photo as we left to ride to the railroad depot. Undoubtedly, it was at that time, while dealing with such a shocking time in my life, the end result had to already be surfacing, known as Bi-Polar-Disorder. It was to be my absolute partner in life from that time onward. The truth was no one had any idea of what would be better defined until years ahead.

There was no one with us, as we were standing in a fog of our own. The emotions were so torn, hope would have been to see all train tickets torn up into pieces and flung into the morning air, so we couldn't stay. Instead, we shifted our weight from one foot to the other, fighting for much needed sleep. There it was, coming around the bend approaching us. I had watched this passenger train come and go for years, but never like this. This was the **Rock Island Road**, coming to take us far away, to our first stop of St. Paul, Minnesota where we would change trains to **the Empire Builder.**

We boarded and in our way we looked off into the darkness for just one we loved. There was no one, so mother got us seated. She looked at me and said, "OK, go walk, look, and say your last goodbye." I stood there peering down and back watching how the tracks behind closed. I took in the grain elevators, our lights as guides that led up to our house. I clung with every part of my being, to hold fast to every familiar person, place, smell, and sound.

This streamline "Carrier of People", leaving all I knew for what was not ever forded was moving too fast for me. The entire journey was to be a collision with what became years later, a time for diagnosis of something I had to relearn how to live more effectively with no matter how many tracks had been traveled.

I know this had to be the event that triggered a behavioral life style.

I might as well have been an architect or a mapmaker from that moment forward. I can't say as to how long, I know for a year or more, I used to lie in bed at night, mentally make myself plot each and every street, route taken and locate the key places that were clinging to my heart. All were amazed at how perfectly I could get around on my three return visits. One day, this stopped and I didn't know it.

That trip was an expedition, of meeting travelers bound to all of their points of destination. There were the fine porters and the conductor who treated us so well, all spanking clean in their black trousers, white starched jackets and chef hats. They became our friends, serving us sandwiches in our regular seats, and for special meals, we visited the dining car. We looked forward to this, as the whole car was full of "Chit-Chat" people, taking seats at their set tables with the finest of everything. We couldn't help but notice the broad array of those entering the Dining Car.

One group of gentlemen came in together standing erectly, but not too tall as to tip the high ceiling of the car with its brightly hung lamps. I noticed one was in a three-piece suit and seemed to be the spokesman for the other two. He had a crisp white shirt and collar with a tight knot at the top of his appropriately matched silk tie-that set off that dark navy suit and black shined shoes. I also saw, how his peculiar round glasses didn't slide off the bridge of his nose. The other gents walked by in their casual Western attire, as to the cut of their tight fitting pants; they were both wearing shined cowboy boots. They sat fairly close to our table so I could overhear their conversation about business and something about ranching.

Further down through the car was this bright laughter coming from a lady dressed rather lightly for the morning hour, almost as though she, or perhaps he had been out the night before. Their frivolity was evident, but not overbearing.

Others already seated had these huge white, linen napkins placed in their laps; some had already received their breakfasts and were enjoying their entrees of the morning.

By now we had taken our seats. I couldn't help but be distracted by the spanning scenery we were passing by as we sat and talked and waited for the waiter to come to our table. Now, I saw what had to be the biggest menu I had ever experienced. Why, it was nearly as long as the width of our table and had several tissue pages to select from. I thought how the trip was really something, but this menu was overwhelming!

I saw what I wanted, but checked with mother to make sure. She knew I always loved pancakes, so I had them along with eggs and bacon and the biggest glass of milk I could remember. All of the water glasses were being filled by one of the waiters.

That was different also, because every one of the staff was a Negro. Their smiling attitude was evident from the first moment of entering the car, taking our seats, to waiting on us at our table, as well as taking care of those throughout the car while we were there.

The lady and her gent seemed to keep up the cackling laughter the entire time. Another family was across from us with their children already at their table. They seemed to be a happy family, as they sat and talked, while their dad was pointing out specific sights outside the window, on the opposite side of the car, where they continued to enjoy their breakfast.

By now meals were being brought to our table. The food brought us to ooh and ah over the plates before us. The waiter asked us if there was anything else we would need.

My brother said, "Can I have some more milk," as he had already finished his and the waiter returned with a fresh glass of milk for T.J. and we were sitting now and eating and having "Chit-Chat" among us.

As the hour was passing, more people were walking and gathering to enter the car for their breakfast. Those gentlemen had been enjoying their steak and eggs and were deep in conversation. I noticed the older one, in his suede, buck colored jacket, reached into his pocket and withdrew his dark brown knobbed pipe and was packing the bowl softly and familiarly with his thumb on the tobacco. I took a glimpse to watch him light his pipe with his matches from the top of the table. After he sucked on that pipe, he left a trail of curling smoke into the ceiling of the dining car. What was pleasurable was the aroma of his pipe. While he was getting set, the other two continued to have comments regarding the fixtures and all within the car. I noticed the plush carpet on the floor when we entered. It was more like a home than a Railroad Dining Car! Of course how would I know, this was my first such remembered train trip.

Although we had traveled during my first grade out to Wenatchee, Washington to meet my dad, I guess I was too young to remember very much about that trip.

While I sat there, I paid attention to the finery on all of the well set tables, with white china platters and all that went with them, including the big bowls for those wanting cooked or cold cereal, or fresh fruit, which T.J. and I had. That was a fine meal to begin that day as we talked and made our way west. Before excusing ourselves from the table we thanked the waiter and heard the cooks say, "Do come again."

I enjoyed meeting and talking with others on board. As we reentered our assigned car and seats, I saw the nice little couple who had that definite accent, which we found was Swedish, as they withdrew their basket which was full of their own food. The lady was so sweet; I enjoyed watching her unfold all of her fine linen, to make a table for them and their morning meal. This was definitely different from what we had just experienced. They had two blocks of cheese, which her husband was grasping hold of and slicing off thin slices along with slices of sausage from a long roll. They had homemade breads and she reached into the basket for their fresh fruit. I remember how they offered some to us, but we said our sincere thanks, having just had our breakfast. Before they ate, the man and woman bowed for a short moment of prayer and thanksgiving for all of their food and God's care. She wouldn't let us miss their fine meal, insisting that we would accept oranges from them. So we sat and ate wedges of our oranges and talked and got to know each other. They and other nearby seated passengers seemed to be the nicest of people.

I was about ready to take a walk between the various cars as I periodically did when one of the Waiter Staff came through asking if we would like light blankets for the morning hour or magazines or a bar of candy.

What was really special was standing out between the cars feeling the wind on my face as we moved north. The glow of the fields of corn and other farms and fields was beautiful, standing tall and erect, line on line, through Iowa.

Speaking of geography lessons, I was seeing lesson upon lesson unfold before my eyes. There were, two songs that were popular then or shortly afterwards that said it for this framing of our lives: *"I Love Those Dear Hearts and Gentle People" and "Far Away Places".*

The three of us were coming from a broad city square, now surrounded by the highest buildings, sprawling city streets, people, noise and confusion. We were quick stepping and rushing to insure we boarded **The Empire Builder** bound for Seattle on time. There was no layover so the tug was on, as mother did exactly that with both of us. Seeing that "Carrier of People" and baggage was such a change for me. She was all washed and shined clean, in the special orange with dark green striped paint emblazoned in gold imprint. The regal white Northern Canadian goat was surrounded by crimson red and a splash of white encircled the goat on the frontal column, to exclaim who she was: **The Empire Builder.**

There seemed to be a contrast between trains through and through for the passengers revealed more elegance as did the train staff.

While traveling to Seattle, after departing St. Paul, Minnesota, we met this man on the train whose name was Sven Johnson. He treated us so special, even to invite all of us to dinner in the Dining Car where those "Chit-Chat" people convened. We spent a lot of time visiting and getting to know each other all the way west.

Upon arrival we went our way to fulfill our true destinations. Where before I was, all eyes moving north, now I seemed to absorb each and every detail strolling car to car.

We had traveled before for a day, sometimes a week or more, but never further than Oklahoma or Texas to see relatives. So this journey was the longest both in terms of time and miles.

How could any young boy not be enthralled at the panorama of small towns and stops along the way moving westward? At one of those towns we stopped at, I turned and asked mother, "Could I step off the train to get some fresh air?" She said, "It's OK, I'm sure it will be good for you." At the same time, I stepped down on the depot landing, I immediately realized we were in much colder country. I took some long strides to the end of the landing and went to the restroom in the station house. Afterwards, I stopped and bought some candy for my brother and some gum for mother and me. Just as I exited the station house, I heard the conductor bellow, "All Aboard," and I made a run for it to make it just in time to jump onto the stairs to the coach landing. I rejoined mother and my brother and they could see I was out of breath. Mother said, "I was afraid you weren't going to get back in time." That was the last time I did that!

The path of this "Carrier of People" collided with the deep snow through Glacier National Park, we had to stop and wait for the snow removal train before forging on to the West Coast. To look out on this deep snow covering all of the country about us, to see how the branches of the surrounding trees in the forest were weighted down with piled on snow was captivating. At the same time, we were glad to be inside the car of the "Carrier of People", held up in this blizzard, to wait patiently for the clearing being made ahead for a safe passage on to the West Coast. None of us could have imagined that our travel was coming to a halt sooner than ever believed.

The morning of our turning south was the morning, I said, "I've never seen such a lake as this before." I soon found that we exited at Everett, Washington and had been looking at Puget Sound and Elliott Bay off shore of Seattle. This move was more significant that I'd known at the time. Our home and more would be nearby. We entered a final dark tunnel, which after exiting brought us to feel a slowing up and at last to feel a slight jolt and bump of the cars, one against the other. All of the passengers gathered their luggage, coats, packages, and embarked from their individual cars.

We walked down the ramp into the King Street Station, to meet my grandmother and her companion who had promised so much.

Soon afterwards, we came to realize our regal stay included our staying in the George Washington Hotel, near today's Plaza Hotels. The hotel was a tall multi-storied building all in red brick that showed its tarnish from the years of wear. We noticed on that first day we were greeted by the whipping wind as we drove up to the hotel. I saw a green covering over the front entrance with monogrammed writing revealing to all entering that this was the George Washington Hotel. We entered by making our way up those stairs through those swinging doors with bright gold door plates, which I later came to realize were really brass.

All on the staff seemed to come to attention when we approached the front desk to ask for our room keys. The staff members that stood out for me were those dressed all in the same color that flapping green covering outside. They wore these funny little round hats with a tie that fit under their chins.

Mother told me after they escorted us to our room, "They are called Bellboys." I noticed another Bellboy who ran the elevator received his instruction from a fellow Bellboy, "They need floor seven." The one running the elevator placed his gloved hands on more of the gold levers and closed the gate like door and we were off to the seventh floor. Everywhere we turned was a new sight not seen before.

When he walked away, mother gave him a tip and he replied, "If there is anything else be sure and call."

When we arrived, I saw carts standing in the hallway and bustling women in different frilly black uniforms and cute little white hats that seemed to be sitting on the very top of their hair. I couldn't quite figure how those little white napkins were able to remain without falling to the floor.

We didn't know it, but we would be staying there for the first week upon our arrival in Seattle. How could we have thought we would be there enjoying all a part of that world? To think the hotel manager, clerks and

Bellboys alike knew us by our names. This was the way we transcended to what would be our new home, school and community.

Chapter 4

Arrival in The Northwest

We became aware that our temporary living condition would never work. My grandmother asked us to stay with her at her home on Sandpoint Way in Lake City. We were too many. Her companion who promised us the world, to draw our attention, never came across with one particle.

He had promised to take us: fishing, hiking, beach combing, taking rides on the ferries, driving to the mountains, to name only a few of the fish hooks thrown out for us to bite on that never happened.

Mother, interviewed for a position at the Boeing Company at their old office on Second and Union in downtown Seattle. I remember sitting on those black plastic chairs and what it was like for the two of us. She had given us strict instructions to be quiet and behave.

A woman introduced herself to everyone coming in and gave each a set of papers to be filled out. They sat scratching their foreheads as if they were trying to figure out some multiplication tables, just like I used to before learning all of my facts. While sitting and waiting we didn't squirm one bit!

At long last, one man came out and asked for mother to join him in his office.

Afterwards, she brought the personnel man out and pointed us out so he would know who we were. And to make sure he understood, she told him, "They're mine and they've never gone hungry. I didn't come all the way out here for that to happen. I'm not leaving without a job." Sure enough, she got a good job at Boeing Plant #2 that day.

Winter was upon us and in the swirling, drifting snow, mother rose at three a.m. to ride her bus to Plant #2, every morning and return at night.

We attended school at Lake City Elementary, which reminded me of the old Virginia Graham Elementary School in Okanogan, Washington I attended while in the first grade.

School busses were arriving, opening their sliding doors so the kids on board could get off and make way into the building to attend their classes.

We made the long walk to and from home to school each day. My grandmother was a champ every morning! She fixed us a hot breakfast, the finest of lunches, and made sure everything fit just right in our lunch buckets. She would always greet us with a smiling "Good-morning", and would make sure we were dressed warm with our stocking hats, coats totally buttoned, that we had our gloves, our snowshoes buckled, and gave us a big kiss, to give us the right send off daily. Then we walked all the way up to where the road curved left before going down the hill in Lake City.

We always had plenty of time even in those snowy conditions. When we arrived at the door of the school we were ready to be thawed out. There was a closet area, where the kids hung their coats and other items to drip and dry, before we went out for our first recess.

That first day was a picture all of its own. There we stood in our homemade shirts blue jeans and lunch pails in hand. I felt as though I was an "Okie boy"! I might as well have stood there bare footed when I was introduced to the class. All was so different including the teacher, who acted like we had come out on the stagecoach or covered wagon. She tried

55

to make me feel welcome and at home, but I honestly had never heard such words as "either or pardon".

As I stood in the front of the class, they gave me a thorough look over. I immediately noticed a girl with ravishing long dark and brown and dark eyes to match. I thought she was really something and in short order I found her name was Sally. We managed to say hi to each other and sneak looks all morning.

I turned out for the basketball team. The P.E. teacher and coach took me under his wings. We kept practicing and playing our games. After making the team, I asked Sally to come to our games to see me play. She and some of her girl friends came. The coach told me, "You'll be a good one in the years to come."

Those were long days that became longer especially in the evenings, when we were constantly told we ate too much and we were in the way. We couldn't listen to our radio programs and my grandmother's companion Sidney, fought mother over everything.

The only place we went was to the Northgate Mall Saturday mornings, where more fights occurred over money and who would pay for the food.

One night it ended, because he hit my mother and struck out at us. She told him never to touch us again and I blurted out, "You touch my mother ever again, and I'll kill you!" This upheaval was the final straw that brought us to look for our new home. It was short order, and we would be moving where the commute would be a thing of the past for mother.

As it turned out, Sven and mother remained in contact. He wouldn't just come and go, with mother, he would always visit with us as well. We went for rides together and to the movies, and one afternoon we went to see *Across the Wide Missouri* starring Clark Gable. It was playing at the Northgate theatre and tied perfectly with our ride before. Mother really liked Sven, but he was an alcoholic who really enjoyed his beer. I believe we would have seen him even more had this not been true.

Some months passed before mother was able to locate our new home and, as expected, we gained friends in the neighborhood. I watched the other kids riding bikes and so wanted one of my own.

My first Christmas gift was from Sven. He told me he had something special for me. Sven went back to the trunk of his car, opened it up and my eyes grew like saucers. There it was, my black, English Racer! It had no special horn, gearshift, or anything like that, but it was wonderful. I was so happy, now I could ride with the kids in the neighborhood.

As I write, I can still see the gleam of Sven watching my joy in receiving this special gift. How I enjoyed riding that bike!

A couple of blocks from our home, was our favorite place where all the kids played, it was a small forest perfect for games and playing Army.

Another favorite spot was the basement. Even with the height being so low I still managed to practice my shots. This required some adjusting to make it work. There were two side- by- side- sinks next to each other used for washing clothes. I had a couple of hard rubber balls that I used to replace my basketball where I shot baskets into the sinks, and periodically I would get my brother to play "Horse" with me, or to scrimmage with me. We had to be careful not to bounce our heads off the beams of the ceiling or jump too high on our shots. You know, it seemed as though I spent hours down there in that bay of tranquility away from the chaos. Even if Sidney was home from work early, I was out of his sight or reach.

I knew I really hated that Sidney for he made it known he never intended to take us anywhere.

When we first saw him upon our arrival, we saw that he was six foot four, a strong build, but he drooped his head down when he walked. I know mother had always taught me to hold my head up high no matter what. He was dressed in his khaki pants and a wool green coat worn by lumberjacks. He was totally balding and had steel blue eyes, which were piercing to look at. During all of the battles his fierce temper would come out of him much like flooding water, no matter what the season. In fact my grandmother stood as best as she could against his rampages that shook the whole place.

Now that I have addressed what I have battled all of my life, I can't help but wonder if his behavior could not be marked as manic. His language was atrocious, anything but right to be used in the presence of mother or my grandmother, not to mention the two of us boys.

I realized how my language sounded exactly as the language heard in our environment. I swore as though brandishing to protect myself and tried to reveal real strength. Strangely, however, I knew that wasn't the true me at all. Within me was the same boy, yet really the exact opposite of my true character or personality.

One night during our basketball season, I arrived home later than expected because we had a late game and I had broken my glasses. He tore into me verbally from the offset. He had a way of belittling himself with the mere opening of his mouth. This time he called me everything in the book. I came to realize, in his opinion, I was some kind of a "special kid", who could come and go when I pleased; furthermore, I was a pain at least to him and dinner had to be held because of me, and the chores were not done due to my being so involved with my activities.

About that time, mother arrived from her day of work. She was always worn out upon arrival. Before I could talk to her, he blurted out how I had broken my glasses. I was going to tell her so not to alarm her, but he wouldn't permit that.

I quit taking any of his unnecessary words, and I told him "Your so called promises have never been real, you're a liar." All of this took place during our stay in Lake City, Washington just north of Seattle.

Mother blew her fuse over my broken glasses; however, Sven phoned that evening. She told him what that kid of hers had done. He calmed her and asked to talk with me. He lovingly reached out to me and told me he would be out first thing in the morning and we would take care of this in quick order. His phone call really helped ease mother's fuming from before.

Sven arrived the next morning as promised. He greeted everyone with his jovial, loving, soft smile, which never seemed to leave his face. He said, "Let's go and see what we can do about this problem." We drove down to Lake City to the optometrists' office.

I was fitted for my glasses and when we left I had a brand new pair. He was grinning and we had a good laugh over mother's fitful reaction. We stopped afterwards and Sven had his usual cup of black coffee and I had chocolate milk, a cake doughnut with coconut icing with nuts sprinkled on top. Then we returned to the house to a much more peaceful surrounding.

Sven touched me so that years later I contacted him again. I called him and made an appointment to meet him at his favorite spot, a tavern he had frequented for years in West Seattle on California Boulevard. I was now a grown man towering 6'3 and ½ " tall and when I walked in he recognized me immediately. We sat and talked for a long time and reflected on that incident where he had helped me so much. He was touched at my coming and shed a tear sitting there at the table. I didn't see him again, but when I'm in West Seattle or near the lumber mills, I always think of him with love and goodness in my thoughts. I always thought he would have been such a good dad.

Many times I recalled what was wonderful about that forest like setting back in Lake City. It was the fact of being clear from the other kids, to sit at the foot of the big old trees, beside the little creek, that carried all of the wrongness away from that place, called home. Not only did I enjoy being outside, I thoroughly loved being there when the rain was coming down, washing me clear of all of that commotion that never stopped.

I enjoyed the gathering of the little creatures, such as the birds of the forest and squirrels scampering about me, which seemed to be there to lift my spirits. Through all of it, I had found a haven that could be mine even momentarily, with the kids romping about playing war or other make believe games. Mine was anything but make-believe! You probably won't be terribly surprised at how I knew I was a lot older than those kids, both in years and in my very own spirit.

The handwriting was on the wall and we knew we were moving to Georgetown, in South Seattle, near Plant #2 of the Boeing Company. Mother was able to locate an apartment closer, so she would no longer need to rise at the crack of dawn and collapse upon arriving home every evening.

Georgetown reflected a browning, as it had been infiltrated by all of the industrial fallout. It was there, I became aware of how people had to live behind those dimly lit windows, shades, in dingy run down old buildings they called their homes. There certainly were "Street People" present even then.

There is real evidence of positive change, in the year of 2000, with offices and complexes replacing the older areas.

What a trade this was for our family.

Both of us were enrolled at Georgetown Elementary School where there was a mixed bag of fellow students. The big game was shooting marbles, so mother bought me a special bag of marbles, I lost to an Indian boy who took his win far more seriously than I realized.

There are all kinds of ways to face one's education. At that moment, I collided with right and wrong and learned how fast an Indian boy can and did move, flashing his deep seeded temper. I was flat on my back with his knife at my throat. If that wasn't lesson enough, our neighbor, the biggest boy in school was in a brawl and laid me out across a desk and probably would have broken my back, but the teacher broke up the fight.

It was time to hightail it and that we did. Consider the school year wasn't quite over and we were on our way to Queen Anne Hill. Not bad, four moves before completing the fifth grade.

Other factors were present in those two story units we lived in, as it seemed much like a place where people were transients. When the F.B.I. came to pay a visit with the manager, who always seemed a bit on the strange side, it turned out he was wanted by the F.B.I. due to his being a Communist. It wasn't that impossible to see that a number of the residents were alcoholics. Our departure came by another falling asleep after dropping his cigarette, and starting a fire in our unit.

All that had occurred prior made me come to think how we had come in good faith, to receive much more than those promissory notes, rather, to better our lives. Instead, we had been confronted by one who had such influence to destroy bit by bit what had been decent, deep seated belief in God and one another. Our self-concepts had been affected and we lost that tender, gentle spirit we carried no matter where. No longer would there be the soft, sweetness that I know I had before. So much of the inborn innocence had escaped my spirit, perhaps never to return.

Mother heard from her boss at Boeing that he owned an older home on lower Queen Anne Hill. This was and remains today "The Old 217 West Republican." That house is still there. In fact, only last night while we were in Seattle for the evening having dinner, Sandra, my wife of some nineteen years and I turned to see what was left from those, days.

Sure enough, there it was among all that growth of expanding business parks up and down the tiers of the lower blocks. All of the progress would surely squeeze that old house out some day. When I stopped in front, I shared with Sandra what the various windows signified. I could see so vividly where the window was that marked the kitchen, the master bedroom, knowing the living room and the kitchen were in the background, as was the little room that had been mine all those years ago. I pointed out to her the window down the alley where the hobo had been asleep in the coal bin and I startled him from his sleep while I was washing the clothes and my alarm caused him to escape through the window and down the alley.

It always does something for me to realize among all of those houses, where so many of the kids lived, are replacements by the maze of new growth.

I have returned to see if it was still there many times over the years. It has remained, even though there was more there then than I would have ever imagined.

We were grateful to have this home. When we thought back as to where we had come from, this was a "God-Send" for us. Sure it was older but we took it, and began cleaning, sprucing up, painting, and readying to move. We remained there through my sixth, seventh, eighth grades while at Warren Avenue Grade School taking me to Queen Anne High. All experienced while there carried on throughout my life.

We walked to what was the old Warren Avenue Grade School, where today the Seattle Sonics play season to season at the Key Arena.

There was the neighborhood gang of friends we hung around with along with my classmates at school.

I remember hearing the girls say from the start as to what a nice boy Gerald Kent was, in fact more than the other boys. Those girls who had shared such complements asked me later, "What ever happened to that nice boy Gerald Kent?" I knew exactly what they meant. Their first feelings shared pointed to the true me, yet to survive required behaviors I had never practiced before.

I was trying to be a good student.

Years later, I knew how much was lacking. The fundamental skills and knowledge were not taught nor learned, as they needed to be, to continue into secondary levels of education.

Somehow, when weekends came and we were together, where time should have been precious, I was away more and more. There was no time to be a young boy, as the collision course with life was impacting me from every side, the same way the tracks converged in my life.

Another fact was true. I behaved strangely from time to time, yet did not know why. There were times of elation and relating to others in such a way to gain approval via telling jokes, or being jocular, to literally realize a soaring in my behavior, yet then came the times of gloom beyond any belief of mine, or others. It was as though I had sunk to the levels of complete despair. Then, was the time I was sure there wasn't one who either perceived it going on or was aware. I always heard train whistles in the night whether there were trains or not.

In retrospect, I can't help but wonder whether these were calls of my spirit, back to those gauged tracks to what was and could have been. Consider, that where we live today, I can clearly hear and am awakened as the trains are arriving and departing Tacoma, Washington every night.

Times and conditions were so different from today. What was different was mother thought nothing of our catching the bus to see a movie, or even to walk together as brothers all the way downtown. We would stop at our favorite hot-nut stand for a mixed bag of nuts, swim at the Moore Hotel, or ride all the way out on the bus to Madronna Beach on Lake Washington for a day of swimming. Usually, longer distances entailed going with our friends. No one thought anything about it, where today parents have to transport their kids everywhere, insuring their safety.

Between the seventh and eighth grades, one evening mother announced she had met a guy that was coming to call. That was the night we met Jesse. He pulled up to the curb in his Ford Victoria, two-door, with a spare tire on the rear of the trunk. He was a handsome man about mother's age and he looked sharp in his suit and vest.

That was about the same time the movie *Shane* was showing. What struck me was how he looked like Alan Ladd, the star in the film. He was a Merchant Mariner off a ship bound for Australia.

After our introductions he said, "Would you boys like to go to the Ringling Brothers Circus tonight?" He already had tickets, so we went to the circus and had a fine time. He was in port so we saw him more and more.

I grew up believing and hoping all would be true in my life, as it seemed to be unfolding in ours then, just as the current song sung by Frank Sinatra, about *"Young at Heart"*. Had you, been there, you would have heard me whistling that song, as I believed we could be, as the lyrics revealed.

Mother and Jesse were to be away one weekend, but left us explicit instructions as to the cleaning of the entire house upon their return. I know my brother and I gave it our all. The entire floor was swept, mopped, waxed, shined and the bathroom was cleaned to shine. The outside steps had been cleaned for a perfect entry. I am sure we didn't get the windows, but the rest was in top shape, including a thorough job done in the kitchen with all being washed, wiped and put away so we were ready. They pulled up and came inside, as we stood at attention with our mop and broom for inspection. We watched mother blow more than her fuse. In fact, she became volatile. She criticized our entire effort, and punctuated it saying, "If you can't do any better than this, then don't do anything anymore." We were hurt beyond belief, and became angered at the shrill shrieking of her voice. All this behavior did was, bring a deep seeded reaction from us, by our saying, "If we can't do it as you expect, then do it yourself!" Here they had gone and done their thing and we didn't go or do anything. Instead, we had followed the agenda to rate this. Over the years ahead, there was always an agenda, which she had prepared. Undoubtedly, that was where I began to practice time management.

Jesse did not interfere and that became commonplace. Each time he did mother would cut him off by saying, "They are my boys." I thought then, and for all the years to come what a grave error this was. It totally emphasized injustice within our family.

Let me take you back to earlier days upon meeting Jesse Boyd.

I'll never forget the first time I saw him with his shirtsleeves rolled up to his elbows. What stunned me was, seeing matted hair, one-half of an inch from the surface of his muscular forearms. The reason this affected me as it did, was due to maturing ever so slowly. Why, I barely had hair on either my arms or legs.

This passed and with it came the good news of their being married.

I can remember how the kids in the neighborhood always laughed at how he stayed at our place, but with their being married, that embarrassment came to a close.

When he wasn't catching the next ship he would be selling. He accepted sales positions always making us think he might remain with us and no longer ship out.

Each time he shipped out or boarded another sales position. It was at such times that he offered me an opportunity to accompany him, which I seldom passed, as those times were always the best.

Not only would he take me on tours of the vessels he was assigned to, but to see his quarters. Foremost were those special moments of following him in his oil stained coveralls, him raising his forearm, to absorb the sweat from his brow, and me listening to him as he explained all pertaining to the tour. I realized I had to pick up my step or he would leave me lost in some portal, unable to find my way back to the main deck supporting the gangplank.

I found him to be darn patient, though. There was so much to look at and take in on those first tours.

When I was older, he took me with him on the Alaska Steam Motor ships he was working on at the time. We made our way down where the "black gang" did their work, including all he was doing at the time. He did much more than show and tell. He explained what he did step by step during his watch. After he was assured I fully understood, he handed me the rag to do the wiping etc., and he said loud enough, for me to hear over those motors and the generator blaring in the background, "I'm going topside to get a cup of coffee and I'll be right back." Before he left, he ran me through everything again, then winked, which was his way of passing his trust, and left me in the bowels of the ship, as the Wiper for the ship at his leave.

I found I didn't dwell, instead I made the rounds checking the gauges. I always remembered how he entrusted such to me and would return later having had his coffee.

He'd be smiling and asked, "How's the Wiper of the ship doing?"

I wouldn't have ever believed it, but the day not all that far in the future came and he helped me to get my Seaman's papers. The intent was for me to be bound for the DEW line on the vessel about to depart. Mother intervened saying, "No, he's too young." Looking back, she was right, as I was only fifteen years old at the time.

Somehow, that concern of his matted hairy body no longer caused me anxiety as before. Maybe I was coming to terms that I was still a boy growing taller every day, but not outward.

The truth was, my father's mother was one-half Cherokee Indian, so I gained one-eighth of that blood. You know what they say about Indians having little or no hair on their bodies?

Many years later I couldn't help but smile over such concerns of yesterday.

Chapter 5

On to Queen Anne Hill

The Anderson's home was two stories high. We pulled up to the curb. When we got out of the car, Sven, mother, my brother and I gathered together; Sven took mother's arm helping her up the stairs that led to a short walk to the front door. We were all dressed warmly, shutting out the bite of winter nearing. Sven pressed the doorbell and Mrs. Anderson answered the door. She had a smile on her face welcoming us into their home. Their family came to meet us, and Sven made all of the introductions.

What was evident was the warmth and glow from that moment forward. All was like a holiday story as the rooms were so comfortable and decorated for the occasion.

Mr. and Mrs. Anderson made us feel welcome, even to invite us into the kitchen, where the delightful feast was being prepared. Mrs. Anderson proved to be a wonderful cook and baker. Our feast included: roasted turkey, baked ham, Swedish fish balls, ludifisk, candied sweet potatoes covered with marshmallow topping, mashed potatoes with special creamy topping, breads beaded with fruit that were from her mothers recipes in Sweden, cakes, pies, raw vegetable trays, fancy jellies and cranberries, hot chocolate, hot coffee, and hot cider, with the swizzle sticks to stir with for us kids.

The dining room was set to hold the wonderful food and the aromas sifted throughout the house. Other delicacies were loaves of Swedish breads, that made our mouths water for one slice smothered in butter before the main meal began.

The introductions would not have been complete had they not included their beloved Airedale terrier, who revealed how friendly he was to all of us.

Mother and Mrs. Anderson were out in the kitchen visiting and putting the finishing touches on for dinner while Sven and Mr. Anderson were sitting in the living room talking and enjoying a glass of beer.

Memories like these shared, always seem to occur as the seasons change. All the facts of this internal battle I have faced during the best part of my life, do seem to go with the seasons. When the rainy and snowy seasons approach, a kind of wintering comes within my spirit, as I always am prone to search more deeply for my true self than any other time of the year. The intensive search always became introspective on all counts, looking deeper and deeper, to draw meaning for myself. An event about to occur while visiting was more than sufficient, for such search into the depths of my self and behaviors. Here were circumstances eliciting both cause and effect.

The Andersons had two children, a daughter and a son older than me. We were warmly received and I found that they attended West Seattle High School.

Before we knew it came the call for that fine dinner of which we sat and prayed over in good spirit. When we first saw the ludifisk we found a refined dish that was always served during this holiday period of the year. Mrs. Anderson made a special entry carrying their favorite to the table. She always served it in a large deep serving bowl. It definitely had an aroma all of its own, which was even more aromatic, upon lifting the covering to release those scents into the air about us. She placed a large serving spoon and explained, "Even though it looks soupy, I've smothered it in cream with a covering of almond on top. Just spoon or lathe it on your platter and wait for the taste we have enjoyed all of our years that I learned to appreciate coming from Sweden." When we went to bite into it, its slippery texture slid down our throats and the entire Anderson family waited to see if we enjoyed it. Surprisingly, we all said it was good and that brought an acclaim from all.

Afterwards, the adults sat around the table and continued their visiting and getting to know each other.

Their older son Gary invited me up to his room to see his favorite collections.

This was really special being with a high school aged guy. I turned around and my brother was right behind us barging in and being obnoxious as always. We both tried to get him to go back down stairs, to find something else to do, and he would have nothing to do with it.

Gary asked me if I would like to see his twenty-two-rifle. I said, "Would I". In the meantime my brother remained and kept blabbing as always. I didn't ask him, I told him, "Get out of here." He would hear none of it. In the meantime, Gary withdrew his rifle to show it to me. He asked if I would like to hold it. I said, "Are you sure it's clear of any cartridges?" He said, "It's clear and safe." I hadn't ever held any weapon before, other than the old Smith & Wesson 38 revolver that the Police Chief of the Enid Police Department, gave me years before. But, for me to know if there was a bullet in the barrel wasn't something I was aware of then.

My brother just wouldn't give up and I lifted the rifle to my shoulder, slowly swung it as to face him, all the time telling him to leave, so we could have a few moments alone. There he stood his staunch way of not moving or giving an inch and I blurted out, "I will shoot" and he disputed me. Now, I was just plain angry and was pointing the rifle directly at him and just as I squeezed the trigger, I jerked the barrel to the left. The blast that came out of that barrel ripped through the wall and undoubtedly beyond the rooftop and furthering its course and altering all it impacted. I dropped the gun immediately, all three of us stood in shock, which brought those below to determine what had happened.

Before I could utter a word, Gary told them what had happened. The remaining moments in their home was the same shock as we exited afterwards. I knew from that moment, there would be no relationship between us as brothers. That seemed to be true time after time in the years ahead. Upon this happening there was no way I could really understand such, but as the years continued, I came to realize behaviors that prompted this overriding lack I had within me.

Such signs were dealing with heightened agitation in daily life, being confronted by having to deal with rejection, or an abundance of negative factors that control all of us. Both of these had been present up in Gary's room that afternoon.

Between, 1961 and 1970, more was in place and continued, until later, when dealing with weapons while going through Basic and Technical Training in the Air Force and later on into my career of Law Enforcement.

Even in 1984 this followed me to the Scout Camp for the summer where a large part of my assignment was to train and help boys meet their requirements, with the twenty-two-rifle on the range. I believe all of this ably prepared me to be alert of one and all as they awaited clearance on the range.

Throughout the years I remembered that terrible incident, which I carried all those years. Somehow, there has never been real healing or forgiveness within my spirit for that rash moment of losing control of my temper, for the price remained to be the highest. When reviewing over and over every act such as this, it is no wonder there became such heated anger between my brother and me, nor was it hard to know that for forty years we haven't had any contact with each other.

To write this story brought me to return more than I would have believed to truly reflect and see the old walks as they were back then.

Our playground of yesterday was only a block and a half away, before crossing Elliott Way, which led us to those Great Northern tracks, the stacked boulders and the salt water breeze off the bay. I was fairly sure that old property would be gone as mentioned previously. In fact, most of the area was now paved over for parking for the workers in the new nearby offices. Then I saw something that almost took my breath away, a creeping vine of a raspberry plant stringing out onto the alleyway, which reminded me of those fresh raspberries that my friend's folks used to grow. His loving mother would spread raspberry preserves on her wonderful scones. The house was gone, but I was convinced I was looking where their back yard had been. I took a deep breath as the moment touched my spirit.

When hearing all of those trains coming and going up and down the track below where we lived, I thought how I stepped off that **Empire Builder** in 1951 onto the platform and was told the towering building and clock heralded King Street Station. Seattle was one bustling city to be sure, especially for us hailing from our home of yesterday in Enid, Oklahoma.

As the years passed, the rain was constant, but winter always seemed to bring a quiet snowfall. Ahead was spring and budding rhododendrons. We welcomed summer and the days of warmth and clear blue skies that always seemed to come in September. Shortly after our arrival, sooner than we would have imagined, we quickly learned how to dress for each season and became acclimated, as we were becoming regular Queen Anneites. Granted those days became more like we hoped, halcyon days for our family, as we settled more and more.

It is my hope today as you read you'll be able to reflect on your younger years and experiences.

While boys living on lower Queen Anne, we had a short head start on today's world of 10, 15 and 21 speed bicycles. Our bikes were stabilized with much wider tires, seats, and had deeper springs for a cushier ride. We used our bikes for pleasure and also for our paper routes to haul our papers to a central point, drop a load, deliver a portion and return to pick up more until our route was completed.

I never forgot the last time I went trick'er treat'n with my best buddy. Keep in mind he was considerably shorted than I was, as I was topping 6' 1" + then. He said, "Let's go ahead and do our Halloween in the apartment's", rising on the tiers of Queen Anne Hill. Granted, we had no business in them, as they were all clearly posted with their **NO SOLICITATION** signs, yet in we went, to the top floor with the plan of working our way down floor by floor. It didn't take that long after knocking or buzzing their doorbells, to hear this one man who answered and said, "I don't mind your being here, but did you have to bring your father along?" This left me so embarrassed and that was my final time to be sure. Well, after all I was only twelve years old!

The waterfront gave us distance and refuge from our homes and all of the upheaval.

At times we would walk the distance to the piers along the downtown waterfront and take in the curio shops and eat fish'n chips at Ivars a must to do even then.

Another favorite past time was to pedal up to Kinnear Park. We lined our bikes up, and pointed the lower level of the park before Elliott Bay.

As we sat there lined up on the knoll, checking the straightness of our line, we pushed off and surged downhill towards the big old maple trees and the carpet of fallen leaves. We kept our bodies low and parallel to the ground as we sped toward the leaves. Then we would hit the brakes and slide freely onto the leaves.

We were just kids, living on lower Queen Anne, where we felt free for a little while longer.

I have to share the last venture with you, for even today I fully recall all of the details and after you read them, you'll more than understand.

This occurred in my boyhood in the 1950's, where some of my friends rode our bikes all the way to Alki Point.

One on a summer Sunday, we packed big lunches, formed a caravan of seven to ten boys and pedaled down to the Seattle Waterfront.

We had planned the trip for some time, so the fervor was growing among all of us as we checked our equipment: tool kit, lunch bags, baseball gloves, and a ball, and a change of clothes for the ever, changing Seattle weather.

We rode down to the older friend's home. When we got there he wasn't quite ready, so we leaned our bikes up against the fence-that bordered the raspberry bushes already mentioned. All of us knew to be extra cautious about his dad's gorgeous Buick Century with its waxy sheen on the maroon paint and the clean white soft-top. While we waited for our leader for the day, his mother came out to say "good morning" in her loving fashion by offering fresh baked scones for our morning start. All of us thanked her in chorus before we devoured all of the scones.

We were off, on the way down to the waterfront and found ourselves riding through a salty breeze. Our pathway went by Crawford's Seafood Restaurant and Ivar's on Elliott Way, overlooking the future Myrtle Edwards Park. In those days, there were only piles of huge rocks and dirt from other projects in the city. There were also the huge oil tanks in the tank yard before crossing **The Empire Builder** tracks where we might see various ships anchored from Pier 70 all the way down to the city center.

We stopped to look at the fishing boats and the fishermen, who were soaking wet from the spray of their hoses they used to clean the fresh catch of the day. We watched them spread their catch out covering the fish in ice and looked inside the waterfront warehouses where they processed the fish. The women workers inside wore weather gear, including rubber boots and scarves and long gloves that reached to their elbows. As we stood looking at the scene of churning water boiling up with white-caps, kicking up logs and pieces of packing crates, spilled oil and various waterfront debris was evident below the walkway.

Then we mounted our bikes and cruised further down the waterfront and though we had full sack lunches stopped at Ivar's and grabbed sacks of fish n' chips and cold drinks. Some of us stayed outside to watch our bikes while others went inside to use the restroom before continuing.

We continued down Alaskan Way, making sure to stop at the Ye Olde' Curiosity Shop, with some of us taking turns waiting outside, watching the bikes, as others went in to look at the rare displays.

And then we pushed off for the West Seattle Bridge, passing the industrial sites along the way as we rode beneath the Alaskan Way viaduct that hammered with traffic noise

Our route was to continue onto the Spokane Street ramp, ascending to the West Seattle Bridge and take in the view of Elliott Bay and its shipping traffic. We fought a cold wind all the way to Alki Point, historically known as the founding point to Seattle. It was there we found a spot where we could lay our bikes down and rest.

Some of the guys ran over to change into their bathing suits and as they waded in and they soon realized how cold the water really was, bringing us to play baseball. The wind was blowing so hard it kicked up the fine sand when anyone slid into a base.

Later we gathered around the old wooden picnic table and spread all of our sacks out for lunch on the splintered, table. Afterwards, we resumed our baseball game and later returned the same route to our homes. You're right; that was one Sunday, among so many others of similar ventures back then.

Jesse and I worked on restoring a small one-man sailboat. The day finally came to launch "our craft". He borrowed a boat trailer so we could transport her, a smart seaworthy craft, of some twelve feet in length, with an eighteen-foot mast. This wasn't any sailboat, rather a craft by design to jib across the river and mouth of the bay near Melbourne and Sydney, Australia. She had raced others in her class and done well.

We got her loaded on the trailer and readied her for transport to Madronna Beach on Lake Washington. The closer we drew near the lake the more excited I became. The day was one Perry Como sang of when describing *"The Blue Skies in Seattle"*. There was an abundance of sailing and motor craft on the water. Jesse had me get out of the car and help direct his backing down to the platform.

Both of us took a last look at our completed work and were darn proud of her, even though we neglected to christen her with a bottle of champagne or a name and a title. She was so clean with new powder blue paint and mahogany trim to the top of her mast that gave her a regal finish. Even Jesse admitted she was a smart craft indeed!

We both put our life jackets on, but it finally dawned on us that we didn't know where I was going to sit.

The design had a four by two rectangular cutout section for a one-member crew to sit, sail and steer. What we did in retrospect was definitely wrong; nevertheless, he tied me to the mast where I sat out facing the bow. This was the ride of all rides as the lake was kicking up a fair amount. Every time he would steer so to hit the waves head on, I would be awash, inundated, foaming at the mouth. I craned my neck to see how he was doing. Never had I seen him in such a state of hilarity. He thought that was the funniest sight he had ever seen. Love and respect must have been present as I just laughed right along with him.

Today is the second anniversary of his death and I can still clearly hear his laugh, giggle and soft snort that day.

We weren't through yet, as he caught a squall and the wind to lose her and over she went. She was fairly easy to up right as she had a centerboard for us to place our weight on and up she came. Guess who got the last laugh seeing the skipper just soaking wet? That turned out to be our last sailing together, as he sold our boat shortly afterwards to one of his fellow seaman taking her back to Australia with him on his return voyage.

We mentioned that day a long time afterwards with sheer pleasure. It was a day to treasure, as all of our plans turned out exactly as we had hoped. The spray of the water and foam have been with me ever since.

Chapter 6

Up the Hill to Queen Anne High

There I was standing on the North East corner of Queen Anne and Mercer Street, out front of the Marqueen Apartments each morning, thumbing for a ride to the top of the hill to be at school on time. This usually worked, as there was this one man who knew all of us, who wore horn-rimmed glasses and a head of hair that had barely been brushed or combed before his departure each morning. He was amiable toward all of us and pulled over in his drab green four-door that we filled with anything from four to six of us guys. I remember his kindness, as he not only got us there in time, but dropped us at the west side entrance, for our early morning classes.

Later, my best buddy George got his license and started to drive his new black 50 four-door Chevy. This way we had wheels to get up that incline each morning. Sometimes, none of those methods worked, so I ran up the hill, and was on time for my first morning class.

We learned this hurriedly as it was considerably different now at Queen Anne, than the previous years. We had assigned classes a part of our class schedule, than at the old Warren Avenue Grade School, and I began to fit in rapidly in my eighth grade.

The friends of yesterday were already pulling away from each other due to interests, choices and activities. We were turning out for sports, clubs, and jobs after school and still saw one another from time to time. Times such as these brought a lot of experiences back even for a moment. This was the eighth grade and already the expectations were evident between 1954-55 at the age of thirteen.

The classes that stood out for me were those never frequented before, such as Mechanical Drawing with Mr. Bergman, whose name I share with total respect as a definite Bird. He was a slight built thinning man, who always wore a three-piece suit of grays and blues with a crisp collar and a tie with a tight knot. He was already graying and wore thin round glasses. One thing became evident, was he knew his subject. This drew us to realize, we could draw lines of perspective, parallel, and horizontal forming what became for some a professional leaning even today.

Mr. Bergman would periodically leave the classroom and all of us, including me, behaved horribly. While he was out of the class, our antics began much like a food fight. Instead, we began throwing paper, chalk, pencils, erasers, and finally took our drawing boards that we used as armor from flying items. This didn't get serious until we began to throw our protractors with the sharp end outward. Fortunately, I ducked down below my drawing desk just in time to miss my hair being parted.

Mr. Bergman reentered to find the chaos and all dispelled immediately. The pay off came for all of us! We exited at his command to the office where we convened with the Vice Principal, Dr. Cushman, who was a significant Bird, above us on his perch overlooking our behavior. He would get to the bottom of what did or didn't occur. It always amazed me how there would be such a rapid concurrence to join others on the esteemed Cushman Cleanup Committee.

Our duties consisted of picking up papers and cigarette butts on the school grounds. This more than confirmed my making sure my behavior would exhibit what it should have been all along.

There isn't a way I could forget Mrs. Simpson, of whom I have thought of many times over the years. She probably knew I was in love with her, and why not, as this was the year of the movie, *On The Waterfront* with Marlin Brando and Eve Marie Saint. Mrs. Miller was Eve Marie Saint's twin, I was sure, as I volunteered to any and all tasks for her. It was my first class in Art and I thoroughly enjoyed it.

The design of the building was '*Upstairs, Downstairs*', and down on the lowest level was Mr. Dates' Woodshop class. He was approximately 5'2" tall and seemed to be the same across. He was a good hunk of a man, who always wore his three quarter length shop coat. Mr. Dates had black, wavy hair, combed straight back, revealing his full face, usually with the countenance of a cheerful smile. We weren't in his class long until we fully knew why he was able to be in charge and control.

He had one basic premise that applied to all in his class. That was capsulated by seeing that every student had five hundred points equaling an "A" upon entering his class. The final semester grade depended on us, including our behavior, whether or not we followed the shop guidelines and the caliber of our work on assigned projects. He was the teacher of total clarity by saying, "It's entirely up to you, if you lose all or a portion of those points, know that will be your grade. However, if you want to earn those points back, there is a way."

All of us waited to hear how this might be done. He turned to his work cabinet and withdrew a shiny, lacquered, hard, wooden paddle, with a contoured shaped handle.

The details were louvered, drilled, cleanly, sanded and finished with a roll into the surface of the paddle, a good one-half inch thick for solid application. This was the medium of getting our lost points back in the book. Each stroke from the master teacher, Mr. Dates, was equal to a hundred points. After this implicit description we watched various members of our class lose one hundred, two hundred and some lost all five hundred points.

It didn't have to be administered all at one time, rather, was left to our choice, all, or one at a time.

My vivid memory was due to having lost three hundred points in one class session. Consequently, I made an appointment to see Mr. Dates after school that day. He asked me, "Do you want one or all today?"

I told him, "Let's clear the slate!" Mr. Dates was fair, as he did all he could to help me relax and assure me he would apply each with the same impact, but each meant I would have regained one hundred points. Never had I been so nervous as I followed his instructions of grabbing my knees and bending them slightly to take the blow.

He stepped back and said, "Are you ready?" I acknowledged, and the next thing I heard, was the whip of his wrist, the extension of his short muscular forearm let fly and, before I could imagine it, I felt and heard the crack of that fine implement across my butt. The sting was like an electric shock that reverberated to my toes over and over. Then he paused and said, "Are you sure you want another today?"

I thought, I had one hundred points restored, I might as well complete all three and walk, perhaps crawl, out of here with my three hundred points and my regained original grade of "A". I made sure he knew this, and braced for the second expression of his fairness in having a built in method to help us. I was sure I knew what the experience entailed, so I grabbed hold and "Wham", the second measure of fairness left me broken out in a cold sweat. Then Mr. D. checked with me a final time.

This time I was thinking what's one final blow after all I've taken the first two. I braced a final time, and I remembered thinking he said, each would be equal. I was sure the intensity was more each time. A final wind was felt just before that finely tuned instrument, impacted, the sorest butt I could have imagined. I nearly fainted and was caught by one of my fellow students. They asked me if I wanted to sit down for a moment. I declined, and took some stretching steps to let the heat dissipate. Mr. D. said, "Now that wasn't so bad was it?" He added, "You have all three-hundred points along with your other two-hundred to equal your original grade."

I can assure you, I walked the straightest path ever after that afternoon of deep knee bends, so to never take such a stance again.

Mr. Dates was a great teacher. We gained exposure that included working on the lathe where we made bowls, handles, and other refined wooden pieces such as lamp bases. We had a major project, on which I worked to present a coffee table, for mother and Jesse. There was just one problem. My table had a unique characteristic. It rocked as compared to a moderate see saw and brought many a laugh.

My Science teacher had previously played Minor or Major League Baseball, and along with presenting elements pertaining to our Science class, he would correlate principles of Science with the game of Baseball. He was another teacher I never forgot. He was a tall man with brownish, curly hair and wore clear plastic framed glasses and always wore a gray two-piece suit, with a white long sleeved shirt and matching tie.

The main reason I recall him was he explained the soundest reason for us not to smoke or engage in drugs. What stuck was a premise for me to follow from thereon. "If you were meant to have any foreign elements, inhaled into your lungs or bodies, you would have had bilging smoke present within your wonderful bodies in the beginning."

As is true for students in schools today, my schedule was quite enough, along with delivering papers, being promoted from route to route, and fulfilling all of my responsibilities on the home front.

New opportunities were discovered that eventually relieved me from delivering the evening newspapers. At first, I helped friends clean carpets and windows of their homes and apartments. Then, I located a job as the stockman at the neighborhood Rexall Drug Store. Along with said duties, I washed the outside windows, did janitorial work within the store, priced shelf items, kept the stock faced, and worked as a shipping receiving clerk in the afternoons after school all day.

My next job was at the corner newspaper shack.

I talked with my grandfather and his partners, and they took me on to help out at the Marqueen Garage on Saturdays. At first they had me clean the office and sweep the garage floor that was splintered and worn, from one end of the block to the other. Never had I held a handle of a push broom for such a long time as I did there. The greatest lesson learned while there was hearing my grandfather repeat, "The work is darn dirty, but it pays a good living."

I found working there in the worst of winter conditions and finishing by heading to christening my hands in the bucket of oily black solvent was not the way I wanted to earn my living.

Before leaving the hallowed halls, of where I learned and gained huge respect of the craft my grandfather and his partners provided for their customers, I made sure to express my sincere thanks to each member of the staff.

It is a certainty every one of them were and remain in my spirit, Birds, all in a line helping so many in need.

While there, I had the duties of providing a fleet of distributor trucks their regular oil and lubrication every Saturday. To say the least, that was a challenge, as my work had to be completed before leaving every Saturday.

When thinking of how I was able to fulfill each and every opportunity that came along, I did this and realized my course had the constant affronting of this unknown condition within my behavior. Needless to say, I would find days and even nights much more turbulent than all of my compatriots did I am sure. Highs and lows came and went as the seasons themselves.

I was able to secure a warmer, cleaner, suitable job as the stockman and the fountain cleanup man at the neighborhood Bartell Drug Store. Down the street was the A & P Grocery Store, where I was hired as a box boy and worked in the Produce and Dairy departments keeping the stock in good shape.

By now I was topping 6'2" tall, and was plain lean, probably due to all of the running back and forth from one job to the next.

My Coach and Physical Education teacher turned out to be a fine friend. It was really something while in Coach White's first Physical Education class after he took roll he made a point to refer to me as

"Moose". That tag became mine and he referred to me that way from that time onward.

Those classes were always challenging. The one I never forgot was when we were in teams and everyone was on his butt. Coach White threw a medicine ball in the center of the court. We played it similar to the game of soccer. The only difference was we had to remain on our butts throughout the game. There was no standing, only scooting as fast a we could, to move pushing with our hands and arms, and kicking the hefty ball from one end of the court to the other to achieve goals and points. Did that give us a real workout!

Jim Daily has been and remains a significant teacher and was a crowning Bird that helped turn the tide, affecting my thought of pursuing furthering education. You had to come to know him, as we did during our sophomore year in high school. I can still see him standing in front of the class with his suspenders that he wore every day. One day he shared with us why he chose to wear suspenders instead of a belt. His story called attention to his father, who made him know wearing suspenders was a must to retaining tight abdomen muscles in the years ahead. There wasn't one snicker.

Our classes were rolling along when he assigned us to select a favorite book of our choice. We were to read it and write a book review. Reading wasn't my favorite, but was about to become more than a favorite, as I found Ernest Hemingway's, *The Old Man and The Sea.* From the moment I picked up the book, I began reading and became enthralled in the story line to the point of carrying and reading the book everywhere I went.

Gerry Bradley

I knew that evening was our families' night to join my grandparents for dinner. Just as you guessed, I took the book and continued to read it before and during our dinner. This was something for me as we were dining at our favorite fish house, Crawford's, down on Elliott Way. What could have been more fitting, to be reading about this, the largest fish "I've ever caught", and looking at the Captain's Plate, I had always ordered.

Jesse introduced me to a Champion Billiards player from Chicago, down at the Marine Firemen's Union. He taught me about the game called Pool. I was clumsy when it came to handling the cue stick. When I first met him, I would no more have thought of featuring him and his life in a future assignment as this book review than could be imagined.

Our family was conversing as usual, where I would have been joining in, now I was bent over the print, captive to Hemingway's style and the story line about this old man and his triumph he had finally caught.

We were ordering our dessert, which I never forgot. We always had a light dessert, which usually was a dish of sherbet. Everyone specified the flavor they wanted. In short, the waitress brought our dishes of sherbet to our table. We were dipping our spoon in, and grandma let out a shriek, due to there being a fly frozen in its place in her lime sherbet. She said to my grandfather, "Will you look at that, well will you let them know about this?" She continued loudly to bicker over our previous conversation and my in- depth reading, which I had to give up on as we were going to leave with no intention of paying the bill after this grave matter on behalf of the fly misguiding his landing. As usual, my grandfather smoothed over the upheaval with the manager before we left. But the friction continued, for we all heard, "Nothing like this ever occurred when I was a waitress all the years before."

The day the assignment was due I turned my paper in along with my fellow students. It was a couple of days later that Mr. Daily stood in front of the rest of the class and began to share the results. We thought he was finished and he said, "There was one paper that stood out above all of the others; and I can tell you, the writer of this paper exhibits, he will be an up and coming writer in the future." By now all of us were just plain curious, even to hear one of the girls pipe up and say, "Who is it?" Mr. Daily said, "It's Gerald's paper." Then, another asked if it was, and he said, "No, it's Gerald Kent's, and I'm going to ask him to come up and read or share his paper with our class." I had never been asked to do anything like this before, but now I walked to the front of the class and he held out my paper to me. All eyes and ears were on me as I read the entire paper. Afterwards, their comments were nothing but, "what a wonderful piece of writing it was." To think that this one English teacher had recognized and given me recognition of the effort made. That moment continued to ring down the hallways as my fellow students exited our class.

Before we were dismissed, Mr. Daily asked me to explain to the class why I took the direction I had taken; I shared my background about my friend from the Marine Firemen's Union, how he taught me billiards and that he lived much the same as the old man in *The Old Man and the Sea* in an old shanty, down on the Dwamish River. When they heard this, they could see how I came to write the paper.

Here was an absolute turnabout for me. From that point forward, I considered continuing my education.

What I learned from this was the importance this would be carried much like a torch, to light my future students, efforts as they progressed in their educations and beyond.

It was winter and we knew from the shipping schedule, Jesse was on his way home. He arrived as scheduled, to find one of the severest snowstorms that turned into more than previous winters, as it lasted for weeks.

Before, what happened, I want to remind you that the same upheaval continued throughout my life time; I never understood or grasped why I had to ask this man, Jesse, talk to me, much worth share events having to do with my activities. While all of this occurred, there was always the drink and the cork being loosened in our house. As if this wasn't enough, he and mother joined each other in their drinking and partying into the night and mornings. The scene would always take a turn in regards to his or their treatment toward each other or the two of us boys.

That was when it became caustic and louder than usual. I have already explained the changing of the wheel and the control that occurred which was totally baffling. As if I didn't have enough to separate, and not have any inclination of what was brewing within me at the same time.

Then this event took place, as I now share with you. Sure, I was between the seventh and eighth grade. You might think, surely he was old enough to deal with the maturation level, which was slower for me in dealing with this subject, even though I was at the same time as discussed, much like George, "An old man", as in *It's A Wonderful Life,* caught between all about to be conveyed.

Saturday rolled around and, between getting from one job to another I finally made it home with snow nearly up to my knees. I went inside and started to undress, and Jesse red faced, giving me all clues I needed said, "Come with me" and he led me to the car. He added, "Get in I have something I want to talk about." I had no idea as to what he wanted to talk about especially in this manner. This was so unlike him. Here we had gone out, and he opened the doors of our Crown Victoria, sitting there buried in the snow. When we got inside the car, we could barely see outside, as the snow had more than blanketed our car. He began by saying or asking about school and that was rare by itself. He even asked about my jobs, and the sports teams at Queen Anne. Then, he asked if I had a girl friend, or if I was dating. As usual, the discussion was question and answer style, which was his style.

I was as lost as our car was under the blanket of fallen snow. Jesse continued and said, "Well if you're not dating yet, I know you will be sooner than you might believe." "I know you don't think you will think of certain things, but believe me you will, and you'll ... and he reached across the dash board bumping my knee, and reached in the glove box. Then he withdrew this paper sack all folded. He went on and said, "Here you might need these, and I know you know what they are. Be sure and use one of these when you do get the idea."

Before I could reply, he turned and opened the door, got out, and walked back to the house, stumbling across the street, in the drifts of snow. Somehow, I lost something so precious due to this so-called talk. I lost what I had of any innocence I might have had.

I sat there under that blanket giving me what was left of insulation from the world. I kind of knew or thought I knew what was in my lap, cradled, waiting for my unfolding the sack, and withdrawing the thin box, that read, Trojan, wrapped in cellophane. I couldn't and didn't open that box and placed it back in the paper sack, and gently folded it as before. I remained sitting there in a state of shock for sometime afterwards. There were no words to say, only disbelief, that this was handled as it was, and the very thought of the way he treated the subject, as coldly and bluntly as the snow and ice surrounding me, was something that left me with a kind of chill that never thawed out for the rest of my life.

Finally, I was able to gather myself enough to get out of the car, close the door, and see the snow jarred off the car onto the ground in clumps. I walked resolutely back into the house, where it was supposed to be warmer. Neither, Jesse or I, acknowledged anything from the moments, nor did I have a lot to say to mother. I walked into my room and opened my dresser drawer and placed the package in a corner, where it stayed untouched for many years.

I don't think I ever forgave him of this hurtful act committed that day in that magnificent snowstorm we had received overnight. This wintering experience shared would always be with me. I had no idea how deeply it had permeated my soul.

All that occurred was to put such special times on hold until he joined us. We were doing as we always did in our family for the coming Holiday season. A difference from our Thanksgivings, leading to Christmas would be having Jesse with us, and not "out on a ship" away from our family.

Our family anticipated, planned, shopped, and wrapped all of the gifts, which became a family effort involving each member.

Through all of that happening was that time, when I as my friends, and fellow students, were changing within all that was deep-seated inside me totally was being tapped beyond any persons belief. This included, reaching out to touch base, where there seemed to be much more in ways of peace and true acceptance, a place where there could be a real home, as I knew was possible, without the disharmony in my own. That view of our home was anything but that described. The home of my heart was constantly in a state of disruption it seemed at every turn every day.

It was here, that I peer back through the prism of glass to recall what it was like one day returning from a day of school. Ironically, both my brother and I were walking in about the same time. Mother was sitting in a chair in the kitchen. We said, "Well another day of school was"…and she blurted out loud, "What's so good about the day, or anything for that matter," Neither of us knew what brought this on at the time. All we were doing was being friendly and including her, then, she continued, yelling at the top of her lungs, "I'm just fed up, nothing is worth it, not even staying alive," when she said this we were stunned, but she exclaimed loudly, "You kids aren't worth it and you haven't been worth it for a long time!" I still remember replying to her, "Mother you don't really mean that, you're just upset." And she went on, "You know I'm going in to the bathroom to hang myself!" I ran into the bathroom to see the rope already tied onto the shower rod. I reached up and quickly untied the rope and rolled it up and hid it. At this, we both started crying, pleading that she wouldn't do anything like that. My pleading, and sobbing, trying to get her to change her mind, was all I could do for the moment. This was such a shock for both of us boys, yet the screaming continued from her, and we were equally crying and pleading with her to not do anything like that.

Both of us through our tears and pleading for her to calm down, and know this wouldn't do any of us any good, brought her to finally quit screaming, and we were able to get her to sit down for a moment.

Now, you can see vividly how out of balance anyone with this God awful condition can get and be far beyond any balanced kind of behavior.

The very thoughts and events that occurred were that that remained in my heart, and I felt as if I was there again writing this event down as I'm doing. It brought me to weep for all that happened that afternoon, even to this day.

Our evening was beyond calm, or quiet, rather, we reached out to mother to help anyway we could. That night my brother and I completed the dishes without one squawk. We were trying with all of our hearts to keep mother as calm as we could, and sure enough she settled down, and nothing more came of this frightening afternoon that none of us ever forgot in all the years ahead.

After the diagnosis already mentioned came the time of resuming my dealing with all ahead, to include therapy. Most important was, the adjustment of my level, so to live a functional life style into the future days, weeks, months and leading into a vast number of years. More ups and downs were mine that confused those about me.

The way mother lashed out on that day many years ago, would be far from the last as it continued in one form after another. Each, seemingly had the same deadening effect upon our lives, that carried through and through toward each of us within our home.

There was to be an unveiling out there in time in all of our lives, undoubtedly in many of yours, that would be a "revelation", empowering millions suffering the *Snake Pits,* that held so many for so long, who in truth didn't need that, not to mention the fearsome "Electric Shock" treatments that were administered. Imagine how this immense finding, on behalf of research scientists would lead to a mere diagnosis, open door therapy, or even group therapy, furthering treatment that individuals could decide to take just as their other daily medications that comforted them from one malady to another. Exactly, a miracle!

Before taking another step forward in this story, I have to say the following: What I desired the most was to be a boy, to have the privilege of boyhood, and foremost to know this was true for that day and that time. As mentioned, there was little or no time for this though. I found I had jumped into the arena of where what I grew to realize was constant "change".

Chapter 7

A Move to Milwaukie, Oregon

All of the ties that were more than binding while having lived there all of those years were to be left behind. We were going to move and start my ninth grade year in high school, back in Jesse's, hometown of Milwaukie, Oregon.

This was painful, for I was engrossed in the community on so many levels. That didn't concern either of my parents, only the stance that we were moving and that was that. What rang through this constant shifting from one place on the map to another was to hear mother declare, "When in Rome do as the Roman's do." Within our eyes were priceless relationships being said goodbye to: jobs I had secured, school work I was working to establish a solid record toward and our home during those years.

Upon arriving in Milwaukie, Oregon, we found this little house not very far from the high school. I had a bedroom with knotty pine walls and ceiling, and we had a skimpy side yard. I still remember putting my football uniform and cleats on, so I could get out and practice my stance, start off the line lifting my knees high and moving those short yards across the lawn readying for football try outs.

Jesse and I had our first real battle there! It wouldn't be our last. He announced, "If you think you're going to go out for sports and not work, and think that I'm going to give you spending money you have another thing coming to you." This was much more than a pronounced announcement, rather what would be the lay of the land from that time onward.

I made up my mind on the spot that I would turn out for sports and work also. This brought flaming anger from within me, upon realizing our family had been treated as a pawn on a board. Long before, I knew I was I called a "principalian". It was apparent we would continue meeting the beck and call of Jesse from thereon. And to think, he had the guts to expect from us as he did, yet resolved all by stating there would be no aid or help.

During the year I turned out for football and basketball. I found in both cases the timing wasn't quite right. I still don't know how the Coach thought I was right for playing guard of all positions, but that was what I kept working to achieve.

There was one throwback to my younger years. I was hit in the face with a baseball bat. That incident and the eye surgery that I had to have in the second grade, related to what was happening to me trying to play football. As a guard you have to block out the opposing linemen.

Along with tackling drills, we were practicing tackling. The coach wanted us to tackle one another coming full force at each other. The protective option left me tackling and the back would run right through my arms. I was going head to head, but just as I was about to make the tackle, I'd close my eyes.

Even though the coach was exasperated with my inability to accomplish the tackling assignments, he had the Assistant Coach work with me, one on one, to instill needed skills. I finally gained the strength to strike out, and bring the runner off his feet. When he was sure I had it, he took me back to the Head Coach who was blockheaded as his haircut.

Gerry Bradley

We had one member on our team who was big as a tree trunk. The Coach had us line up against each other. First, it was my turn to run through him. I did just that and he found he was grabbing the same air I had before. This was more than he could deal with, so once again the Coach lined us up against each other and the mission was mine to tackle him as he ran toward me. Needless to say, we took our stances across the line from each other and broke the scrimmage line. I saw this hulk coming at me, as I had broken a grimacing pace and just as he was to collide in my extended arms, I reached out and closed my eyes and went slamming down on the turf. He had galloped beside me; the Coach threw his ball cap on the ground along with some scalding adjectives with sheer disgust.

There was another fact that I was dealing with everyday that was worsening. To thoroughly prove my awkward stage, we were doing drills in the stands running the steps and to this day. I don't know how I could have fallen through the bleachers scraping the inside of my right knee. This abrasion was deep enough to scab over each day and was scraped off by the end of the practice session.

Fortunately for me, our neighbor lady happened to be a nurse. I finally went over so she could take a look at this abrasion one evening after practice. She was stunned as she saw how the infection was well on its way to setting in, bringing her to cleanse the wound thoroughly and to hear her say, "Your football days are over, as this is very serious and must be taken care of from here on." That was one nurse I didn't question and the very next day I turned in my gear trying to explain the cause to the Assistant Coach. He really understood where as the Coach muttered under his breath as I walked out of the locker room.

I can't be remiss, by passing all whom I played and studied with, while pursuing both instrumental and vocal music. You are the instructors, coaches, and mentors who made phenomenal marks on me. I would never have received any of these opportunities had it not been for one band teacher that cared enough to take me on a tour in the music room, housing all the old clunkers. There was one battered silver sousaphone sitting on the top shelf gathering dust, awaiting one such as myself to come along and reach up and pull the horn down long enough to check it out. More important was, my taking the mouth piece and placing it over my lips, to realize I had found a much better fit that led me to years of enjoyment, studies, competitions, new hats, and vocal music, including years of voice training.

The instrument was more fitting for my aperture. I spent my first semester during my lunch hour with Dick Hammond, the band teacher, learning to play the horn. The second semester, I became the first chair tubbiest and had excellent opportunities to compete on the state level, at the University of Oregon. I continued playing through my Junior College days.

You know how some years seem to crawl along until the year has swiftly passed? This was such a year that included finding work, at the barbeque pit restaurant down by the river. The job kept me for the most part down below in the kitchen, washing pots and pans, peeling more potatoes for fries than I could count.

At the same time my mother was working as a waitress. The reason I recall her being there was due to my seeing her again as I had back at the "Chit-Chat Café" years before. I vividly recall one afternoon while I was up to my elbows in potato peelings. I heard this man sitting behind the counter making advances toward my mother. He grabbed her by the arm; I came flying out of the kitchen telling him, "Keep your hands off my mother." The owner butted in and said, "You can get out of here, after all the customer is always right." I told him, "Clean your own pots and while you're at it, peel those potatoes at the same time." Mother pleaded with me to quit and go home. She wanted me to know she would be all right. I took that ridiculous paper chef's hat and apron and threw them in the owner's face as I slammed out the door.

I am glad this anger surfaced, as it seemed to do much more than flash, at times I would more than simmer, specifically, dealing with out and out frustration, stress, and heightened agitation. In each case I would either withdraw totally or fume in a slamming behavior. And it always seemed to be true as to the constant agitation.

I was still in the midst of attending classes through the week. The football season was well underway and I was playing in the Pep Band at those cold, wet games to be followed by the school dances.

My study sessions continued, as did my polished skills by all senses of the word.

I found the dance lessons during the school period to be just what I needed. I don't know how I struck up a conversation with one of the Cheer Leaders, she seemed to like me and set out to teach me to dance. We became good friends all the time knowing she was going with one of the Senior Yell Leaders and a star football player of our school.

Due to all of the transferring all the way into my senior year, I perceived I was a lot like Sal Mineo, in *Rebel Without A Cause,* as I was somewhat lost in the constant shuffle from place to place through the years. And as I reflect, all of this was more than cause for me to flare as mentioned.

Afterwards we were on our way back to our classes for the afternoon. I always looked forward to our band class. Then I turned to my English class.

Miss Morgan, my English teacher, a tall blond, dressed in her sweater tops and her flaring skirts, stood there explaining prepositional phrases, clauses, punctuation and interrelated elements of grammar. She seemed to radiate with a sincere smile toward all of us.

The real memory was I remained after each class to help her anyway possible. Our classroom was down stairs and the windows were the type that swung out and upward, which she left open for ventilation.

One afternoon she asked, "Would you try to close the windows?" I replied, "I'll give it a try," as she was unable to do so herself. I stepped up to the window, and knew the skill of turning my palm upwards, so to be able to break the stickiness of the armatures holding it tight. I hit it once, twice, and the third time I miss hit it, and a cracking of the window followed with my wrist being cut in the process. The cut was deep enough to cause it to bleed; Miss Morgan let out a screech at the sight of the blood. I didn't find her much help, as she seemed to go into shock, but the scream was cause for another student to come running to help and give me first aid.

Afterwards, I walked over to our family doctor's office as they were expecting me. There I found out what a waiting room was. The afternoon continued and I sat waiting and waiting, and I began to hear the staff closing the office. I stuck my head outside of the door making sure they knew I was still there. Were they ever embarrassed, and I knew if I hadn't done that, I would have spent the night waiting for the doctor to treat me. Consequently, the doctor came back and tended to the cut.

Even in my bound state, I inquired as to my being able to deliver the Oregonian Newspaper. Talk about timing. The winter that comes up off the Columbia River Gorge hit with a gust overnight. There was no way I could forget, how I was out the next morning in the dark deep drifts trudging up those hills, delivering newspapers on my route.

I couldn't help but think how Jesse had offered to go out with me one morning offering driving lessons. Both he and mother had been out for the evening and returned in the late morning hours, to greet me upon my rising to deliver the papers on my route. Of all times for Jesse to say, "I think I'll go out with you this morning on your route." I was totally surprised, to see him walk out with me with the snow on the street, and say to me, "hop in.". My route was down on First Avenue and its parallel streets. He knew this and didn't hesitate while driving me to collect my papers at the paper shack, then to proceed at my instruction as to the beginning of my route. What became my memory of that morning was hearing him say, "Pull over." Here we were headed down toward City Center on First Avenue. He blurted out, "It's time that you learn to drive," and I replied, "I can't, I haven't got my permit or my license." He repeated, "That's alright, you want to learn how don't you." Of course I wanted to learn, but here on the snow-covered streets during that early morning hour didn't seem to be the right time. His insistence brought me to change seats with him and he became the passenger, rather driving teacher, and I was in the driver's seat. He coaxed me to go ahead and pull out onto the street and continue driving through my route along the way. As you might imagine, I looked back to make sure no one was behind so the way was clear. Believe me I was timid, and slowly drove forward, listening to Jesse tell me to continue. Then he added, "You're doing just fine." What got me was, that morning of my first driver's lesson resulted in my feeling the assurance that I could do it and it was terrific to hear Jesse, my instructor say, "You did a great job and you'll be able to get your license soon and drive on your own." I was amazed at the entire situation, the evidence being the result of delivering the route in half or better the time than all the times before, whether during the afternoons or on the Sunday morning route. Jesse proved to be patient and the same great leader, or teacher, during the total experience. Remember the sailing he and I had shared together? Well that morning together was similar and one I didn't forget.

Now, I was doing everything possible to get up those icy, snowy streets, to deliver the newspapers on time there in the neighborhood in Milwaukie, Oregon where Jesse had grown up and gone to school.

Winter continued throughout the area. Just as soon as the thaw began, I brought my Sousaphone home with me; I still remember how understanding my mother was when hearing her say, "You aren't going to keep that horn in this house, just take it out to the garage if you must." So I bundled up and took my horn out to the garage and continued to practice.

Once again, here was a more than understanding reaction on her behalf, at the very thought of my trying to better my path for the future. I didn't bring it home anymore after that! Her behavior was enough to thaw out any storm and ironically it did.

One classmate told me how he earned his money by caddying over at the Waverly Golf and Country Club. So the next Saturday I joined him and he showed me the way to the Caddy Shack.

There, I received my preliminary instructions and soon found myself carrying heavy leather bags of a foursome for my first eighteen holes. I can still remember what a long day that was as I dragged home afterwards. I received some good tips, though, I decided I would be back on Sunday and realized I just needed to get in shape. Those I caddied for were patient, since they knew I was a new caddy.

I remembered how two men I was carrying clubs for came over and revealed I was causing a shadow, as I was standing holding the pin on the wrong side of the pin. Another party yelled good and loud as I had already walked down toward the green, and heard "Fore", and I looked up and saw this white dot flying toward me; I fell flat on my belly to have the ball pass where I'd been standing. From then on, I remained with my party. Those I caddied for included a noted Grocery Store C.E.O. and his associates. On Saturday afternoons I caddied for their wives. Consequently, at days end, I was exhausted.

From this experience, I knew the day would come when I would be playing this wonderful game with a certainty.

Before school was out, came the moment of reflection when some of my friends invited me down to Oswego Lake across from the school grounds.

What they did was swim out to this old timber raft. I told them I couldn't swim that well. They told me all they did was dive off the raft after they got out there. So I thought it would be safe and went with them. We swam out to the raft and after we were on board, they started pushing each other off the raft. They were wild and began to shift their weight to tip the raft upside down. I kept diving off and when I would get back on board, they would tip it over again. I knew the only way was to dive off to prevent the weight of the raft from falling on me.

The last time I dove off, I swallowed something foreign, sewage, or something gross, and I began to slip down. As I sunk, I kicked with all of my strength to resurface, and clawed at the water with sheer desperation. I surfaced and yelled waving my arms for help. They ignored me and I went down a second time. Now I was panicking and trying with all of my might to surface. They laughed at me and continued their antics, dove off the raft and down I went this time to and never forget, vividly recalling every aspect of my life before reaching the surface for the third time. I screamed, and was flailing my arms above the water, which made them realize I was drowning. All of them jumped in to pull me out of the lake, which came so close, to claiming my life.

I never forgot what it was like when they pulled me from the water and laid me on the surface of the raft. My body shook and quaked on the raft's surface. Some of the guys were panicking, jumping in the water, swimming for shore as fast as they could go, leaving me on the raft.

I screamed for them to not leave me out on the raft alone. Finally, two of them swam back with a long two by four for me to grab hold of and kick to shore. None of those guys owned up to the horrible moment, instead left the timber and turned leaving me with the plight of grabbing hold and kicking to shore. Just to get back into the water was more than I could do, yet I knew that because they were out of sight, I had to or I would be stranded on that raft to intercede the Willamette River. I dipped down into the water sliding away from the raft grabbing hold of the board, pushed off and kicked more furiously than ever before in my life. When

I reached shore I walked out of the water; I didn't go near water for years I'll assure you.

There was irony in that incident, as I received a summer position at the Junior High School pool, where I could have worked all the way through my years in high school every summer. That would inevitably lead me to either a neighboring college or University to further pursue my degree.

Chapter 8

A Summer Not To Forget

Before the end of the school year arrived we knew we were returning to Seattle.

First, we had to see Seaside, Oregon where Jesse had worked while in high school at the Standard Station.

We stopped atop the bluff at Ecola State Park, overlooking the sprawling beaches of Cannon Beach, where we saw those driving their cars down the beach by the mile.

Ecola State Park was fogged in, bringing us to take cautious steps so not to frighten the deer that we could have fed with our hands.

From that moment, which was comparable to the moments back in that forest in Lake City, I was still able to make some sense of all of these moves we were making. It was a shock for my grandparents when we returned to, say the least, as my brother and I would be staying with them for the summer.

Jesse and mother were headed for Southern California where he was accepting a full time position selling cigars. This was a transfer from the work he had been doing while we were in Milwaukie, Oregon.

That was the summer where we helped out any way we could, including helping with the weeding of tiers of a rock garden. Furthermore, we gave a hand when it came to shopping for groceries, which took quite a lot to feed us two boys.

My brother and I walked to catch the bus and make way to Madronna Beach on Lake Washington for the day. After our day splashing, practicing our swimming, eating hotdogs, drinking Pepsis, having snow cones and always finding we had a stain of grape or lime on our faces, we returned home.

I made sure to return in time for I had to work at the paper stand each weekend. My paper stand was a faded green newspaper shack where I stood selling the Seattle Times, New York Times, Wall Street Journal, and the Post Intelligencer. I sold papers to those on foot and those stopping their cars long enough to roll their windows down to make an exchange. I always thought of them as the whisking part of the trade. I could hear them slipping into position, on the rain soaked pavement, aligning themselves to gather the latest news of the day and whisk back into traffic.

I learned lessons that summer never thought of before. One such lesson was on a Saturday morning. We had just returned from buying our groceries; I was carrying groceries down the back walk with my grandfather Henry behind me. My grandmother was walking to my side and I didn't think. I cleared my throat and spat across her walking path. I always knew Henry had a low voice of authority, but never like what I heard that moment. He said, "Young man, do you know what you did?" I wasn't really sure, I thought how I had spit and knew I was in real trouble. He commenced to chew on me up one side and down the other as to what does not happen, especially before a woman, much worse across my grandmother's path. I fully knew what he had been conveying and immediately apologized to my grandmother.

Before the summer was over I helped Henry rebuild the front porch of their home. I hadn't done anything of this caliber of work since roofing years before. I recall what a satisfying feeling he and I had over the finished job, just as my dad and I had all those years ago.

During the entire summer, I walked and caught the bus to the paper stand, where I spent considerable time in knowing it was nearly time for dinner. Sure enough, there was my grandma and Henry rolling up with that pleasing grin on their faces. They had dinner all prepared for me; I can still remember tearing the foil away shortly after they rolled on to take their evening ride or return home. The overture was one of love and respect as they made the effort to bring me such a dinner every evening while I was there, pedaling the papers. Furthermore, it was the same as sitting down to the fine meals prepared by my grandmother, as the very same wonderful ingredients were there for me to munch on and pass the papers to my customers as well. It never failed that the meal included the meat and potatoes, baked rolls, vegetables and milk to drink along with either a fine slice of cake or pie. That definitely fortified me for the rest of the evening before turning for home.

Before we knew it, we would be boarding the bus together, two brothers bound for Southern California. We both told grandma and Henry how grateful we were for their caring for us all summer. We boarded the Greyhound to Santa Ana, California where we met the folks at their new home.

Upon arrival we were met by both of them. Jesse was telling us of the heat and the constant sunshine in Southern California. They didn't dally along the way. They were excited for the moment telling us all that was here in this area. We were tired from the trip and wanted to rest. As usual Jesse had other activities in mind for us. As we grew older the beck and call always seemed to be there, bringing more confusion and certainly disruption for us, at each point of time and place. What no one knew, including me, was all of this constant upheaval was really the last thing I needed, or for that matter, at any time in the future in my life. Nevertheless, there seemed to be more at every turn in the road.

Two major elements were a must and needed to be fulfilled every day. The first was to insure, that I had ample physical activity every day, the other was to be certain to get my daily sleep.

These are as vital for those that have Bi-Polar Mood Swing Disorder as living an organized structured life style. That would have been a wonderful help in the future years that lay ahead.

It wasn't long after we arrived and mother introduced us to their neighbors, which included this woman and her daughter. The daughter and I were the same age and liked each other from the start.

I didn't let any time slide by, rather hit the street immediately the next morning, to search for a job. Along with searching for work, Jesse took us with him on the road while he was selling. He wanted to show us Laguna Beach, and the San Juan Capistrano Mission, the orange groves, and beach tours as well.

The next morning I was out early and returned around one that afternoon, to exclaim I had been accepted for a position at the Sears and Roebuck store. They laughed at my enthusiasm, telling me it didn't matter because we were leaving for Seattle the next morning.

I found out afterwards, that Jesse had quit his job due to a dispute with the manager and he would be shipping out in the near future.

The shock wave was something I never became accustomed to; after all that had happened you would think I would have. Such agitation was precisely what I found out years later was anything but the best for me. What would have proven best would have been to have much more stability, and the opportunity to place my feet on the ground, which would have helped immensely as I dealt with all within my very being.

Soon after the finds I realized that the same agitation, disruption, unsettled state of living or its results triggered, behaviors that accompany all, with Bi-Polar Mood Swing Disorder.

Something was setting in or in truth had been for some time from all the events that were so unsettling. If they had not, they would over this trip up the coast highway.

When you took a trip with Jesse, it was always one way, his way, with few or any stops in mind.

To travel with him required holding the whole way; even to think of stopping to go to the restroom was more than he could stand.

This particular trip was more like a streamline train out of control. Late the first day he finally reluctantly stopped so we could go to the restroom. We ate greasy fried chicken and we slid back into the back seats of the car and were off like a blaze in the early evening hours into the night. It was the night of all nights! We were all sicker than we had been in years. Would he stop? Absolutely not! He kept driving into the night of all nights on the ever shifting, and changing, highway. He finally stopped! When he opened the car doors we rolled out of the back seats so sick, which began long before any available sacks were found and used. All three of us, including mother were sick, from that chicken dinner we had before.

After we left the shoreline, it was the last time we would set our feet on the beach.

Ahead was a Greyhound bus which he was determined to stay with on every hairpin curve. We kept the windows down and hung our heads outside, to contend with this maniac behind the wheel. He finally had to forego keeping the same pace through the day as the bus in front of us.

Upon arriving at my grandparents, they were baffled as to our, return.

I made up my mind I would never put any others through what we had experienced. Furthermore, it would be a long time before I rode anywhere with him after this kind of treatment. What I was left with was a question. Were we only to be a Bedouin family while together?

Imagine that as a boy even attempting to settle down, study, put any form of roots down long enough to feel we might settle at long last was anything but possible. It would have proven a miraculous moment indeed had we remained long enough for another day, week, or month, not to mention year.

Chapter 9

Back On The Hilltop

The entire journey north brought us back to where we had been.

Lower Queen Anne Hill became home, for me when my family moved to 217 West Republican Street in 1952. I was eleven.

Our house had a peaked roof with gray and black composition shingles on the outside walls; the porch was painted gray and the top panel of the door had a stain glass window along with a brass doorbell that had to be turned for the ring to be heard inside.

In those years, I explored the base of the hill; the shops and shopkeepers, became more than business people. They were more like family friends.

Green's Tavern, a historical log cabin, sat on the corner of West Republican and Queen Anne Avenue North. Directly across the street was Chick's Shoe Shop. Chick was approximately 5'10" tall with broad shoulders and muscular arms that testified to his former power, in his younger days in the ring. He always wore plastic framed glasses down on his nose as he did his work. Everyone always knew he was friendly to all who entered his shop. Framed photographs and posters hung showing him in various prizefights. He was Greek, dark complexioned, and beginning to show gray at his temples.

Next to his shop was the Uptown Theatre on Queen Anne Avenue owned by a woman who I'm afraid all of us kids drove crazy on the weekends with our shenanigans. She grimaced every Friday evening knowing upon our arrival we would throw our long legs over the seats in front of us. Some of the guys headed for the balcony, while the rest of us spread throughout the theatre to yell out comments and make squeals and groans during the film. We filled up on popcorn and candy; afterwards, we would walk directly a cross Queen Anne Avenue to the Freeze to grab a milkshake, hamburger, fries and visit among ourselves before heading home.

Just up from the Uptown Theatre was Cathay Gardens, our favorite Chinese restaurant where our family met and enjoyed excellent food.

Down from the newspaper shack on Mercer Street was my barber. Bert knew from the start how to cut my hair. He would cut away and talk with me and revealed his interest in my activities at Queen Anne High School. Years later I heard of his passing. What saddened me most was I never told him that he looked like another barber who became a famous vocalist, Perry Como.

On the corner of Mercer Street and Queen Anne Avenue I worked at the Rexall Drug Store where I washed windows in the coldest months of the year. I can still feel how cold it was as I dipped the squeegee into the water.

On the same side of the street on Queen Anne Avenue, Annie and Johnny, who owned the shoe repair shop, were our good friends. They were wonderful people. Annie was always chic in her sweaters and skirt combinations, seemingly always with her hands on both hips. She sparkled with her make-up on to the hilt, the eyeliners absolutely perfect; and she was usually chewing gum. Out would come Johnny, her husband, with his stained apron. He had black, graying, sweptback hair with an oily look, tanned skin and a sweeping mustache. Both Johnny and Annie weren't much more than five feet tall. Johnny was an avid fisherman; his trophies and sports photographs hung on the wall revealing the weight of his catch over the years.

Where on the corner of Roy Street and Queen Anne Avenue was the store that sold bicycles along with all their regular services: selling tires, mounting, replacing mufflers, etc.? I remember it was the store where I pointed out the bicycle I wanted and, as you guessed, that bicycle was mine that Christmas.

Directly across the street was the Marqueen Apartments, a large brick building where families resided to be close to their work and downtown. Around the corner on Mercer Avenue was the Marqueen Garage, a big barn like structure with a wooden floor that made a slapping board on board sound as clients rolled in for service.

Across Mercer Street and Queen Anne Avenue was the Van de Kamp's Bakery, which enticed passersby on their walks up and down the Avenue.

The seagulls were soaring to their highest heights and would drop from the sky lighting for more morsels in sight. On the block of Mercer Street and First Avenue North, Bartell Drugs served lunches, coffee, milkshakes and ice cream leading shoppers into the photo department, the ladies fragrance section and other departments that met the need of the shoppers from about the Uptown area.

One day I would work there, as a stockman.

I was also a future employee of the A & P Grocery Store on the corner of First Avenue North and Republican Street.

Across from the Uptown Theatre was Charles Sabin's clothing store. Our family traded for years. A few steps away inside of the Mecca

Café, reminded me of those aisles I walked while on board **The Empire Builder.**

Above, was a network of electrical wires to which the trolleys were attached, buzzing to our ventures or to my friends' homes on the various tiers of Queen Anne Hill. While sitting in the trolley you couldn't help but peer out the windows yet hear above the background the conversations of all of the people riding to their destinations. Sometimes, if the driver took a corner not quite right, the armatures would disconnect. When this happened, the driver gathered his heavy-duty gloves, ran back to the rear and grabbed hold of the cables, reconnecting the armatures with the wires above. Then he ran back and took his seat, closed the expanding doors and we were buzzing on our way again.

What really hit me was, the fact that all of the thoughts of familiarity came like the same rapid-fire thought process that I vividly remembered when nearly drowning in Milwaukie, Oregon.

The patterns were revealed, in the behaviors practiced our household. The constant switching of cars on the tracks as we continued to move up and down the coast in pursuit of ships, ports of call and sporadic jobs taken by Jesse.

That wasn't so in all cases as we were engrossed in all of our studies and vast opportunities offered and accepted.

This was my sophomore year at Queen Anne High School. Soon after returning, I got back in touch with my friends of yesterday. They were very surprised to hear I had returned, as they were more than certain we were either in Oregon or California. Change was ever present in our household, as none of us knew where we were half of the time.

It was during that year that I found my life was becoming much more social. Classes included, Mr. Daily's English class where he recognized my effort. From there, he put me in touch with the Student Teacher, who gave me additional instruction before class writing poetry.

I'll bet as you read on you're able to see I felt more at home while in school than any other place or setting.

At the same time, I continued the work I accomplished on the tuba while in Oregon. I signed up for the school band and the concert band. It was a short period of time afterwards that the band teacher asked to see me after class. He began talking to me about my becoming the bands Drum Major and explained what this meant and what I needed to do to be ready for the assignment. He gave me the instruction books, whistle, and baton to be used for the assignment.

I knew the perfect place to learn these commands. Once again, I returned to the haven of yesterday, Kinnear Park, down on the lower level. I still vividly remember walking proudly to the park with book, baton, and whistle in my hand. Upon arriving I walked further down into the base of the park where we had previously slid on our bikes. Now the assignment was a serious one, which I was determined to learn rapidly before returning to our band class.

I took my book and laid it out on the ground anchored by two rocks so the pages wouldn't flit and disturb my attacking each position sequentially. First I read them and was sure I had a good understanding of each. Then, I followed each with the baton and whistle commands. As I began to grasp each command I continued to practice each phase to have them engrained in my mind. I returned and by Sunday I was gaining competence to report to our band Director that I was ready to accept his directions.

He asked me to show him the commands, before any of the band members arrived. He was quite impressed at my mastering them as I did in such a short time.

Before class was over that day he announced he had news to share with the class. He said, "Gerald Kent is going to be our band's Drum Major." Then he explained how all of this had come about. My fellow classmates acknowledged their pleasure in the assignment.

Our band director asked that I stop back in the band room after the day's classes. Although the day ended so quickly, I did as requested. He said, "Here's your shako and your band uniform which you may take home. It's cleaned and long enough to fit you and this garment bag will protect it on your way home.

You should have heard everyone that night, as I had to try the uniform on so they could see how it looked on me.

Talk about Birds, both Mr. Daily and the band director had touched me in very special ways, with equal challenges that would be with me for sometime to come.

The year was a turn of events that included all the work I had put forth during the previous summer.

I decided to take typing that fall as one of my classes. So, I took my money earned from the previous summer and bought my first typewriter. Along with the machine, I selected some related materials so I could begin practicing. I devoted the time to practice daily before the start of the school year. In the end I had taught myself how to type. This was to give me an edge for the class.

As it turned out, there were only three or four boys, including me, in the class. The girls were working to attain the necessary skills which I had been working on all summer. We took the instruction that was tied to what the teacher called "Our timed write exercise." All of us did just what I became familiar with both on the track squad and later while coaching girl's track and field. We heard, "Take your marks, get set, go," and the bang of the starters gun. All you could see were flying fingers on the keys doing everything in their power to take the honors. At the end of the exercise the teacher found mine was sixty-five words with no errors. Now the secret was out among the girls in the class. My buddies just laughed as they looked at their results.

It's peculiar how all of us find our way. That motor skill definitely proved to be very positive. There was no way I could have imagined I would close the year typing one hundred and twenty words per minute on manual machines.

If I had been told this skill would lead to more than ever anticipated, such as positions after graduating and on into the United States Air Force, and I wouldn't have believed it.

The school year continued and I was working at the A & P Grocery on the weekends and continued working as the stockman for Bartell Drugs at the base of Queen Anne Hill.

Our weekends included participating and supporting our team in all of the football games at the Metropolitan Stadium. Before we appeared, our band practiced the daily music, marching, to become a precision group.

It's like being there again, even as I write, feel, and hear how we were scurrying from our classroom down the steps, carrying our music and instruments, so our band would represent our school well. We moved forward on the street so classmates above could check us out. When we struck up with our school song, we knew there were some listening to *"On the Hilltop, Yes, you know, We're, Here."* We didn't anticipate how many additional options would be offered to us in the future.

We marched and worked diligently on our formations presented during the halftimes, as did our football team, while competing vigorously each week. Bonds and friendships were formed among us.

Every Friday afternoon we were all in uniform, down to our white buck shoes that gave us the look we had earned from all of our work done each week.

I soon realized there was one member who was petite of build, much like Audrey Hepburn, with shining short cut hair, and bright flashing eyes that definitely drew my attention. At first both of us were timid, but as we were in the band together and were seeing each other regularly, we became acquainted.

As time passed we became more than friends, rather boy and girl friend. I hope she somehow finds this book for the message shared is one I long ago wanted to convey to her. Our dating included she and her mother, inviting me to their home where we sat at the finest table prepared by both of them, to enjoy each others company and the finest of meals. Such times usually came during weekends.

I knew how much I cared for her when I would hoof it to their home in the blustery wind and pouring down rain for a fine afternoon with her.

That period of time in our lives was awkward, as I didn't have my license or my own car to get back and forth; however, this didn't stop our seeing each other.

All the preparations continued with our band. We were outdoors on the street polishing our ranks and related skills, readying for our invitation for the annual Band Day at the University of Washington. At the same time our band was preparing for the *Annual Christmas Parade* in downtown Seattle.

This parade became a competition between each high school band present. We found on that particular day we came up short and were selected as the second entry.

I'm not sure what it all meant when looking back at the flurry that came with the snowstorm we had throughout our overall area that year. Such conditions made the days long, no matter how early we rose to start another, day in our schoolwork or keeping up with all of the activities. Due to sliding from one activity to another, there wasn't time to turn to the home front duties as in the past.

We as a family found we were being elevated up to Tenth Avenue West just north of Upper Kinnear Park. This was more than any of us could have hoped would come for our family.

We stood and peered out on the view at Pier 91, where the Naval Base was and out on Elliott Bay, taking in all of the traffic of the ferryboats and the shipping lanes, with the incoming freighters to track the arrival of Jesse's vessels.

I know as I write, it wasn't the entities, the time, or the place that was of essence. It's the patterning of all personages as they either did fit, or misfit, within my life through those years, which came to be as vast as the leaves blossoming and falling. It had nothing to do with their size, looks, or points on the leaf itself. What was, prominent was the placement and behaviorally how my deeds either attracted or pushed away any opportunities of gaining any form of a balanced way to continue.

At this time in our lives all of us were experiencing, even trying on for size, those whom we came to meet and began to know. This didn't occur only with those with we attended school with, but rather with all we contacted throughout our lives. No matter what school activities we attended, such as PTA or the All City Affairs, we met new people and had moments of thoroughly enjoying the music as we practiced our steps across the floors.

Due to my membership, we as members of the Seattle Chapter of Demolay met the Jobs daughters at Saturday evening dances.

I realized long ago that all of it was like a natural turn of events. There was an exception for many of us; that was how all of these events were far too much to adapt to, such as when the music took a swing toward the Bop and the Stroll I found as perhaps others did my feet just wouldn't move to the beat where some seemed to flow with no problem or effort whatsoever.

I came to live and respect our home and where it was located to the point I would bound up those flights of stairs from Tenth Avenue West, eastbound toward Queen Anne Avenue, to the base of the final set of stairs which took me within blocks of being at school on time. This was the best feeling in the whole world!

I can see how you are sitting with anticipation as the seasons are taking their natural change. You can sense there is soon to be another shift in the clouds, the mood, that was always effected by the current carrying those damnable ships, that carried much more than the trade, rather, the sense of rhythm of our lives, within our families' mood and ability to treat such trade winds about to hit us again as a family.

Chapter 10

Return to Queen Anne Hill

Prior to the ending my first semester in my junior year, Jesse and mother announced we were moving again to Northern California. There never was any discussion before or after, just a dogmatic statement expecting all to comply. Input from all members of the family was anything but as we lived with dogmatism and declarative stances. I was always in a state of calamity. No consideration was taken to our lives or all we were involved in past, present, and future. Upheaval was ever present! All I could gather myself to do was ask why and what brought them to make such a decision. As always, it was due to better shipping opportunities that would lead to quicken the turnaround so Jesse could more readily ship out again.

Consider that we were living in the best apartment we ever had in our nomad movements up and down the west coast. We were totally entrenched at Queen Anne High. Our state included being a part of the environment of fellow students, friends and activities equally established. Mine included making a break through by realizing I planned to attend the University of Washington, where I was being considered to become the future Drum Major of the University of Washington Husky Marching Band. Prior to this possibility, I had been the Drum Major while attending Queen Anne High and later received the additional honor of becoming the All City Drum Major representing Seattle, Washington.

My development as first chair tubbiest had continued. I was employed while attending school working at Bartell Drugs in the afternoons, and for the A & P Grocery Store on weekends.

I was a member of the Seattle Chapter of Demolay where I was in line to proceed through the chairs and become a future Master Councilor. My friendship base was so extensive that I would find myself on corners downtown and friends would call my name just in friendship. Our band already received honors at the Annual Christmas and Spring Parades. Further recognition came from our appearance in the Centennial Parade held in Victoria B.C. Academically, my work in school was rising to levels where I could look at aspirations of going to college.

I have never said this before, but I was developing pride, where we, lived on Tenth Avenue West. Living there, overlooking Pier 91 and Elliott Bay was a far cry from past days. There the seasons were always about us. The fall and winter months brought the ever- present fog enveloping the ports upward to the pinnacle of Queen Anne Hill.

Nights were a figurative piece repetitively played by the foghorns. All described became home and at last I had deep feelings of being home. Nevertheless, even though all of these ties and familiar points on the fabric of life were real now another dogmatic shakeup was before me.

I shared all of this with a dear loving family, who were my friends. In fact, had they been able, they would have adopted me long before. They felt just like I was another son of theirs. The family immediately responded by inviting me to remain with them and graduate from Queen Anne High or while I attended the University of Washington or a neighboring college. I planned to continue to help as much as possible. Their oldest son Harold was my closest friend and our current Master Councilor of our Chapter of Demolay.

I had known his family for many years. Ironically, I was introduced to his mother by my mother as they worked together. Harold's mother would ask me over to help clean her home and do various odd jobs. She always paid me very well to help me earn my way. The work ethics learned and practiced came early; I definitely credit them to my mother. If there wasn't enough going on then, to have to face the constant factor of my mother's intense jealousies of others was more than enough.

Mother and I began discussing this future move. How could I be anything but abrupt with the years of lacking candor I had learned and practiced? She said, "You're moving with us," totally disregarding my detailed reasons to remain. It went like this, "End of discussion." She continued, "Where else would you go, and don't even think of living with your grandparents." I told her, "I wasn't planning on living with them, I don't need to as I have received a loving offer to stay and live with Harold's family." At this she became ballistic! She blurted out, "Either you will go with us, or you can go and live with your dad in Salt Lake City." She was both bellowing and vehement to the point of stabbing me with her final point. At the same time there were painful memories that occurred and were carried for years afterwards.

I just reread a letter written to me by mother from years ago, revealing a differing angle to traumatic happenings during my junior year in high school. This is the perfect time to share all that was deep inside of me brewing more than anyone would have realized or for that matter cared. The rash behavior on her part then and in the future had definite end results, affecting our future relationship to be sure.

This was my dad. While she was in a rage before we left our home in Oklahoma, I watched her rip all of his photos from my Baby Book.

A phrase written by my dad said more than even he would have imagined by having said and written, "For better or worse." Think of how deeply this penetrated me from thereon, while I had looked at and read the content, but I never had really seen this before. Undoubtedly, we don't see or hear as Jesus said, until it is the right time. The whole sentence said it all. "I thank God for your coming to be with us for better or for worse. It doesn't seem to matter which." The truth of the story I found afterwards was he didn't even want me in the beginning.

I pleaded with her to not do this, because it would be something she would regret. Even today there are remaining corner tips in my baby book. There has always been this part of the story missing due to her selfish, immature behavior, and now you surely are aware as to the tie to this mental illness mentioned previously in the foreword of the book.

As always, she would reiterate over and over making sure her point was clear. She said, "You have one month to make up your mind." I replied with sheer hate, "I won't need a month, I know exactly what I'm going to do." She tried to tone down saying, "I know how you feel, go ahead and consider it and let me know at the end of the month."

I immediately made contact with my dad explaining the entire matter to him so he could respond. As the month which seemed shorter than either she or I could imagine was drawing to a close, I had already arranged for my move to Salt Lake City, to live with my dad. None of this was discussed directly before the end of the month and their departure date for the San Francisco Bay Area. This time we both remained coolly silent. I told her, "I'll be leaving and will be remaining with my dad." There was an evident chasm that remained longer than either of us would have imagined, as though I knew about a deep part of her I had never known before. I found it cruel and lasting! You see, when having to face moments such as these, they are safely tucked away for the reason that were they to show their face again, it would be a last and final time.

You know my statement nearly killed her! She never shed a tear. I had already checked out at school and bid all friends, teachers, mentors, grandparents, and activities similar goodbyes from many years before.

This was the time of youthful rebellion, sometimes with more wisdom than was accepted. It was the time James Dean and Natalie Wood and Sal Mineo in *Rebel Without A Cause* struck out to find their ways just as all of us were doing.

Before all occurred, Jesse and I were confronting each other more and more. One time I told him, "Why don't you grow up, for God's sake, I'm a sophomore in high school more mature than you have ever been." You can imagine how well that went over from then on.

Never had those tracks coincided as at this time. I grew more in every dimension in that one short month than I could fathom. I moved each day that month as caught in a constant fog. There was no one to turn to, not even my grandparents, as they were well aware of all that was going on within the home of our hearts. The night before I completed packing my clothes and personal effects as time was fleeting.

My mother and my grandfather took me to catch the bus at the Eighth and Stewart Greyhound Bus Station. Our embrace was awkward at best. I boarded for Salt Lake City, which was to be my new home. You know, there wasn't a mile that I didn't want to get off that bus. I have never felt so torn and fragmented as I did. To fill my mind, and my aching heart and soul, I pulled out the latest novel on the market, *Peyton Place*. When we stopped in Idaho, I came so close to turning around and returning on that already traveled road to end this entire saga. I felt every route was closed, so I continued. I was far too distraught to sleep. Late into that final night on the road all of my fellow travelers saw what seemed to be a huge light in the middle of the highway ahead of us. As we proceeded and closed on that light all became even more curious as to the source of this oncoming beaming light. Finally, we approached and slowly passed what turned out to be a house ablaze with all of its members and the fire department attempting to fight this destructive force, causing others to lose their home that night.

I know the reason all these years later-I vividly recall that specific incident. It was due to realizing there was a shredded home by a similar destroyer of not only a home, but the very members of that home. Both were equally destructive, with one immense difference, one home could be rebuilt and allow that family to settle, where another could realize this inflamed state for all the years to come.

We arrived in Salt Lake City, Utah on time. All I had heard about this sprawling city seemed to be true. The streets were the widest I had ever seen and the cleanest.

There was a definite halting, stalling on my part, to even stand and gather my effects disembarking. I knew I changed considerably since seeing him while I visited him many years before. Then I was twelve years old and on a two weeks summer visit. This was during his hospitalization in the state sanitarium in Clinton, Oklahoma where he was being treated for severe Tuberculosis.

Now, I stood shy of 6'3" tall and known by my Physical Education teacher's nickname "Moose". I stepped off that last step on to the ground, hesitantly took a quick not to be noticed look and spotted him. It was apparent he wouldn't have noticed had I drifted off into the crowd into the city streets. He didn't even know who I was.

That has to be the price of abandonment never to have sent any support or any communication all those years. He had one of his friends with him. Introductions were worse than awkward; they were stilted at best. I had to gather my luggage including one of those original trunks I had sat on, to close and make our way west. There had to be something to that trunk, that was well worn from its banging on the tracks of life, which had become an old friend accompanying me in life.

I was fatigued from more than the journey. He told me he had made arrangements for us to go to his mothers as she was looking forward to seeing me. I hesitantly replied, but agreed even though I would have preferred to have some time to rest from the trip. What I found coming from him were more demands immediately after stepping off of that bus.

Needless to say, that evening was a fiasco, believe me, I heard about it afterwards from all barrels. Keep in mind I still had not seen his place of residence or where I would be living. How many hours had I been there, and already I had been absconded for not being able to freely call his mother my grandma.

Here is a perfect place to stop for sheer clarity. I had not seen his mother since I was in the first grade. When we were on our return trip from the year we spent in Okanogan, Washington and were bound for our home state of Oklahoma, we purposefully routed our trip so to stop in San

Francisco, California to visit his mother before turning home. Our visit was short and the last time I set my eyes on this woman.

To think at the age of seventeen between 1957 and 1958, I was finding the drive home was in total silence. That silence enveloped both of us as having sunk to the deepest and darkest levels of any sea.

We arrived at his home. It was one of those old boarding homes, rangy both by stories high as it was in volume, reaching out to the alleyway or area used for the residents to park their cars. We entered and he became excited introducing me to all inside finishing coffee and dinner. Others were milling about in other rooms. The introduction included meeting the house manager and the owner.

By this time, I was beyond being physically or emotionally spent. He took me upstairs and showed me his room. All the time I had been anticipating this would be our room.

I was soon to realize he had made arrangements for me to have my own room across from his. I entered what was to be my room. He showed me about and then said, "You take some time, get settled, then we can visit some more before we call it a day."

I turned and he was gone; I was standing there in this room of which I know I left a portion of my spirit. What was to be my room was located at the top of the stairs on the right side of the hallway. There was little light and the entire room was cluttered with stacks of this and that, collected since who knows how long, certainly long enough to be weighted down in dust and clinging spider webs. I walked slowly with deliberate steps over to the window, and immediately stopped, as being held by an unknown force from seeing more grime and caked on filth on those pull down, old fashioned shades, than I had ever seen. I was stunned into a total shock that encompassed me from beginning to end. I not only knew I couldn't stay in that room, I knew I was in more trouble than I could have ever imagined. I was so overwhelmed I couldn't even move. Tears flooded my face until I had lost my composure. I walked out into the hall and clutched hold of dad's friend. I tried to explain what was the matter and I found he more than understood me. He went and explained the entire matter to my dad. So we were able to sit and talk through the whole position as our pictures were far from the same or even similar. A change was made that night as we shared his room.

When I rose the next morning he had already left for work. I went down the stairs and was asked what I would like to have for breakfast. The landlady was nice to me and we sat and talked for sometime. She told me, "Your dad will be returning later to see if you would like to ride with him for the day." So when he arrived, I agreed and we were off after lunch in his Volkswagen van used for his deliveries.

Since then every time I see any Volkswagoneer, I can't help but think of that afternoon and all that was a part of the experience then and afterwards.

The afternoon was spent riding to get to know each other some, delivering the laundry and cleaning to his customers.

What best described the afternoon was how I was positioned as sitting on heaps of laundry bags, wrapped in the smell of newly cleaned garments, and the flapping of the tickets on his book in the breeze, which already had the smell of the coming snow.

There was a definite crispness in the wind as there was in our comments, back and forth with each other. We would share a mention and we forced a grin from time to time. I knew what he was trying to do, but how can anyone force everything into such brief moments that were not there all those years before? We made a quick stop so I could get a cold drink and continued on to the end of his planned route for the day.

A significant part of our discussion or talk during making his stops was to hear him say, "What are you considering for your future as to how you plan to make a living for yourself in the years ahead." I told him, "I've made full plans to attend college and believe it is going to take me in the direction to write or perhaps teach." He listened about as lightly as those leaflets blowing in the breeze. Then he added, "I think it would be a good thing for you and I to own our own Dry Cleaners in the future; I was kind of counting on you or hoping you would want to do this with me." I added, "I think this plan is fine for you, but it definitely isn't something I would be interested in. No, I'm going to go after my degree and seek what I've dreamed of for a long time."

I realized this totally crushed his bubble or plan and soon found the true reason for this talk.

While we ate dinner, he shared the adventure we had that afternoon with interested parties at the table. He and I continued visiting. Even though both of us were on a treadmill of trying, I definitely was torn between one home of the past and trying to fit into another at the same time.

I had already asked about what school I would be attending to hear only casual mentions. I shared about my deep involvement with Demolay and all of my other activities of which I was entrenched in and out of school. The more I conveyed the more I knew he had been in the same shock, totally ill equipped, to his having done nothing to get me enrolled including picking up the paper work.

He knew nothing about raising a boy or otherwise. I knew I would have to do everything including register myself in school and beyond.

Evening came and after dinner passed, he asked me to go out with him for a walk. This was one of the most pleasant times we had since my arrival. But in no time at all, he began to query me about everything from the start to the very moment itself. He abruptly told me he saw that I was quite the one to readily swear; I didn't show any respect for his mother and I had been nothing but trouble since my arrival.

So add all of this to the previous cruelty I had thrown in my lap prior to my arrival, where the streets were as clean and wide as heard of, then to be absconded at every turn and to have to deal with what had been a bit of "a high," just trying to share my background and warm up to this stranger who wanted me to refer to him as dear old dad.

He went on and said, "You have questioned everything that occurred and it's evident you aren't going to engage yourself like "Son –Father or Father-Son" relationship. Before I could answer any of these accusations he added, "Are you planning on working and contributing toward your living costs?"

At this the dam broke! I began saying, "Before all of this came up I was going to talk with you about the possibility of you and I locating our own apartment where we could have our own lives together. But, it's more than apparent you never had anything such as this in your mind from the start. You've had your say, now it's my turn. As to my contributing you have no concerns and no wonder you had such a plan for our so-called dream to work together as you mentioned. I've been working two and three jobs for years while attending school. And I will continue to do that and more. You made your last mistake, as you aren't equipped to raise any child. You didn't want me here in the first place or you would have arranged for my enrollment in school. I have had nothing but one demand after another since I stepped off that bus. You need not wonder anymore as to how much contribution there will be for when you return I won't be here."

He spun away and that was the last I heard from or saw him. I packed immediately and sent a wire to my grandparents explaining all that had happened and requested Henry to meet me at the bus station when I arrived.

To think only one-half of my junior year lay ahead. So much of my life had been like one tiny petal of a hanging flower, hanging and spinning as by a thread of life, before falling softly to the ground.

No further contact was made, nor did I see him again until twenty years passed. One Saturday morning, I was returning from buying groceries and I turned to see that he was in the car next to mine. He was a much older man even more slight of build now. That undoubtedly was due to his ailing body and spirit. It took everything within my being to be decent, gentlemanlike enough, to invite him and his friend that helped me so much before into my home.

I determined hurriedly that he had no real intent to ask for or to see me. He had already been to see my grandmother with particular intent to confirm whether my mother was alive and the whereabouts of my brother.

I terminated the visit; after all, he had never crossed the great divide to visit before. He still didn't have one care, only wanting information so he could have approval from his "World wide" church to marry the woman from the boarding house.

He died when he was seventy-three. That was twenty-two years ago. I attended his funeral held in Salt Lake City where his body was on a slight hillside. Over four hundred came to pay their respects. I felt there was little or no weight to what had been shared by his minister so I acknowledged the request to say some additional words. I told about a noted philosopher, Bertrand Russell, who made mention to the fact of his dying and realizing how rich he truly was as he was able to raise ten fingers. Each of those fingers stood for a friend; to have ten true friends made him a rich man indeed. I added, "J.C. would have marveled as he had to be a rich man to have so many loving friends present at his funeral."

I have always recalled the hush among all when I uttered those words. There were few if any comments afterwards, but those words still hang in the sky between Salt Lake City and here in my acquired homeland of the Greater Northwest.

Upon my return in 1980 my grandfather and grandmother welcomed me lovingly with open spirits. They never questioned as to the intent or the reason for the reversal. When I finally was able to tell them the details they were aghast. I regrouped as though nothing had occurred, attending my classes of which I had been in the midst of only days before.

I have never forgotten the generosity on their parts upon my return to their home. They took me up to the loft where my bed and the entire room was spotless waiting for me. I asked if this was to be my room? My grandmother said, "Honey, this is your room as long as you stay with us."

However, when mother and Jesse heard of the return on my behalf, they took the harsh stance of the whole thing being put up by me in the first place, in order that I could have my way. This accusation carried over the miles and years as they repeated such to me for literally years to come. Deep inside at the level of my soul I felt and knew I had been wronged by both, as it was apparent no matter what or how many times or ways I tried to convey what the true experience had been, they would never signify their trust again.

Chapter 11

My Senior Year to San Rafael, CA

All that lay ahead from that point in time had to be like the ebb and flow of the tides themselves as they both pulled due to the great force of the lunar surface. There was the constant rushing to shore which best described the story from this moment forward. Before leaving Queen Anne Hill and all that had been home for all of those torn years, there was a portion of time that was much the same as the torn sign board back on the bowery route where I had delivered papers.

Another habit or behavior would show its face from time to time. That was related to Jesse and his arrivals home after each voyage. Sometimes items would somehow appear; anything from a case of fresh pineapple from the Hawaiian Islands to decorative pieces that enhanced our home, ranging from his showing us the revered God Hotei, or the importance of rubbing his wooden belly for luck, to lamps and the like. It didn't concern us until he would show up with some appliance. Mother caught on to his antics in no time and told him repeatedly that he would get caught and would end up going to jail or worse. What was worse would have been his losing his Seaman's papers and licenses to resume shipping out as usual.

When thinking all of this through, it didn't take a Sherlock Holmes to figure out how all of the finds were secured. Our family ties and gained understanding included realizing Jesse had more than an impish kind of behavior that showed itself clear back to the earliest days.

I always remembered how he would walk up to us and kick at our shins and say, "Got your boots on?" Another trick was to catch us as he was lighting his cigarette, then to reach out and say, "Did you know a match burned twice?" I never could understand how he thought that was so funny.

At the same time, all of the holds that had been held up by mother as she claimed us her sons, which kept him from overtaking such arenas of discipline, were going by the way of the waves he rode upon from voyage to voyage. I was realizing to have any attention seemed to require much of the same kind of behavior.

Many years later I was proud to state I no longer drank as I got all of that out of my system long before. In fact when I was fourteen and fifteen years old, due to my size, the guys I ran with for awhile would have me get my overcoat for one purpose. Before mentioning this, few of us, including me, thought of the ramifications related to any of this that occurred. I may have been younger, but I was the tallest and the biggest, so they would pull up out front of a store and I would enter. The rain was pouring down hard, in I would walk with my collar turned up, squinting through the drops on the lenses. I walked back to pick up two cases of beer walked up to the counter, lowered my voice as far as possible, paid for the beer, and told the clerk, "Stay dry." I walked back out to the car and loaded the beer in the trunk as all of the guys sat waiting for me.

They opened the car door for me and I got in the back seat with a couple of them. We drove down the road, they laughed at how "smooth" in their words it was to see how I would pull such off where they couldn't even think of doing anything like that. Our destination led us down under the Garfield or the Magnolia Bridge in the night. There we were all together ready to do our drinking. I had secured the beer and one of them had dipped into their old man's liqueur cabinet, to bring Canadian Club Whiskey along. Some were smoking their cigarettes or cigars, chug-a-lugging as fast as they could, and pouring the whiskey and beer on top for Boilermakers. So the evening went from my delivering the goods to imbibing as we were doing then to find that most of us were well on our way, the wrong way. I know those were the first times of my really getting drunk and sick into the night.

More importantly, the future medication diagnosed leveled my behaviors and revealed I couldn't drink at the same time. It was vitally important to always remember how the two conflicted. Consequently, those days in the past were to come to a stop.

I had joined The Order of Demolay between fifteen to sixteen years of age between 1956-57. I soon found there was quite a lot of the same kind of drinking that went on, much the same as before. One night I vividly remember coming home from one of our dances in sad shape. I found the same brotherly ties deeply broken years before, as I awoke to hearing him tell how I had come in plastered that night.

You know something? There was irony regarding all of this as all the years before we grew up hearing, "If you want to drink, then drink at home." Tell me the majority of our behaviors don't come from the environment we claim as our homes.

My last experience of drinking way too much was one night before having to rise early the next Saturday morning, to go to work at my job at the A & P Grocery Store. The entire day was one hangover, which I paid for every time I heard someone speak or crash a grocery cart into another.

That cured me! From that point on I drank only with real reserve, even after joining the Air Force, where they called me "Two Beers Bradley".

After I had joined Demolay, I was able to get George and others that had been classmates and friends of the past to join the Seattle Order. This turned out to be a good direction for all of us.

It seemed George and I went everywhere for quite awhile, even the night we had dates clear over in West Seattle. There was only one thing amiss and that was his transmission didn't have a second gear. We went anyway. All was going great until we got to the Spokane Bridge ramps and we were about to merge into the lane of traffic to carry us across the bridge to pick up our dates. We looked outside the window to see this woman next to us who wasn't about to budge and give us the clearance we needed. I looked forward and saw the concrete pillars ahead of us. I yelled, "George we're going to hit the pillars if we don't..." and we collided into those pillars.

I looked at George to find he was cut on his lip, with a broken tooth stuck in his lower lip. My leg had pushed our radio through the dash. What was serious was, this was the same leg that I injured when I had been hit by a car pedaling my bicycle. We missed picking up our dates! We were taken to the hospital and I still remember mother coming to take me home that night. She said, "I'm sorry you had such an accident. We asked George if we could take him home and he replied, "No, I think I'll go out on the town anyway."

At the same time, my best buddy Harold and I cruised up and down and around the blocks of Fourth and Pine in his 48 maroon Dodge, checking out the chicks to no avail.

The summer between the sophomore and junior year was the time we spent our free hours on the shore of Lake Washington where one friend, a member of our Demolay chapter, lived. All of this and other activities were before my final departure from all that meant so much during those years.

At the end of my Junior Year I would be joining all of them. Mother was regaining her strength, as she had been sick that year. It turned out she had cancer and was fortunate to have all pronounced cured three years later. Her need for blood transfusions was paramount. I definitely remember how vital it was. Here they were down south and I was with my grandparents.

The only way I could see to help her was to go and make it known among my fellow Demolay members as to the definite need. I asked them to contribute and found important lessons that night I never forgot. As it was pronounced by the Dad of our Order, "Anything such as this is out of the question." I know none present that night forgot my response as I said, "If we as an Order can't reply to something that has such a significant need as this, then what good is this organization."

I know you can recall how I had my first blows with Jesse when we arrived in Milwaukie, Oregon over my thinking he would help me with my spending money. All this time I had done nothing regarding turning out for any sports while in school.

Upon settling in with my grandparents, it seemed as though the track season was directly ahead of us. I made up my mind to turn out for track. Due to all that was happening with mother's health, I was told I shouldn't go out for any sport as it wouldn't be right to spend any money due to the condition my mother was dealing with away from all of us.

Well, unknown to any of the family, I did go out for track and thoroughly enjoyed every aspect of it. Granted much of it was experimental, but I would find in the future during my senior year at San Rafael High, I would be on the track team and later while attending Allan Hancock College I would run Cross Country and Track.

I kept running and attempting to throw the shot put and kept control over all of my gear, with the exception of my track spikes. I couldn't find a decent place to leave my spikes so I left them stuck through the springs underneath my mattress. I should have known that wouldn't work with the fastidious house cleaner my grandmother had always been.

We were pacing ourselves in our next to last meet of the season. I was in third place and we were approaching the final turn. There on the infield was Jesse who had come to see me run. As always, it wasn't for that at all. He was there to tell me that my grandmother had found my spikes and not mentioned it to me, but she was plenty mad to say the least. I know you won't be surprised to hear this was the first time he had ever attended anything I did while attending school.

All of my waves of good-byes were real and I knew it. I wouldn't have the opportunity to graduate at Queen Anne High with my class, which was very hard to say the least.

Next Stop San Rafael, California

Once again, six months later, I was boarding the Greyhound bus, but the attitude was greatly improved from a similar scene some six months before. I was on my way for a complete shake up of my entire being. As I sat there leaving the driving up to the driver, I had only time to think of my new home, to contemplate all that had happened those years living there in Seattle and specifically there on Queen Anne Hill, at the high school, with my fellow students, friends, teachers, even mentors. They would accompany me much farther than to San Rafael, California, rather into all of my life. When this became the most apparent, was in knowing how vital it was to account for all when I finally wrote this book.

My thoughts march ahead to just prior to graduation when I remember everyone was announcing their plans for their future years. My plans were united in that my very finest friend Alex and I were planning on leaving for Europe, after working that summer to gain the funds to spend traveling through Europe. Others were making their final plans before going to the Colleges and Universities of their choice.

All of our hopes had been made to attend commencement and our Senior Prom. Being the born optimist I had become, I know I realized it important to share our plans of leaving for our trip to Europe in full detail.

Some may have been aware they saw a tilted behavior. Ironically I was anything but aware of this. Instead such announcements became even more noticeable.

The entire year was similar to the flurry of snowstorms experienced while on Queen Anne Hill, plodding up those stairs every day, to get to class at Queen Anne High. At first, so much of me was still there, rather than in San Rafael. I kept making long distance calls to Beth and finally realized after our last conversation that she had met her guy while attending classes at Washington State University in Pullman, Washington. From then on I began to see what was on the other side of the wave right before my eyes.

I was fortunate to find an opening in an Art class. Our Art teacher welcomed me from the start. Before I knew it, she had me working with pencil and charcoal. What stood out were the combat boots I chose to draw and kept over the years framed.

The last sight I had of them was in my grandparent's basement where they were proudly hung.

That class was perfect as we were freed to try every medium possible. It was there I became even more familiar with other students in the class. Stan became my good friend before the end of the school year. He had spent his year playing on the Varsity Football team and the Swimming team.

The summer of 1958, prior to starting my senior year, I familiarized myself with the community going out and walking from one end of the town to the other. All the time I was seeking a job for the summer.

I found myself at Gil's Drive Inn where I received a position to work as a salad cook. Beside me throughout the summer was "the Cook," who turned out to be an on-going subject among the staff. He wore the same white uniform that I had including our chef hats, the real thing in his case, and mine a paper cap, while working over the food being prepared. He was the topic of conversation. The entire staff merely tolerated the gross behavior of the old cook. He cursed one and all, and griped, regarding any and all errors made daily by various members of the overall staff. It wasn't that difficult to see how he intimidated the girls on the staff.

One day he had been on my case one time to many. I called him on it by telling him, "I've got you figured out totally. You grumble and curse at us about everything and pump your chest out and frighten those about you, but I know the truth; under all of that behavior is a heart of gold to be sure." He laughed and said, "You're the first to tell me off in a long time and you sure do know who I am alright!" From that moment he became quieter, calmer, and became my mentor when it came to teaching me all of the skills apart from the cooking assignment I had. Our work became as slick as the burgers he and I wrapped and passed to the staff to place in the bags for our customers.

One evening, I was helping with the clean up which included emptying the vat of hot grease from the hot dog bin. I had a good grip on both of the vats and I walked across the floor, pushed the screen door open and stepped outside on the cement floor. Before I knew it, I had slipped on the greasy surface. I did all I could to balance myself to pour the grease in the catch can. I just couldn't quite pull it off. I was able to get the vats to the edge of the can, but my left hand was on the lower end and the grease was pouring down over my hand. Somehow, through all of this I was able to hold on to the vat and pull it up and away from the barrel. When I looked down at my hand, I watched the layers of skin curl up and peel away from the flesh. I don't know to this day, but I kept my sense and grabbed for clean towels and wrapped my hand to keep the air off the burned flesh. Through all of the constant pain I yelled to one of the staff, "Could I use your car to go to the hospital?" She said I could and gave me her keys. I jumped into her car and drove to the emergency entrance of the Hospital a few blocks away. I still remember when the doctor entered and found the burned flesh and said, "You're the bravest burn victim I've seen in some time." He took care to prepare the burned areas totally wrapping my hand and gave me instructions to come back and have it looked at in a few days, to get the wound completely wrapped again.

That night I parted company with the crew at Gil's and that really signified my fellowship with the cook. I went in later to thank him and the staff for the experience.

What came at San Rafael High included: teachers, classmates, classes, and interrelated experiences that were binding throughout the year.

It is clear as the day itself, that as my hand became better, I was finally able to remove all of the bandages and feel the fresh air again.

I remember how everyone that night at Gil's turned as white as our uniforms and how amazed they were at my being able to keep my wits and care for the accident I had.

The first day I found myself in the foyer of the main hallway. I knew I was a new student arriving as a transfer student among all of them, of whom I came to realize had attended school from the elementary years through junior high and now were in their senior year at San Rafael High School together.

I was much more than a new student among them, yet noticed how swiftly they observed me. The gathering from the first morning throughout the year was much the same. There were several groups representing themselves taking their portion of the turf in the center hallway before starting another day of classes. The groups were Key Club, the Sportsmen, and the girls were the Ra Ravas.

When any new transfer student appeared those mentioned had their opportunity to size them out. I knew from the first morning I had better blend in as quickly as possible.

Fortunately, those mornings merged into another just as the classes did and friendships began to be made day by day.

147

At a later time, after years of having graduated from San Rafael High, my wife and I were attending loving friends, parents' fiftieth anniversary. While there, I took my wife on a tour of the same walk taken back while attending my senior year.

One home we spent time in after moving from Lincoln Avenue where we were literally across the street from the high school, was what I showed her and where I parked my car before I left to enter the Air Force. The space was still there minus my car.

From that time onward there could be no excuse as to my being late for any class.

That promptness carried to where I would line up to run the various events while on the track team that spring before graduation. And this time, I didn't fall through the bleachers as before, while attending Milwaukie Union High School.

One of the research tools that helped bring it all back and aided my accounting for all included in the story line was the keeping of my yearbooks.

The year brought definite differences such as remaining away from any cleanup committee while attending Queen Anne High back in the eighth grade and making sure to not have contact with any board of wisdom or point saving measure.

The year was constant adaptation on all levels. Our Philosophy teacher, shared much more than Philosophy, rather the works of a current humorist such as Shelly Berman, which brought much laughter during our classes.

The very word and action included in adaptation, was much the same as a close friend. Over all of the years the resounding complement has been: "How in the world you are to no matter how low you become, to soar upward every time, and take on more and more is amazing." Such has to fall under exactly that of adaptation, which was needed, particularly, long before receiving any diagnosis or any medication to aid in seeing to my leveling off. When asked how were you able to do it no matter what, I have always said, "I just toughed it through."

Both the writing of this story, and you the reader will discover each event in my life. I hope you'll become aware how I jumped into the arena I refer to as "change", was what I strived to do the entire way.

Our Gymnastics Coach gained all of our respect by the fair way he led and taught by example. I still remember he was short, wearing his white pants and shirt, and stood wearing his wire rimmed glasses, holding the clipboard, in his crew cut always a bit grown out and frazzled.

When I came to appreciate these who had taught me then, I found I was working through all of the preparatory elements leading me to teach as well. They marked me as I hope I did some of my students later.

I've never how forgotten how our Health Education teacher, who made sure so many facets of his class would be practiced from then on in our lives. His caring spirit radiated among the student body.

The civics teacher had a tough job trying to gain and keep our attention on the subject of California Civics, which helped us understand a great deal about being citizens then and into our futures.

Our band director and I seemed to meet at a stalemate from the start. He made me understand there wasn't room to become one of the Drum Majors, as they already had their Drum Majorette!

I continued my work on the tuba for the year. As you read, you'll find how adversity was seemingly always in front of me on the path taken daily. This was another blow for I had worked so hard to become the drum major and was hoping to carry all of it and more on to the University of Washington's Band.

Oh no, here I was caught up in this parental decision to move again and again to meet their needs. I know it has been evident from thereon that this has been so like a battleground throughout. Yet, as the director of the band said long before, "The beat went on."

A standout for us was our senior English teacher, who had a very close friend, Robert Culp, from their Hollywood days together. He had one glaring objective, which became ours; that was readying us to take our entrance examination for the University of California at Berkeley. He worked with us for the entire year with this in mind. There wasn't a day that passed that he didn't reveal, he had worked the copy machine to death, by bringing another set of trial test forms for us to complete. He insured we gained the knowledge that related to each facet. I knew as all of my fellow students, that the heightened moment for him would be for us to exclaim, how we had passed the exam and gained entrance at the University of California, Berkeley.

I remember taking those tests and finding I had missed passing the test by a mere three points.

Another teacher who came to be a good friend of mine was the Life Science teacher. I know I was anything but her favored student due to my constantly keeping our class in a state of hilarity. When looking back, I know now that behavior was due to the rising level of a manic phase. The poor woman wanted to pull her hair out I'm sure.

When you received your yearbook, you passed it around for one and all signatures, which seemed so important. Believe me those signatures became even more pronounced, when pondering them in later years as I have before writing this chapter. What I did realize then and even more now were the faces of the broad array of friends I was able to gain in that the final year.

Before proceeding through the seasons, hallways, classes and every experience that occurred, I thought of a significant event before starting school.

It came directly after my burn and the healing process. Some of the neighborhood kids were going regularly over to the Dominican pool on a daily basis. So this opened the gate for me to try one more time to swim. Those I went over to the pool with introduced me. I was able to explain the fear or phobia I had when it came to being in water. I couldn't have hoped for a more empathetic staff of life guards. A couple of them began to work with me so I could break down the barriers that separated me from being able to swim at ease and even dive off the low board. What came was just getting into the water. The lifeguards emphasized that I should just relax while in the water. Consequently, I kept easing down at the waters edge and began to hear what the lifeguards were conveying to me. They urged me to just dip down under the waters surface. I could see this was a process of easement and familiarity of being in the water.

This continued and the scarring from the burn was healing. I was beginning to enjoy being at the pool basking in the rays of the California sun and before I could believe it, I started to swim across the width of the pool. That led to my swimming the length of the pool daily. It had just taken time and I sincerely thanked the crew that had worked with me from the start. Here, I thought I would never be back in any water ever again.

The summer of 1958 was coming to a close, and I would be in full swing in school proceeding through my senior year to graduate along with those to be introduced.

At first my not working was understood, but it became a rub especially with Jesse and me. Jesse was selling again after I arrived. I wasn't to go with him anymore due to my first job secured at Gil's, to take time to recover, and rapidly found I was walking down Lincoln Avenue with the palm trees on the medians up and down the street much different from our years in the Pacific Northwest.

How prominent my home state of Oklahoma had been for me, to be surpassed by my living in the Pacific Northwest, now to find we were in the Northern California Bay area.

I walked back and forth to school daily and returned to find more and more friction and bitterness between Jesse and me. We rattled back and forth with each other constantly. Both he, and my mother, hung on to their belief that I had fictitiously made up the whole story so I could return from Salt Lake City, to remain with my grandparents as I had until joining them. Only they could dream this up as they did. The truth was, neither of them got their way on this move of moves!

My wrong was in succumbing as I had, not working out some effective plan to remain at my grandparents or better yet, to have taken the offer to live with my truest of friends who offered me the finest of opportunities of living with them from that point onward. They were more like my parents than anything that had come before.

What a way to begin the school year, particularly my senior year.

I didn't think of the achievement of regaining the ability of being able to swim as a posture for that year.

I have already previewed the Birds, such as the instructors I was working with in my assigned classes.

My attention now turns toward my fellow classmates through the year.

I can't recall exactly how I became acquainted with Alex, who was a running back and a member of the Sportsmen's Club. All of the members that knew Alex were on the same team, but he was definitely a guy who became a perfect friend for me.

Before I was forced to move again and again as already described, an event place during my sophomore year in 1956. I became a reader and began to write. An even more emphatic occurrence came from my reading. I picked up the volume of *A Man Called Peter*, by Catherine Marshall. Reading this account of his life, I came to realize that being 'tapped on the shoulder' or to be called by the 'the Chief', had occurred in my behalf as well.

Peter Marshall's call was quite evident while he was in Scotland in his younger years. The more I read of his life and ministry the more I realized I had to be receiving the same call from God himself. His tap was "by the Chief," which was the way he referred to the Lord. And much the same as Peter Marshall, I found I carried His tap gently and totally from thereon. It didn't seem to matter what came in the constant waves lapping at the shore in my life. I knew His presence with a certainty.

Then in 1958, how emphatic all became after asking "Why," and anything interrelated when trying to communicate with Jesse. As if there wasn't enough to deal with due to the transition, now to find he was unable to be queried or called on the brink of the truth, that he hauled us up and down the coast for years to meet his needs. I further told him he didn't care a bit. At that he struck out at me and grabbed at my collar and lifted me off the floor, threw me not once, but three times to many against the wall. All the time I was seeing the glaring hatred piercing at me through his blue gray eyes; I felt those muscular arms doing the throwing. He threw me one time too many! As I came bounding off the wall the third time, I pounced on him and collared him and, threw him on the wall. He fell to the floor. I stared at him with a deep seeded hate and yelled at the top of my lungs. "Don't you ever touch me again"! He never did.

After that, I called Alex and he came over and we got out of there for the rest of the evening. Our friendship grew from the start and I knew it was to the chagrin of his fellow Sportsmen. He wasn't the kind of guy that was coerced by others as to the actions he took or didn't take. Even to this day when I look back at his and my photograph, it's hard to realize what drew us to become friends.

When any transfer student finds where I was that year, I can't help but ask how did we, I, get through it. I know, in my case, the name of the game was emphatically accrediting my actions. When this became most evident was in knowing that it took three fourths of the school year to even have a date. That by itself was anything but easy, when thinking back to my previous years in school, when I knew so many people, dated, went to all of the school dances, and later the student's parties at their homes. Now I felt like a dunce in the corner of the room.

Not only did I spend time in the company of Alex, he introduced me to his family. They were fine to me from the start. At first Alex introduced me to his mother, and one evening his dad and his brother Jeff came in after a long day at their automobile agency. This was the first time for me to meet them as well.

This was their schedule, as they would remain late every day to close down their business. All of them readily accepted me as one of the family, as had the loving family back on Queen Anne Hill, who I almost lived with in my Junior year. Alex's dad and brother had their drink before dinner and Alex's mother would have prepared a fine dinner for them to enjoy. We sat together on the evening that *Bonanza* was on T.V. I thoroughly found Alex's dad a delight as he would laugh at the story of those grown men on the ranch depicted weekly.

In the meantime Alex would show me around or play his flute downstairs. He got his Bongo and Congo drums out and I would take a try at the percussion background. Alex was talented musically and had a flair for poetry, but at the same time had gained background that I was sure others in school would never have known. He was caught up in the vocal talent of Johnny Mathis and we listened to every album he had by him. Along the way he brought me to appreciate the fine, feathered friends in the sky. He was introduced to all of them and drawn to the Audubon Society, particularly bird watching, which he began to include me in as we went out to see any and all new species.

Where our fellow students were in the midst of whatever activities they might be involved in over the weekends, he and I would be off for the cliffs and huge rocks out toward Bolinas and the coast. Our intent was to locate, another specie from the overall area not seen before, along with the coloring of its plumage, its call or song from among the pines. Then, we stopped in the engulfed silence, peered through the binoculars to see and credit that seen and kept an analog of the species we witnessed.

From such an afternoon he took me back to something called home, when entering I would hear from mother, "I suppose you've been

with Alex all day," in her ugly rude manner. Long before I had come
to know how she treated those I knew, with a wrathful kind of tongue,
depicting her jealously toward any I spent any amount of time with no
matter whom at the time.

The first time I really saw such hatred on her behalf was back to
those junior high days while living at the base of Queen Anne Hill.

I found the bite of her tongue when I mentioned Harold's mother,
years later while in high school serving as a Preceptor, with my affiliation
in The Order of Demolay, she was ruthless, cutting to the quick of my
soul.

Each year we sponsored a very special evening where we welcomed
our mothers to our banquet. I invited her to join me at this occasion. Her
reply was, "You can just ask Harold's mother, for I won't be going." How
many times I was grilled to the flank with her obnoxious inability to be
gracious and open to such opportunities. I spun before her not saying a
word, rather immediately went over to Harold's home, and after awhile I
explained this to them. The end result for that evening gala was for both
Harold and I to escort his mother to the event.

Before continuing let me say the previously mentioned behavioral
tendencies are related to Bi-Polar Mood Swing Disorder. How do I
know, you ask. I am aware, as I have realized that sameness comes when
I periodically forego taking my medication. I have learned this tends to
bring to the surface intense annoyance, shortness of patience, temper and
hatefulness. Real growth has come when realizing such signs, signaling
for me to stop and take my prescribed medication knowing momentarily
such thoughts, and actions will dissipate.

When thinking back to such serenity, the next morning while attending class it was time for our P.E. classes. I had another lesson to learn that day. My finding while in the class prior was seeing how a lot of the guys would wear the sweatshirts of their choice. I thought I could wear my maroon cut-off sweatshirt, with the flying gold Q on the front, for having been on the track team at Queen Anne High. That shirt turned into the topic of conversation as my red coat had the first day. Of course I didn't think of the proximity of San Quentin Prison when I wore it. Needless to say, I retired it after that experience. One thing was a certainty. They couldn't say I wasn't an individual no matter what they thought.

While the football season and games were going on, I became acquainted with another family that I would know for years to come. I decided I would go out for basketball that year. I practiced every night until there was only the light from inside of their home, to allow me to continue working on all of the fundamentals. My intent was to do more than make the team. I fully intended to excel with my shots, dribbling, driving, lay-ups, shots on the line, taking long shots from all areas of the court. I didn't ever hear one negative mention from any of that house as they realized my seriousness.

Experiences were as rhythmic as the bounce of the basketball itself. Our P.E. class now included our playing basketball daily as well. One day while we were scrimmaging in our class I remembered a definite collision on the floor. As it turned out the collision wasn't accidental, it was glaringly intentional. Somehow, I had my back turned on the court and the next thing I knew Le Roy deliberately ran up and over my back, laughing and smiling with a grimace. There was deliberate staring down of each other on the floor until I got the ball, then I dribbled with all I was worth, and walked right up and over his back and his shoulders, causing him to feel much of the same I had felt moments earlier. You're right, he didn't like this one bit. With words exchanged afterwards, I was able to make him know, I had never been walked on by anyone else and it wasn't going to start now.

I recall how he listened, but more importantly, I had gained a friend, as I did "the Cook" that summer. From that point he and I got along rather well.

The year was flying by and I located a job for the weekends in a furniture store where I did everything from clean the store, deliver and assemble what was delivered.

Another opportunity came to sell shoes for a shoe store in town. There was nothing like tending the ladies, as they always knew exactly what shoe or shoes they wanted. The only thing was, it took taking every box off the shelf for them to convey such a wish. What became evident was the continual view of the curve of their legs, and the delicacy of their feet being forced into a smaller size in every case to meet their hidden desires.

It didn't take that long before realizing I was anything but a caterer to the needs when it came to their feet and the paths they took.

I always was able to see the tiniest of Birds, places, events, and happenings; foremost, to envision that not visible to others no matter how deeply they looked. Take for example among all of the Birds along the way, the years, turns in the road and those I came to meet, one editor I wrote with of one newspaper. He said more than ever hoped for, then or into the future. What he said was, "Gerry Bradley sees things. More importantly, he sees things in people, things that other people would miss…he writes about them…and shares his magic with that seen and the words to describe such views."

Three other guys became my friends referred to as "the Three Musketeers". They remained darn good friends all the way through our graduating and beyond.

It's a bit ahead of the time frame, but when thinking of them I have always remembered their coming to one of the proms. It wasn't that tough to recognize their arrival because we were waiting for them and their dates of the evening. We looked down the street and all of them arrived at the gymnasium in their family school bus, now painted purple for the night. They pulled up like any limousine, opened the door, and out came each couple all decked out for the evening. Their dates were beaming and a bystander couldn't tell if they were in shock or embarrassment, but all three of the Musketeers were in their black ties and stood with their derby hats on for the evening. These three never made you wonder for there would always be something entirely different every time we were together.

The basketball try-outs were coming up and I was somewhat nervous, but knew I had prepared and was ready as any of the others turning out for the drills ahead of us. The coach blew his whistle, we all gathered and he explained how the turnouts were organized, leading to a final decision at the end of the weeks work. As we progressed through the drills, leading us to scrimmage at the end of each session, we would play with all the skill we had to offer. No assessment was passed to us until the final day.

Consequently, none of us had any inclination as to who was to be selected. I had been on the track team previously while attending Queen Anne High, but I had never been through anything with the amount of rigor we had been going through in these try-outs. We had fulfilled all asked of us and were standing or were seated waiting the call from the coach. He began to call out certain names one by one. The mystery became even more pronounced as we knew there would only be so many on the team. There were two more positions to fill and the remaining guys waited with real anticipation. He called out Bruce's name and Bruce turned to the coach and said, "Coach, Bradley, outplayed me the whole way in every phase, he should be the one to be selected for the spot on the team." The coach replied, "You're my choice," and I butted in and said, "Coach just carry me so I can learn the game, even if I have to sit on the bench the whole season, I can learn and hopefully have a shot at playing on the college level later." He responded with, "I've already made my decision," and he slapped his clipboard and turned to walk away. I never forgot his non-caring spirit displayed and shall treat the subject later in the story.

I walked away to hear Bruce call for my attention and say, "You were treated wrong, for you are a much better player than me and the try outs showed it." Along with that phenomenal opportunity went the final results that those on the team I came so close to making won the N.B.L. (Northern Basketball League) Championship that year. Somehow, you never recover in truth to such hypocrisy in your life and it is even worse when you have to face it at such a young age. What was so damaging was this was a very significant way I could blend and become a true part of those about me.

This brought a floodgate opening within me, for the tears were soul-felt tears that saturated my spirit from then on.

To think that not that many years later would be a weekly show on T.V. about being able to claim a deep seated fantasy from within.

Undoubtedly, that was one of those fantasies I would have given anything to have had the mere opportunity to test within myself. I would have been the first one to admit to myself had I realized I didn't have what it took. But, you the reader, will be amazed at how many quests of the same stature would be mine yet to come. In truth, they far surpassed this particular caring moment I would have given anything to be able to change.

When reviewing all of your comments and photographs from my yearbook of the *Searchlight* for 1959, I was able to arrive at truths to share and complete this portion of the story line. In retrospect, I do recall reading comments what stood out then and now as the overall positive support from each of you. I was and remain today pleased at the end results, as I was a transfer student at a tentative time, to gaining much of your respect and most importantly our friendship, while we all worked toward our goals and objectives preparing us for our morrows.

I can only hope you found and kept to heart comments that depicted: "You're a credit to anyone who knows you, thanks so much Ray Simms; may you know how proud we were to watch you continue into your career."

Before going further, I owe a long past apology to three women I left in a trail of a wonder. My hope is that if they read the story and put the pieces together, they'll be able to understand what put me up to inviting three of them plus one to the Senior Prom. I know my actions were wrong then; I can assure them it was due to my having a condition that they now can better understand. That still didn't excuse my intentions and I hope each of them can look at this and better grasp what I am trying to explain.

There are those I have wanted to see for so many years, Dr. Tony Rubilletto, our previous Student Body President, is definitely one I have thought of many times.

Do keep in mind that you my fellow students were Birds in the truest sense, for all the ways you touched me, others then, now, and wherever you are.

Not only did we have this year of years together, it was terrific to enjoy them for two years after we graduated.

The reminder from our Philosophy teacher came when he said, "We the teachers, learn considerably more than our students."

There has been deep hope when considering all of you, whether your lives turned out the happiest and as full as you would have hoped.

How I thoroughly enjoyed the humor from your comments, whether you knew it or not, your caring spirits shone through at a perfect time. One perceived even then about my moods. From the moment we threw our mortarboards from the top of our heads we all entered into new plateaus of our lives. We had the memory of our festive evening out on the town, rather the city of San Francisco for our Senior Prom, held in the esteemed hotel on Union Square.

Before we joined each other for a night beneath the crystalline chandelier, the steps we were about to take would be as boundless as the fragmentary light shining. To think that before our arrival, we had dined at our favorite restaurants. Some joined on the Wharf, where others went to China Town, in our case we took Alex's suggestion and convened at Skipper Kent's for dinner. The majority of us had the houses favorite of Lobster Flamedour. As we sat there in the high back wicker styled chairs, some were already eating and the rest of us waited and began to think the lobster must be coming from Maine, as it took quite awhile. When they brought it to our table it was worthy of the wait. They sat this huge brimming platter of Lobster before us all inflamed. To say the least that was some presentation. We weren't sure if we would need the fire extinguisher or not in order that we might try the delicacy in a timely fashion and still have time for a few dances into the evening.

My date was Abbey who I had attended classes with throughout the year. Negotiations were in order for our having the evening together, already mentioned, but after all said and done, all parties were able to attend and enjoy their evening as well.

The friendship between Abbey and me came naturally, and slowly, which was perfect for both of us. She knew from the beginning her stylish ponytail did me in daily while in class. This ponytail of hers was cylindrical in that it was possible for me to slip my pencil up through the inside of her ponytail. All it took was finesse. Abbey finally realized what I was doing and would turn and smile, rolling those big brown eyes at me. I held off asking her to go on a date waiting for the Prom ahead.

And after the fiasco that I got everyone caught up in, she did her part of negotiating, and we realized we would be going together after all.

At the same time I was completing the track season. She and her girl friends came to the track meets. We had to study for our finals to graduate and I was realizing how I had friends I hoped to have at the beginning of the school year. After a wonderful evening at the ball, we drove homeward to sit close together under the stars, before taking her up the hill to her home.

Ahead of us the next day, was our Senior Day held at the Novato Golf and Country Club. Everyone was tired from the night before, but we guys went out to play golf while the girls lounged around the pool and rested; some spent the time chatting with each other from the night before.

All of this activity was so like being in another world for the moment, which flashed back to the real world rapidly afterwards. Most of us were going for our summer vacations. Others were going to enroll early for the summer sessions where they would be attending college or Universities the coming fall. What we came to realize most was our paths were transcending in such a way that very few of us would remain in contact from thereon.

Yet, my hope is if you read this, it will bring some of us back in contact with each other again. What occurred to us is what occurs to all graduation classes that have been so close for all of those years, much like vapor we all take a turn and find we're out of sight and soon wonder what happened to those days and all of those friends of ours.

This is the way it was without any hesitation. Imagine you were out with the gang the night before and came in at a reasonable time and bedded down, to have a regular night of sleep. At three o'clock the next morning, a time never to forget, Jesse threw the door of our bedroom against the wall in a surly bolt, then atypically, he bellowed in the same manner a Chief Petty Officer would aboard a ship to the sailors standing on deck, with the roaring wind and the rise of the bow of the ship as it hit the slamming waves of the sea about them. And before we could believe what had happened, as we barely could even open our eyes, to this announcement, "Get out of bed. We're moving this morning." Keep in mind as always nothing had been discussed so we at least knew of this move or any change. You would think by now we would have been shellshock long before, but I definitely never adjusted to his outrageous behavior.

As we merged on into the summer of 1959, Stan, his parents, his sister Mitzi and I came to know each other more deeply. We had moved again and this time over to Meadow Avenue only houses away from Stan's home. From the very first introduction, I was accepted into their home, just as Stan and all of them were in ours. I wasn't home much as we were always in the midst of doing something together. Those activities would include throwing the football up and down the street, to working out with the weights out back on their patio and being fed by Stan's mother whether it was sandwiches, chips, and cold drinks, or to sit down with their entire family and friends over the most sumptuous meals you could imagine.

I received word about the passing of Stan's mother and after sitting and thinking, I immediately thought of all the wonderful ways she would make sure I was welcomed every time. I couldn't help but remember the pride she took when unknown to me, she seized my favorite Q sweatshirt and cast it away. When I asked about it, no one could remember seeing it anywhere. She got the last laugh on me over that moth eaten garment!

And yet, graduating from San Rafael High in 1959, we joined friends on an outdoor floor known as the "Rose Bowl". We danced on those boards with the lights strung above our heads in the branches of the Oak trees and swung with a wonderful inborn stepping, to the swing of the band music each and every Saturday night. This came after all of my turbulence, of the previous years, even as I was now merging into my junior year still at Queen Anne High in Seattle, Washington.

Stan and I were always running here or there in his 50 green, Ford. The summer in fact the next two years, were more than light moments as I was working. Stan and all of our friends were earning the funding needed, either for college in the fall or, in my case, to depart for Europe with Alex as planned.

Alex received a great opportunity of working as a forest fire lookout in the Willamette forest up north in Oregon. I was hired locally to work for a local dairy as a dock man and milkman for the summer. Stan worked with his dad at their neighborhood butcher shop, out on the Miracle Mile on the way to Larkspur.

It was directly after graduating from high school that I joined the ranks of grown men wearing bib-overalls. They were to train me. I would be working beside them loading ice-cream trucks and having my own milk route to tend to two days each week.

My route was short in the sense that I delivered to the Muir Woods Café in the forest well known by tourists who were drawn to this historical spot at the base of Mount Tamalpais in Marin County, California. That was my first stop where I introduced myself to the owner, who was an enchanting woman.

They knew I would be delivering during the morning two times each week. After establishing my regular call of the café, I would always be asked to sit afterwards for a cup of coffee and a big piece of apple pie. As I sat and visited with the waitresses and staff we became more acquainted. I was able to share with them my goal to join my friend Alex to make our way to Europe in the fall.

One foggy morning, as I cautiously made my way down into the woods for the morning delivery, I pulled in with my truck and parked by what had to be one of the historical giants on the forest floor. As I entered the back door for my deliveries, the owner asked me to do her a favor. She said she knew her automobile was in the way of my delivery truck. And added, "Here are my keys; would you mind moving my car?" I told her, "I would be pleased to," not realizing her automobile was the glimmering Silver Rolls Royce. I was stunned by the experience as the door opened more quietly that any car I had ever heard before. I was concerned that my uniform was clean enough to get in and move without leaving a smudge of dirt on the exquisite interior, of that luxurious upholstery. I closed the door and hardly heard the latch of the lock. I placed the key in the ignition and turned the engine on to hear a finely tuned powerhouse, then checked the rear view mirror, to make sure it was clear to back up and park the classic automobile in a better parking spot. Afterwards, I took a gazing look at the exquisite interior, speaking of ambiance, and opened the door cautiously, then exited, closed and locked the automobile door. I walked back to my truck thinking I wouldn't have ever guessed, I would be driving such a vehicle when I left the yard to make my deliveries for the day.

When I reentered the back door, I sat the milk cans down and smiled as I handed back the Rolls keys to the owner. She smiled back at me and I was sure she knew this had been my first such experience. She said, "After you complete your delivery we have prepared you a sandwich and your needed piece of pie which you have certainly earned this morning." I thoroughly enjoyed every bite, thanked all of them and wished them a fine day. I let them know that I would see them again on Thursday's delivery. I can assure you as I drove up out of the forest to my second and final stop on my route I continued to think about this unique opportunity that was mine that morning.

My second stop was ahead of me and as close to the top of the mountain as possible. My delivery was at the Air Force Radar Station. The product was for the staff atop the mountain keeping vigil on the skies. This delivery included the balance of my load and dairy products to hold them until I returned on Thursday. Then, I collected the empty cans and crates that had to be returned to the yard in San Rafael. Just as in the forest below, I came to know the Mess Sergeant and his staff atop the mountain.

What came was the true challenge of the route. That was driving down the mountain and having worked since three-o'clock that morning. To stay awake was more than I could manage. In fact, one morning I jerked and saw I was headed off the side of the roadway, about to roll through the tall grass, the same as the wheat in those fields in Oklahoma and Kansas, which would have meant a descent for any milkman. I awoke and slapped myself in the face saying, "I needed that," which awakened me. I rolled the window down and stuck my head outside of the cab to remain wide-awake with the breeze blowing in my face. In case you're wondering, I made it safely to the yard. What a morning that had proven to be. Before departing for both the forest and the top of the mountain came my major duties of loading my assigned eight wholesale ice-cream trucks, then on to make deliveries on my route.

I found my fellow workers to be fair, hard working, men, seeing that their products were available for shoppers and homemakers alike. I worked with them at three a.m. each morning beneath the lights of the yard. All of us were stepping lively to meet the eight a.m. deadline so the drivers got on their routes daily.

I was to work with another man not much older that me. He was six foot tall and revealed he either got his workout there or at the neighborhood gym. He had black hair parted on the left side and seldom was a hair out of place even as hard as we all worked. He proved to be a good friend that summer.

All of them had told me about "Frenchy or Froggy", another staff member, returning from his vacation. He returned that day and shortly afterwards explained, "Our day will be a full one." He finished his sharing and a piggyback trailer arrived at the yard. His exclamation was simple. He and I would be unloading the ice cream into our refer box.

That day consumed any and all strength I might have had. I found him to be a tower of vigor and in contrast I was limp at the end of unloading thirty-seven thousand gallons of ice cream. I can still see him standing solid as a lithe built, bona-fide Frenchman, on the docks ready to unload another load. I crawled away disheveled and soaking wet. I still remember hearing his laughter at my prowess assisting him that day.

There was dignity in those hard long hours spent with men I have never forgotten.

While all of this was going on, all of my buddies would drop by to find me sleeping through all three of my alarm clocks. They got the biggest kick out of me either looking like a zombie or totally unable to rev their engines up loud enough, for the blast of their horns to break me out of that deep sleep. The only problem I had was rising at that ghastly hour to return to work. Seriously, I tried everything. Stan and I finally resolved this by playing tennis at night until time to return to work. Our game couldn't help but improve under those lights, and afterwards Stan would drop me by the yard for another shift, but on time.

That experience came to an end and I secured furthering professional opportunities in the financial district in San Francisco.

My first position was with the Industrial Indemnity Insurance Company. While there I became a Stockman-Mailman-Multi-Lithe Print man, even chauffeur, for the C.E.O. while there.

Everything seemed to come to a close one day while I was in the midst of meeting all of the days printing for the regional Vice Presidents. I looked up and saw my tie being drawn into the press. Fortunately for me, I grabbed a pair of scissors just in the right amount of time to "snip" and be freed from such duties.

Before leaving, I made sure one early morning, in fact at 5:00 AM, to report before others arrived for the day of work ahead. And, unannounced, I took the elevator to the floor where one Vice President's office was. I entered his office, sat in his chair, removed a cigar from my coat pocket, lit it, then leaned back in the chair and lifted my feet up on the top of his desk. It was at that moment I proclaimed I would be there, at that level in the future. What was ironic regarding the moment while there, was the proclamation I made, to and for myself, of making a said amount of money, within my future while working in the Financial District in San Francisco. Needless to say, had become hooked while working there daily and wanted nothing more for my future.

Then I became a clerk for the Inbound Freight Department at Grace Line Inc., of #2 Pine, only blocks away from where I left the remains of my snipped tie. However, there was one experience I have to include, as it was more than memorable. I have thought of it many times throughout the years. As mentioned I was also the chauffeur for the Chief Executive Officer and President for the firm. One day which I never forgot was the day he called me and asked me to go over to Abercrombie and Fitch to pick up his golf shoes and other equipment, then to go and get the car, a

Mercedes Benz that was nearly as long as the block itself. And he added, afterwards meet him out from of our office for he needed to go down to the boat to collect more needed items. Consequently, after the collection of his items, I pulled up front to see him exit and open the automobile door, to greet me and say, "Thanks for helping me out, now let's continue on to the boat." As I pulled away from our headquarters I thought here I was eighteen and acting as one to take the direction in much the same way, "On James". I realized what my responsibility was and did I ever think my God the last thing I want to do is cause anything such as a scratch on this automobile. Fortunately, even thought this was the first such time I had been called to meet his need, I continued as he directed me to continue across the Oakland Bay Bridge. He said, "There's the boat," and I looked down at the wharf I saw "the boat", a ninety-five foot vessel. One more thing was necessary and that was, we have to load cases of liqueur, then we'll be on our way out to my home to deliver the booze for our evening party." I pulled up beside "the boat". He and I mustered by boarding and began taking cases of the delicacy for his party mentioned. Upon completing this he said, "Now we can be on our way out to Marin County where I live, drop off the booze, then you can return the car to the garage in time to get the mail out for the day and be on your way home. Needless to say he wasn't aware I lived up the road in San Rafael from his home, so it entailed my retuning and fulfilling the days final duties. Afterwards, I made quick steps down to the Embarcadero where I regularly caught the Greyhound bus that I rode every day to and from work. All the way home that night I couldn't help but think of my first trip to "the boat".

A good friend of mine was the owner who worked his shoeshine stand across from Grace Line Inc., where I worked for two and one-half years before enlisting in the United States Air Force. It wasn't difficult to catch sight of him as he had the whitest, curliest hair, a round, brownish-black face with wide- open eyes, seen through his clear plastic, framed glasses. His glasses were such that he had a time from keeping them from slipping down the bridge of his nose as he was talking. He would keep pushing them up and continued his conversation with me seated up high in his special leather chairs, with those metal stands to put my feet on top of, while he lathered my shoes with the sweetest creamy paste, coat on top of coat. He had a soiled apron from a whole lot of shoes he had polished. I always enjoyed talking with him especially when he began to use those special rags, ending with a nice pop in mid air. The reason he became my friend was he was pointedly, interested in all I did, in the district and beyond. Afterwards, he would reach out to shake my hand with the colors of the rainbow engrained in his palm from all of the shoes he had shined. Believe me, he was a true Bird! He kept all of the executives of the area shining with pride every day.

Upper executive levels of management became my friends. This included invitations from my boss, to go and work out at the gym he worked out in only blocks away from our office.

Fellow employees from various South American countries were on our staff. It was a pleasure to work with them and learn their customs, their language and ways of doing business.

Upon the staffs realizing I was enlisting in the United States Air Force, I did more than perceive their respect for such a decision.

I returned from lunch and was asked by one of our Vice Presidents to come and join him for a chat. He was approximately my height of six foot three inches, but somewhat bigger in all proportions. He always wore three-piece suits. His hair was white and swept straight back, leaving considerable forehead. What stood out most was how he looked a lot like Charles Laughton. He wore glasses and worked behind a three-sided partition for privacy. There was only one hitch, he spoke loudly whether in person or on the phone, which was usually drowned out by all of the activity throughout our office. When he sat in his big brown leather chair, he would lean back and would always have a cigar in his mouth, which was evident by the aroma throughout the office.

He had always marveled at my typing skill from day one. He and I were fluently talking and better getting to know each other from that time onward.

This time he asked me to join him for one of his cigars, which he had never done before. I knew he wouldn't have a lot of time, but he made every moment count. He never minced words, but wanted me to know how much they would miss me due to my decision. I had always known how he was solidly behind my proposal to work half days and attend my college classes in the mornings.

Now as all Birds, he leaned forward and spoke with a caring smile to make sure I got the message, He said, "You've got too much on the ball to remain in the transportation business." Then he all but left his perch to share about a successful friend of his that had done this selling peanuts and candy. As it turned out he was making sure I knew where it was, "It was in sales!"

Before enlisting in the Air Force in November 1961, many of us had some fine times together, that we could recall later in all of the destinations we were bound for in our lives.

We remained in contact during that first summer after we marched down the aisle to receive our Diplomas. There was time for us to swim and have picnics, go dancing into the night at the Rose Bowl on Saturday nights, take drives out to the coast in West Marin County, where we spent the day combing the beaches and running in the surf.

On one of those trips out to the ocean, Stan and I went alone and had the hair brain idea to descend down to the beach below. All was perfect until we had hiked over to the cave like formations down the beach and we lost time in regards to the tide coming in on us. The waves were rolling in at a rhythm, not noticing it was usurping our territory that we stood on only moments before. When we finally realized our situation was serious, there was only one alternative to take. That was to retrieve our gear as rapidly as we could and make a direct path up the cliff. We were climbing and breaking a trail up through the bramble bush, which clung to us to the point of making us wonder if we would make it or not. At the same time, we turned and looked and realized our path was the only way we could take or we would have found ourselves awash or worse. Both of us had our shirts off and were wearing our hiking shoes. The more we climbed, the more we were sweating, beating the brush away to make a clear passageway. I noticed my chest was ablaze, in a reddened hue, and we were yelling back and forth at each other as we were closing to the edge of the cliff. Stan turned to me and said, "We made it, and it couldn't have been in a better time."

Upon breaking the top level, we were able to see our car, so we walked over and loaded into the car. All the way back I kept itching and scratching. By the time I got home my entire body was on fire and itched constantly. It didn't take all that long afterwards to know that brush we had been climbing through to the top, particularly, the sections that were cast in the bright red colors on the branches were Poison Oak. After we knew, what we had a dose of we got the lotion needed to rid ourselves of the overall condition and outbreak brought on by our climb through all of that brush. The lotion didn't do the trick as we expected. One of the neighbors told us to use white gasoline. So we went out and obtained some and began to dab saturated cotton balls over all of the inflamed areas. A few days later the condition improved and was soon gone. I can assure you we didn't repeat this experience again.

Stan and I decided we wanted to have ten-speed bicycles. We found a cycling shop in San Francisco near the Golden Gate Park and selected the bikes we both wanted. Before leaving that day we had selected our bikes and equipment. A few days later, we returned to pick up our bikes and had no idea how frequently we would be out in the country riding, enjoying this new mode of travel and recreation we had selected. Nor, did we have any idea the length of trips we would find ourselves taking then or that I would soon be in the midst of pedaling down the coast of California.

Abbey and others were still about so we enjoyed going to movies and weekend dances before Stan and other classmates were on their way to the campuses they would be attending.

Alex's and my plans were shifting, due to my not being able to earn enough to meet the costs of our planned trip.

Before bidding all a true farewell, I want to take you back prior to our Thanksgiving within my senior year. Our family had moved into our second dwelling directly across from San Rafael High. The pattern wasn't that different as Jesse was both shipping out and selling. It got to the point it was difficult to know what came first. A reckoning regarding a behavior that turned out to be constant and that was the slamming of doors!

Jesse and mother had a definite debacle over I don't know what. What was prominent was seeing and hearing him say he would just leave. Here it was just before Thanksgiving and he was packing again, not for a sailing or selling trip, no, he was on his way. I remember how disruptive this was for all within our house. It was especially so for mother.

I am certain you became aware of her tirades long before. They were particularly prevalent when Jesse would be on the road selling and that jealousy factor would always surface and bring a compelled kind of behavior of her either chasing him up and down the coast physically or via numerous and heated telephone calls. I abhorred all of this and would always be drawn into the center of the actions between both of them. This time I told her, "Let go, he's not worth it, why should we let him ruin our Thanksgiving or our Holiday season anymore."

Oh no, she was frantic, especially after knowing he was staying for the interim period down at the neighboring Motel, on the south side of the canal in San Rafael. Before it was over with, she had all of us down there begging and pleading with him to return. I was against this the whole way. His behavior wasn't worth it, and I told her so. In the end, he returned and somehow we had that Thanksgiving together.

The summers of 1959-60 at the age of eighteen to nineteen, Stan and I continued playing our tennis matches at night. He dropped me at work where I continued into the mornings under the lights of the yard.

Our evenings included running long distance on the roads about San Rafael, lifting weights and going out on double dates.

Rainfall isn't only prevalent in the Pacific Northwest, for when it rained there in the county it was a deluge.

I had purchased our families' 58 Volvo.

One particular night after we went to a movie, I drove up in the hills above Larkspur to sit and neck into the early morning.

The ruts up there on the hill were deep and sure enough we got stuck. It seemed as though it was due to such ravines of red clay we found ourselves stuck. It was no time and we had mud top to bottom, which saved us in the end, after being out in that mud attempting to free the car and all of us. There was no way the parents of those two girls could argue with us, as we stood, caked in red mud all over our bodies and clothing. Needless to say we didn't take them out again after that.

I had turned nineteen in 1960, and entered the fall quarter at the College of Marin in Kentfield, California.

Prior, I was working at Grace Line Inc., in San Francisco, and made the decision to attend night classes at the University of San Francisco. I worked at my desk in the Inbound Freight Department and would make a run out to the campus to be on time for the first class. It wasn't long afterwards that I knew I shouldn't have signed up for Medieval History. The woman that was the instructor was very versed as she stood and lectured of the days of Charlemagne, which I realized I just didn't have any foundation in for such studies.

After the length of the day and attending classes what lay ahead was impossible. By the time I would roll up to the house it was well on its way to ten p.m. I would pull up, enter and find something to eat, go out to my room knowing full well it was time for me to study. Somehow the need for sleep took precedence before rising for another day of the daily routine.

It didn't take me long to know this wasn't going to work. At that, I continued working daily and let the classes go by the wayside.

Alex and I began, prior to graduation, going down to Sausalito where we met friends and shared our music with those present. Here we were, Alex playing his flute and bongos with other musicians and periodically I would sit in on a session and play either the Bongos or the Congo drum. This sharing always paid well as we provided the vibes; the onlookers would keep us in our beer while we sat with them.

Without vibes in the night, it would be the four of us sitting, enjoying the glowing embers of our campfire at Samuel Taylor Park where we would go for our evening picnics. That memory is one I carried for years and a considerable distance into the future.

Before I officially enlisted to join the Air Force, mother and I got into our most heated battle. We all leave sooner or later, but I was hanging in, or trying to, before leaving for my enlistment. This was the final blow when it came to the mouthing on her part and exhibiting the same currents of needless jealousy. She didn't know when to remain silent, or to shut up, or let whatever die.

That night I packed all of my effects and slammed everything into the car not caring one way or the other. I didn't have any place to go and didn't care one bit. I slammed the door, as I was accustomed to seeing and hearing all of those years. The hostility was to the point of my becoming physical and striking out, after years of abuse, so I cleared out that night. I drove up the street and rang the bell and Stan's dad answered the door.

I didn't know mother had frantically telephoned their house telling them what had happened.

That was the night I never forgot. Stan's dad came to my rescue. He took me aside and we just talked. He didn't preach. Instead he reached out to me, as any son would hope a dad would. Long before they had made a decision and let me know they felt I was much like a second son for their family. The mainstay was his treating me and talking with me as a man, helping me to know that sometimes such does occur with the women folk of our homes. I will always remember hearing him, say, "Now boy, do you understand the overall situation?" I told him I did. By now the tears were flowing down my cheeks; he gave me a big loving hug which was what I needed most of all. We talked further and before the night was over I told him, "I'll go back since I'll be leaving for the Air Force shortly." I never felt I could either forget or thank him for the love he shared with me that night. Such loving measures were present on all of their behalves from the start.

When you think back through the previous years and experiences, you have long before realized a common element of always seeing how I "was adopted" or about to be family upon family, never my own though. Such trauma was within my very being, always a companion no matter where I was on the track. It may be a poor analogy. Then again it may be perfect when peering back, to find all of it was just as that old trunk, which I sat on while trying to secure its hasp for the journey. And within the contents, a part of me had to deal with all of the continual end results-no matter where. What never left me through every destination was that I was a guy that finally received the diagnosis, a truth that it could be cured, or at least leveled off, to enable me to live at an even keel.

So I coasted back out front of the house. I slowly got out of my 54 Ford and walked deliberately across the lawn and mother met me at the door. Neither of us said one more thing; we reached out and hugged each other. I unpacked my car and took all of my gear out to my room. No more words were shared that night, for that matter, right up until my departure for Basic Training, and my new life ahead.

A memorable evening lay ahead, that was to take my Sis, as I referred to Stan's sister, to her Senior Prom. This was an honor for me and turned out to be a grand night for the two of us. She and I mentioned it many times afterwards. Her classes' festive event was held in the same hotel where our prom had been held. We went for the same grand dinner before attending the ball. What was tops for me was seeing how happy she was over all we shared that night. No brother could have been more proud of his sister than I was of her that night. Stan's parents took pictures before we left for the evening.

All that was left was to say all of the goodbyes to all I worked with, all of my friends, and to be totally surprised with the going away party by all of them. The morning of my departure was much like a still photo being taken to carry from thereon.

Stan had agreed he would drive me over to the Oakland Army Terminal, so he waited for me out front; I stopped at the door and hugged mother and paused and asked her, "Why now, just when everything seems to be coming together as it was meant to?" I kissed her and walked out to Stan's car and set my case in the back seat. I closed the car door and I didn't look back as we rolled on down the street for all that was in that song that would stand for the life ahead of me, *"Off We Go Into The...Blue Yonder"*.

Chapter 12

Enlistment in the U.S. Air Force

I enlisted in November 1961. There, I found tags while completing Basic and Air Police Technical School. They included: Airman Second Class, Airman First Class, Security Guard, Head Launch Control, Security Clerk, Confinement duties, Patrolman, Visitors Control, Sentry Dog Handler, Base Police and Desk Sergeant during the Cuban Crisis.

I first arrived after having spent six months in the coldest time of the year at Lackland A.F.B., Texas attending Basic Training, then to Advanced Basic Training, and finally the most lengthy trip taken by any of my fellow Airmen receiving their orders and travel pay both home, on to their first stations, I stood in line to collect my travel pay. The guys that had become the best of friends, after all we had been through, shook hands, hugged each other and shared parting words. I know it had to be due to my having been the Flight Commander in Basic Training and Air Police Technical Training, that I had an added opportunity to know every one of those guys.

Our first point of contact was November 1961. We immediately found the fifteen of us, including me, were from California. The remaining, were from Massachusetts. Our flight totaled eighty-five Airmen. Now talk about a mixed bag. I can still feel the bus ride after they picked us up at the Air Terminal to transport us to our future home. It was extremely cold that morning. We came so ill equipped with our light beige raincoats with no liners, which caused that cold Texas wind and foggy condition to permeate through our marrow. We started to pull up to the fence line and

Gerry Bradley

even though it was near impossible to see, there were dark blotchy bodies of what seemed to be masses moving in a peculiar fashion. We were sure we had arrived.

The bus stopped and the Sergeant in charge of us for our transport, made sure all the boys were wide awake as he bellowed, "Welcome to your new home", Lackland A.F.B. Texas. Then we stepped down off the bus and we came to realize, these blob like shapes we had gazed at before were flights of men just as us. Well not quite, as some seemed much further along just by the counter of their marching, turning, and sharp precision drill within their units.

We couldn't have arrived at a better time, as it was time for breakfast. I noted, how one of the members ran sharply down one side of the flight inside the chow hall to report their flight and the number about to eat breakfast. Each flight would walk in single file with hats off tucked under their armpits and would slide down the line together. Directly before them were a number of metal trays, which they would grasp and place flatly against their chests, until hearing the cooks make it known, what the choices were for the hour. There was no limit as to how much we could select. In fact, we could go back for seconds if we liked. Before we even gathered for this wonderful meal, which all of us needed, we met our two Technical Sergeants.

They informed us to "Fall-In," and after much jostling and clumsily revealing how green we really were, we were ordered "At Ease". This one Sergeant who was slight of build stood there and you know who he reminded me of, Johnny Carson. There was one major difference. He seemed to lack any of that humor! We soon knew we were looking at our Technical Sergeant Handy. We were attending Basic Training Phase I. The

182

other Sergeant was coarse and considerably younger. They informed us no matter where we were, if spoken to, the first word from our mouths would be "SIR", and nothing else. A few sharp commands were mentioned and then we heard "Ten-Hut", "Right-Face", "Forward March", "Hut-Hut-Hut-Hut", "Flight Halt", finally "At Ease".

Then the Sergeant explained to us, "We are at the dining hall where you will eat your meals." Before we heard anything else, one of the guys broke rank and began to enter the chow hall. We found the Sergeant had the ability even that early in the morning to be heard loud and clear. In fact that fellow Airman came to realize what a gross error he had made. Sergeant Handy raised his voice to be sure to gain his attention. He asked, "Where are you going?" He replied, "I was just going inside to get my breakfast." Our fearless Sergeant walked up to him and said, "What did you say?" And he repeated it again. Our Sergeant asked him one more time, "What did you say?" And before the young Airman Basic could blurt out any more, the Sergeant said, "Airman Puke"…"When you're spoken to the only word that will come from your mouth is 'Sir,' is that understood?" "Yes Sir!" "What did you say?" and he replied, "Yes Sir!" so to be heard by all of us, I am sure every Airmen already seated or still shuffling through the line heard him and remembered such a moment of their first time to the Dining Hall. Our flight began to march in and line up for our first meal upon arriving at Lackland A.F.B., Texas. All the time we heard snickering directed at us in our civilian fashion, opposed to their customary haircuts and uniforms of the day. We tried to ignore their razzing us and continued down the line answering, "Yes Sir", at each selection, to include a new one for the most of us, "S.O.S."

Gerry Bradley

Later we determined the true quality of such a dish. We selected our coffee, milk and juice to be eaten with out entrees. We took our seats wouldn't you know it. I was at the end of the line when I joined our flight at the table. I no more than raised my fork and the Sergeant we had already come to know bellowed, "Flight #3727 Fall Out."

That went down to be the shortest repast called breakfast I had ever imagined. We did anything but shuffle sidestep as we exited. You're right none of us discussed what we had just experienced. We immediately heard our Sergeant command us to "Fall In", "Ten-Hut", "Right Face", "Forward, Huh", which we did together carrying our bags and other light effects in our left hands. As we marched constant training commands came which we soon realized we were going to learn or else. "Flight Halt." The Sergeant began to give additional instructions as to each individual command. He kept repeating that the first and the last word he or they expected to hear from our mouths was, "Yes and No Sir".

Had we thought back to only an hour or more ago, we wouldn't have believed so many commands could have been thrown at us. It is a certainty we would have believed if we wanted to get anywhere; this was the way we got from one point on the base to another. After more familiarity of our new environment, constant marching and coming to realize how much better it would be when we received our uniforms, and hopefully a warm jacket or coat, we were picking up the pace and gaining some signs of becoming a true flight.

All about us were other flights marching and drilling, appearing they were headed for an assigned destination. We were marching in what seemed to be the same direction as we continued to pass the same building over and over, but achieving more unity.

184

That morning passed quickly and there was a brief stop at what would be our barracks for the remaining weeks. While there, we were assigned to our individual rooms. There were two bunk beds across from each other and one desk at the head of each for the use of both men. We had two commands: "Locate your beds in each of our rooms and take all of your valuables, and lock them to have them upon return." Then we heard a familiar command to "Fall In", and "Flight Ten Hut", "Right Face", "Forward March", this time into the cold, blustery, wind blowing southward across the Texas, plains from the north, in Amarillo, Texas. Those from the northeast were better prepared, as their coats were more suitable to hold out this biting cold. However, we from the Golden State of California were anything but equipped and were freezing our butts off, not to mention our cheeks. That was the benefit of our mode of transportation, it kept us somewhat thawed out step by step. We were ready for our return to the chow hall when we found we were destined to the building that we passed long before. During that time, there had been many of our flight who were able to reply, "Sir, Yes, Sir", and then we would march some more.

Sure enough, it was drawing close to the noon hour and our flight marched directly to where before, we heard, "Flight Halt". One member of our flight had been selected to be our chow runner who ran and reported our flight and number for the noon meal. This time we filed in single file just as before, but there seemed to be less commotion. Every one of us made it through the chow line! We sat and ate, which took no more than ten minutes, instead of having only my fork to my lips, I was able to eat most of the food on my tray before hearing, "Flight 3727, Fall Out".

Having the warm food in our stomachs helped ward off some of the bitter, Texas chilling wind hitting us smack in the face, as we continued marching, learning additional methods of how to turn and move more as a trained flight should.

We were pulling together and beginning to feel some pride in our accomplishment. Were you to have looked and compared us from this our first morning, our heads were higher, more and more erect and ready for a new command. We drilled "Flight, Ten, Hut", "Parade Rest", "Right Face", "Left Face", "Forward Huh", "To The Rear Huh", "Right and Left Oblique Huh," "Forward Huh". The afternoon of our first full day continued exactly as described until returning to the chow hall for dinner.

We heard a command during the latter part of the afternoon of "Flight Halt," directly in front of our barracks, to "Fall Out", and "Take Your Break", which was the last before the end of that day. We didn't waste a moment of our break as we introduced ourselves to the latrine at the end of the hallways on each floor. It seemed as though everyone slumped in a spot and crashed until hearing our Sergeant enter the barracks and bellow, "Flight 3727", "Fall Out", "Fall In".

More orders were given to clarify, we were going to dinner and would return, and have a Flight meeting" inside our barracks.

Finally, our path was directly to the dining hall. This meal was anything but relaxing, yet we were given a generous portion of additional minutes to enjoy and to converse with each other. It was an opportunity to know each other before hearing the all familiar "Flight 3727, Fall Out", "Forward March", "Mark Time Huh", which we did at "Quick Time", all the way back to our barracks. Upon arrival, a new command came,

"Parade Rest", then the Sergeant repeated some of his previous speech as to what our evening would entail.

During the day we received our issue of linen, blankets and pillows. We took specific instructions by the Sergeant in front of all, as to how to properly make our beds that evening. This method was applied toward everything. First, was the group instruction, then we practiced with the Sergeants observing. Either we got it, or the beds were torn up and dumped on the floor, and then we would be ordered, "Do it right."

It seemed as though the key elements were the hospital corners and their tuck, then to tuck the sheets down each side. The reason for this particular tightness we found was, the test of dropping a quarter in the middle of a made bed, and watching that quarter bounce off the blankets to see it could be done.

That night it seemed to be just a bit more familiar so one of the men spoke up, "Sir, there are many of us wondering when we can smoke." The Sergeant replied there were two commands that would answer that question. The first was, "The Smoking Light Is Out" then he reiterated, "The Smoking Light Is Out". He continued with the next item on the evening agenda. He called the flight to gather around to hear, "We're about to have a party, G.I. Fashion, tonight."

We soon became aware that this party consisted of another type of cake and ice cream It included buckets, mops, scrub brushes, Ajax, window cleaner, paper towels, lots of hot water, and an introduction to our flight's buffer for our barracks. Furthermore, he made us aware that this party would continue until the barracks was in inspection order for the coming day.

Gerry Bradley

It took us no time to organize our effort to get it completed as specified. We were sure that this party being thrown would bring us to a place of rest and sleep for that first day. Afterwards, the younger Training Instructor returned and checked our work, and clarified sections that still needed upgrading. Finally, our first day of Basic had come to an end. There wasn't one of us that could explain how worn out we were from the total day. But before we totally sacked out, the Sergeant wanted us to know another command that might be heard at any time. That had to do with our now assigned barracks guards that would stand duty throughout the night. He might blow his whistle once, twice, or three times and yell, "Fire-Fire- Fire" if this was to occur we were to fall out in mass formation to the front of our barracks.

This action was timed, and required considerable practice to get the time within the structure that meant all were safe within our flight.

We finally heard those blessed words, "Lights Out". Had anyone been listening, I can assure you, there was little, if any, whispering heard that night. All were asleep as we heard in our sleepy eyed state, "Tweet-Tweet-Tweet- Fire-Fire-Fire" and everyone wrapped in their blankets made way to exit our barracks, but far to slow, and were we made aware of it. We no more than hit our heads on the pillows, and the bellowing command of, "Fire-Fire-Fire", was more than enough, to motivate us to move as never before. In our formation, we were informed, "that was better, but it would have to be faster in order to save every man of our flight."

Then, our Technical Sergeant shared with us how one barracks just like ours, had caught fire one evening and few if any got out, because, they took far too long to exit the structure. Now, they had our attention, and we knew we would move as never before from that moment forward.

Had you been an eves dropper peering into the rooms from thereon, it wouldn't have been a surprise, to see legs extended outside their blankets with either shower clogs or brogan boots on their feet, so to evaporate from our barracks for any drill.

Reveille was called to fall out for the morning roll call and the raising of the colors. We had ten minutes to shave, before falling out to march to chow each morning.

However our Technical Sergeant via his inspection saw how one among us had not shaved. He emphasized our shaving was a must every morning.

Undoubtedly, any experiencing the same can recall how one guy or another always seemed to learn slowly, if at all.

Wouldn't you know it, the second morning the same Airman had not complied; the consequences included hearing, "Airman, return to the barracks and get your razor." He soon returned with his razor in hand. Before we returned to our barracks, we, rather he, soon found what a dry shave was. Believe me, the razor like moment wasn't forgotten by of any of us from thereon.

Our Sergeant said, "Ten Hut", "Left-Face", "Forward- Huh"; this was the first time we had made that turn. We knew we were directed toward a new group of buildings. We heard, "By The Right Flank Huh", "Flight 3727 Halt".

The building was the base barbershop so we knew what was coming next. As was true for all stops, we were to file in a single file, to wait for our turn before taking our seats. The barber was anything but that family barber back home. He said, "So you're here for your first Air Force Cut". As we talked the barbers used their clippers set for a burr cut for each of us. All we heard was a constant buzz passing over our heads as we sat in a state of shock seeing all of the locks drop to the floor. The floor was covered with a stack of colored hair of every hue imaginable. There weren't any individuals within our flight afterwards, instead there was one true flight with the same haircuts, as our individuality passed as quickly as the hair we saw fall to the floor.

Our activities were much the same including our stops at the chow hall. That afternoon we stopped by one of those buildings we had marched by many times. We still had our civies on and were eagerly awaiting our issue of our uniforms. As we marched in the clerks were yelling at us to give them our sizes for the first article of our uniforms, our fatigue jackets.

We took off the civilian coats and jackets and put our fatigue jackets on with real pride. Our flights Technical Sergeant told us, "It's time you begin to look like a flight." Even though that was all we received then, there isn't a way to tell you how warm I was, in comparison to the way I had arrived in that raincoat with no lining.

I'm sure the feeling was psychological, but I felt warmer than stepping off that bus the first day in the crisp morning fog to report for the beginning of my career or time of enlistment wearing the new fatigue jacket with a lining to break the cold, windy morning air.

The days and weeks melted into another as we attended classes on everything including: the U.C.M.J., Uniform Code Of Military Justice to guide us and to obey, to weapons we would carry then and into our future assignments, the gas house, obstacle course action; foremost, to unite as one unit or flight in all we did.

The "Smoking Light" became lit sporadically after the first three days. That became quite an ordeal, it being lit and being out. I became quite familiar due to both.

The Sergeants drew me to the side and shared their decision of having selected me to be the Flight Commander. That meant when they weren't present I was in charge of our flight of all eighty-five men at all times. It also meant that whatever was in effect prior to their departure stood until their return.

When this came to a head was over the smoking light being out. The men that smoked were agitated with the compliance of such orders. They were more than sure if the Sergeants weren't there, they should be able to smoke. The tension regarding this order was too much for all of them.

On the weekends we could walk freely to and from the chow hall. I had already finished eating and was walking in front of several of our guys to find another group waiting outside by the garbage cans. It seemed as though they had a party in mind for me. One of them from Massachusetts, built thickly, confronted me with their decision to kick my ____, due to my not being more flexible with the smoking lamp and its privileges.

I tried to reason with them but to no avail. I told him, "You can swing all you want to, but don't think I'm going to return any blows." I also said, "All that will come of this, will be jail time for whoever started the fight or begins to throw the blows," I repeated again, "You can swing all you want, but forget thinking that I will give you the pleasure by striking back, because I'm not going to jail for your not being able to smoke."

I braced myself up against those garbage cans and he squared off in front of me. I saw the first punch come flying. It was like a flick of his

191

wrist and I felt and heard "crack", directly on the cleft of my chin. His punch didn't even make me flinch. That was my error because, he was more, angry over that and took another punch at the targeted spot of the cleft of my chin. This time it rocked me a bit and he was louder than ever, as I stood my ground waiting for him to quit. The third blow came harder and swifter, with a real shock that nearly knocked me down. He finally looked at me with disgust and said, "You're not worth it!" The entire group stalked off in disbelief.

I can still see the ring on that finger coming at my chin each time. You don't wait to be hit when someone is wearing his class ring or otherwise! Nothing was ever mentioned by any of them or me regarding the incident.

The next morning upon the Sergeants return I requested a meeting with them and asked for clarity regarding the smoking policy upon their departure. It was agreed that the smoking light, as expressed to convey whether the smokers could smoke or not, would be lit, if they were no longer present. You can guess what the result was upon this being announced to the entire flight. I can assure you those guys never forgot their flight commander regarding any future maneuvers.

All being shared came during the early days, we served together, when I had to step up and act as I had on the Sunday outside the barracks, regarding their privilege to smoke or not to smoke. The end result became the silent respect they paid to me from that time onward, and now all of us were boarding our busses headed to our homes and assigned stations.

One more event took place while completing Basic Training. This took place at the site of the walkway outside of the Chow Hall. The method was to file in for each and every meal. Every time our Chow Runner and I were the last to file through; I unfortunately found my patience fraying to the point of reaching out one evening while waiting for entry for dinner to merely tap the shoulder of the Chow Runner. I had no idea this would be considered as an affront to the fellow member of our flight when lightly tapping his shoulder, to feel myself in mid-air being flipped as a circus performer to slam down on the concrete walk. The next thing that was heard was his blurting out, "No one will ever touch me as you did and get away with it." The result was for him and others standing in the line to find I was frozen on the ground with jammed back muscles. The next thing was realizing he and fellow Airmen were making sure to take me to the Emergency entrance of the Lackland Air Force Base Hospital for needed care. I never forgot when the doctor came in to care for me and asked, "How did this happen Airman," for him to hear my reply, "Doctor, I slipped down the stairs." He certainly didn't believe me, but didn't pursue it any further. His diagnosis was I had severely jammed the muscles of my entire back. Then he gave me medication to relax the muscles during the night. That was the night I came to realize the last thing I would do was tap anyone ever again on the shoulder, especially a guy from the fair state of Pennsylvania or Massachusetts. I never mentioned this nor did the fellow Airman that had more than enough ability to throw as he did. Here, was another example how the entire flight had an example of my being their Flight Commander and the manner I stood behind all of them.

Remember the guy and the ring? He came up to me with tears in his eyes and grabbed me with the strongest hug I could have ever expected. He said, "You're the finest Airman of the whole lot," he went on and said, "I'll never forget the wisdom you exhibited to all of us during that incident." By now we were both hugging and having a tough time saying, "The best of luck and do well at your future training and assignment." We all knew we were far closer than any of our schoolmates or friends back home. The majority received tidy sums in the hundreds of dollars and I held out my hand for my amount to receive, ten cents. I only needed to ride across base on the Base bus to the Air Police Technical Training School.

Before being received into the school, we had to spend three weeks in P.A.T.S., Personnel Awaiting Technical School. Due to my previous assignment as the flight commander and the recommendations passed on, I continued as the Flight Commander. Consequently, I resumed my second management position. I was to communicate with all job sites and assign the men daily to their tasks.

While involved in each level of training, I found real memories from two events. Foremost, was the beck and call for: "Mail-Call". There wasn't a day I didn't receive mail, as my mother made sure I had a letter every day. And the other was, in knowing we could attend Chapel Call every Sunday. Needless to say, I didn't miss it, for there were the truest moments where I found tranquility that led to a perfect way and place to gain: strength, aiding me on each step of the training that lay ahead.

Those were long weeks for all of us. Before we knew it, all related to becoming an Air Policeman was concluded along with graduation and the parade grounds were ahead of us.

We received our certificates and our orders had been processed. I still remember being told that I had a choice of the following: First, was Thule, Greenland where there was a girl behind every tree, if you could find a tree; Second, was Okinawa; Third, was Base Police in Paris, France; and finally, Vandenberg A.F.B. California. Needless to say, my choice was undoubtedly absurd, but I had been away from my home state of California long enough, so I accepted the last choice.

My first six months between 1961-62 were much as that promise given by the Recruiter in San Rafael, California who declared we would be home for Christmas. The only thing was he didn't say what year.

A similar sight was seen when finally taking some time on a weekend pass from the rigors while at Basic and Technical Training at Lackland, A.F.B., Texas and going to town in San Antonio, Texas. When I did go, I had planned everything so I would have a fine time. The way I prepared was to set up my own Chinese laundry and polishing services for my fellow Airmen.

In the meantime, my fellow Airmen would take off for town every weekend and behave in such a way to emphasize why the citizenry of San Antonio, felt as they did regarding G.I.'s.

Their weekends would be spent drinking all the beer they could hold, and upon return there were always those having to drop their heads over the commode, if they made it in time.

I remained getting my gear in order for the coming weeks duties and inspections that had to be attended. The guys within our flight were delighted to have anyone but themselves polishing and pressing their uniforms. Each weekend I took their uniforms, boots, leather gear, and readied theirs and mine, then collected from each. I kept this going until near the end of our training. When I had earned enough, I didn't make it known I would be going to town over a planned weekend pass. In fact, I waited for them to take the first bus and purposefully took the next one. When I arrived in town for the first time I scanned the city and found a fine restaurant in which to dine.

Some of my fellow Airmen from our flight caught a glimpse of me through the window. They couldn't stand it and had to come to acknowledge that I had come to town. They razzed me, but I continued eating my five-course dinner to include the thickest steak any of us had seen for sometime. Before they left, I made sure to see them lick their lips, as I ordered the tallest piece of lemon chiffon pie I could, for I knew they had already spent the best part of their earnings.

Some of us decided to catch the latest flick with Glen Ford in it. The movie was *The Four Horsemen of Apocalypse*. Most of them split for the taverns or returned to Base.

I had seen this dance hall earlier so I decided to go dancing. It was a spacious dance floor that shined, awaiting all to step and swing their partners. I went up to this petite, Mexican American young woman, and asked her to dance. She said, "I would love to." I escorted her to the floor for our first dance. I remember when I took her in my arms, I was considerably taller and she was like a willow branch. She was the tiniest woman and had the same tiny sweet voice and seemed to enjoy both our dancing and our conversation. We continued dance after dance.

I found she had been in love with a Lieutenant and was waiting for his return. She told me more regarding his being shipped out, but he couldn't convey to her the location due to his assignment being restricted. I let her share this story and more about herself.

I recall while we were dancing, I finally said, "Ma'am; I hope you'll take this right, but you sure do smell fine." She laughed at that and we took a spinning turn. Then I took her over and offered her a cold drink as we sat down. We realized that it was getting late so I offered to escort her home.

She had told me that she was a nurse in San Antonio, and must get to bed, as she would be back on shift the next morning. As it turned out her apartment wasn't that far from the dance hall. I took her to the door and she said, "Would you like to come in?" I accepted and we went into her apartment. What stood out was the tidiness throughout. She had her nurse's uniform hanging over the door to her bedroom. We agreed how nice the evening had been from the start.

She asked me, "would you like some breakfast," and I told her, "I'd love it."

At the same time, I was vividly remembering what I had seen before going to dinner that evening. It stood out on the sidewalks, where the shop owners were bartering to sell their wares to fellow Airmen, when none would buy, they would mutter and curse under their breath at "those cheap Airmen".

I also recalled walking up to the front wall of the infamous Fort in History, the Alamo. I hurriedly realized there was only the wall standing and historical markers depicting its importance, one hundred years before.

The real significance of that walk was just ahead of me. Off to one side of the walkway was, a sign that read, "Dog's and G.I.'s stay Off The Grass" and seeing this was a stigma, when thinking only moments before, store keepers were frothing at the mouth to take all they could from all G.I.'s, while there for the given moment. I've never forgotten the hypocrisy broadcast on one lawn in San Antonio, Texas.

We could see and smell that breakfast was nearly done. We sat down and paused a moment for her to pray. Then we resumed talking and better getting to know each other. By now we were as relaxed as fellow classmates, such as the girl back home she had already pictured. I told her all about the girl and how all had come to an end before I enlisted.

We realized there was in essence another in each of our cases. Our breakfast was really good, but the hour was getting late. In fact, I would have to find a place to stay for the night, as the last bus had already left. We came to mutually agree that she would sleep in her room, get some bedding out for me, and I would sleep on her sofa. The arrangement couldn't have been more perfect. Before she went to bed she told me, "I'll, drive you back to the base in the morning and return to work at the hospital."

Morning arrived much sooner than either of us could imagine. We got up and took turns in the bathroom readying and left for the base. On the way, we exchanged telephone numbers and decided that after the day of work, she would call and come out to pick me up so we could spend the evening together.

My fellow Airmen were, a bit curious about their Flight Commander arriving that morning as I did. I just let them wonder.

As agreed she phoned and said, "I'll be coming out soon, so be ready." My, she was prompt! I could feel every eye on us as I went out to meet her in front of our barracks. I got in her car and she turned around and we began to drive away from all a part of attending Air Police Technical School, Class # 3628.

This time she showed me much more of the city and eventually stopped, at a favorite Mexican restaurant, La Fonda, where we had a superb meal. Then we walked along the river that runs through the main part of town where the quaint sidewalk cafes were located. We were talking the whole time. Finally, I asked her, "Would you like to have a cup of coffee and some dessert?" She thought that sounded perfect.

She shared she was currently on the same shift and had made a decision that she was sure I would appreciate.

I came to realize she was the sweetest little branch I could ever have hoped would come along. We really got along and found we had so much in common including our mismatches. I couldn't help but wonder what she had in mind. She had decided she really didn't need her car as the hospital was within walking distance. To help us, while I was completing my work in Technical School, she was going to loan me her car. That way, I could freely come and go from the base and meet her each evening, either at the hospital or at her home. I was stunned at such a generous gift and a workable plan for us. We agreed, and that night she was able to get more sleep and for the first time, I felt more relaxed than I had been for sometime.

You can imagine how the scuttlebutt spread among the men when they saw I had my own car. I heard several of them say, "Can you believe it, he wouldn't even come to town, as he was doing all of our gear and making money doing it, then he came to town and look at the result."

We continued the same course throughout; the respect we paid each other brought us even closer, as we held tight, helping each other at a time in our lives where such care was so needed.

I never forgot the last evening she and I had. We knew I had graduated and we were being shipped to our stations with a leave home first. She drove me back to the base where we sat for quite awhile and reached out and held hands. All the time we were thanking each other for everything. We had become friends like a brother and sister and we agreed we would let it lie there, as she was convinced that her Lieutenant would be back in touch with her in the future.

I couldn't have hoped more for any person than I did for her that this dream she had of her Lieutenant, would return in her near future. We reached out and hugged each other and she kissed me for the first time. I could see she was starting to cry, so I kissed her one more time, and opened the car door and closed it gently. She began to roll away; I never saw her again.

This was another Bird without a doubt. How I hope after all of these years she somehow becomes aware of this book and my feelings then and what she meant to this Airman who waited sometime to come to town and find such a beautiful, weeping willow branch. No more had I found her, than she bid me farewell.

We met outside to say goodbye to those about to board their busses to their homes and report to their first stations both abroad and stateside. We would find ourselves performing duties from: security to administration, to standing on some gate or walking a beat on the streets of a foreign city, not even contemplated. Before that moment of departure occurred, we had a brief moment to hug, shake hands, paying the earned courtesy to each other for the work already accomplished for the months we had lived life together.

Our bond with each other was formed the very first time we were given a true break from the days-studies and physical training, to take a break. Break we did, by lighting where we landed and immediately positioning our backpacks next to each other and falling asleep for ten minutes or more, if granted such an opportunity. It was that leaning on each other that gave us the support all of us needed.

Where I was anything but a whiz when it came to learning the nomenclature of our weapons, another would patiently take time after assembling theirs and help me, or another, who was having a similar problem. That teamwork was precisely what did more than aid each other at a given moment, rather, that was what gave us the unity of a team and made our flight strong.

From there came real comradeship, love, respect for each other and our total effort to complete every phase of our training. Now that we were seeing each member board his bus we realized how close we had become through every aspect of our training. We were caught up in the assignments that came for each guy.

Before I boarded my bus I made sure to get around to every guy, as I had special time with each, whether it was in training, or before, while we were in P.A.T.S. together. Then it came my turn and the sincerity paid by all of the guys was the best, which carried me for a long ways into the blue ahead.

The buses took us back to the airport in San Antonio, Texas. It was there many months ago we had arrived to attend Basic Training. To think I was about to step on to the plane of my dreams that would take me back to San Francisco, California near my true home in Marin County. That was one flight I thoroughly enjoyed from the start to the finish.

I could feel our descent and just before the pilot announced, "We are about to land at San Francisco International Airport," I looked out both sides of the wing and began to see familiar sites such as the Oakland Bay Bridge.

The plane dropped down over the bay and before we could realize it, we were taxiing down the runway slowing, taking a turn leading to the terminal. Then the plane stopped. The Stewardess said, "We hope all of you have enjoyed your flight and we'll look forward to serving you in the future."

I grabbed my brief case and dress hat to make my way down the stairs. I had waited for this for sometime. When I was at the last step, I stepped out on the tarmac and made sure I was clear of the other passengers, so I could bend down on my knees and kiss the ground with delight to be home at last. I took in a deep breath of the salt air from the San Francisco Bay. Then I went with one of my fellow Airmen and we stopped to have a congratulatory drink before pushing on to our destinations.

Afterwards, I went to the luggage area to claim my duffel bag. I lifted it up and over my shoulder and headed for the exit where I caught the limousine bound for San Francisco. That ride into the city was a delight seeing all of the sights I had missed all of those months while away. We were downtown in no time. I asked to get off at the Greyhound Bus Station where I checked my duffel bag in one of their large lockers.

Then I caught a bus and headed downtown into the financial area of the city so I could surprise my mother while at work. Mother wasn't aware as to my arrival. I walked in the lobby of the Continental Life Insurance offices and caught the elevator taking me to the eleventh floor where she worked. Her staff saw me first, so I gave them the hush signal and walked directly up to mother's chair. She turned, and cried, immediately saying, "My baby is back home." That was a special moment for us, and one, we mentioned many years later with each other.

Her staff was equally glad to see me. We visited, but she still had time to complete her tasks.

I decided to return and get my bag at the bus depot, then catch the bus at the Embarcadero for San Rafael. In no time at all mother returned home from work and Jesse happened to be home, not off on another ship. That evening I remember hearing them say, "What would you like to do this evening?" I replied, "I just want to stay home and visit," and that's what we did into the hours of the coming morning. They wanted to know all about my training, literally every phase. So as the hour grew late, I continued to share all of the details regarding: Basic Training, leading me to attend the Air Policeman's Technical School, down to how I was able to fit everything in my duffel bag, but what was best, was they sat and listened with real interest.

We spent quite some time of those twenty-seven days of leave together. I had ample time to visit and spend time with my friends. There was definitely a gap among all I had so deeply cared for before leaving to join the Air Force. It was quite evident that our center of interest had changed.

More and more I knew I was under foot, where before we went everywhere together all the time. Now their work was academia, mine had become serving our country. When you think of it that way and at the same time on day twenty-four I was hearing my parents say, "It is high time you get on to your base as you eat too much." That may have been true, but it really was damaging to hear the similarity of the messages from them and my friends. To think there remained three more days before reporting to Vandenberg A.F.B., California. Such brought me to recall the same harmful reactions throughout my growing up years.

So not to be underfoot or to eat more than they had expected, I packed and readied to make way to my first assigned base. As had always been true of me, I was packed and ready to leave the next morning. They told me they would take me down by the San Francisco International

Airport. I had already told them I would hitchhike down the coast. Where most parents would have taken pride in seeing that their son or daughter was safely taken to their new College or University setting for their future years of their lives, not my parents; they did as they had said. We visited some and upon arriving to the most congested area of the Peninsula by the airport, Jesse pulled over where I would have the best place to catch a ride. I got out of the car, hefted my duffel bag, briefcase and said thanks for the ride, and told them the stay was great. They signaled and were back in the flow of the traffic heading for their turn-a-round home. I stood tall with my gear at my feet and my thumb was at the same attention to gain a ride south. .

I had plenty of time while waiting to catch my ride down the coast, to ponder over the one heightened discussion I had with them while I was home.

One startling fact was that my 1954 black Ford was missing when I arrived. When we finally got together that was my first question. They typically and curtly replied that they had sold it. I retorted, "You did what, without even asking my approval after all it was my car." From there the heat was scorching. Here, I had just arrived home after all of those months with anticipation of being able to clean up my wheels and drive again. Furthermore, I intended to drive on down to my new base. The big question was "why", again bringing me into the arena where I had spent much of my time before graduating from high school. They replied, "It was in the way!" Before leaving I had purposefully parked it up next to the house so it wouldn't be in the way as they were telling me. I was so upset and they knew it. I told them it would have been one thing to do this discussing it with me before, but to do it at a whim, much the same as in the past, to meet their needs was wrong. Not only did they not have any idea as to my planning to drive my car to Vandenberg A.F.B., they didn't care one bit. It seemed as though we would never get off this for my short stay. Here they had sold my car; I had no car to get on and off the base or otherwise. This was another explicit example of what I had been captive to environmentally all those years before. I had to clear out for a while and that is exactly what I did. I can't tell you how many times for the remaining three-and-a –half years while stationed at Vandenberg A.F.B. I thought of this travesty.

After returning from all of my training between 1962-63 an event took place while on leave back to Seattle, Washington and to my old Queen Anne High School, I paid a visit to see my Physical Education teacher from back then. When I opened the door to the gym, he looked up and bellowed across the floor, "Hello Moose". We had a fine visit bringing him up to date. I will always remember that bellow on that day and the way he drew me to him. After that amount of time he still looked a lot like Walter Mathou, he even had the same bent over look at the shoulders, which were wide carrying one tall frame. I couldn't think of him without seeing him in his gray sweatshirt, khaki pants and his whistle around his neck. You see he was a big part of the institution and long before he became one important Bird.

Now, I have shared an extensive portion of my life's experiences; however, this segment in time was without a doubt, one of which I could only say, "I just toughed it out." What really blows even my mind is to think it was without any medication, diagnosis, interrelated help or aid. So I am left with one deep question, "How was I able to accomplish all of that, and still be 'goin' on, and on?' Quite honestly, I had surpassed far beyond the blue thought of in the beginning phases of enlisting as I had in November 1961.

GERLAD KENT, LOVED THOSE HATS

GERALD AT 18 MONTHS WITH MOTHER

STEPS WITH DADDY'S HAT

A RIDE IN DADDY'S PEPSI TRUCK

VISIT TO MY GREAT GRANDMOTHERS

SUNDAY'S BEST 3 YEARS OLD

MOTHER AND HER BOYS

EARMUFFS FOR FALL

BROTHERS IN SUNNY OKLAHOMA

CARRYING CASES GOING PLACES

RIDING IN MY RED RYDER WAGON

ROUGH AND TUMBLLE COWBOYS

WAITIN' BESIDE DADDY'S PEPSI TRUCK

STANDING WITH GRANDMA JOYCE

FIRST GRADE DAYS

FIRST GRADE 1947

HOT SUMMER MONTHS

OUTING WITH GRANDPA HENRY

WITH BUDDIES HIGH SCHOOL GRADUATION 1959

ALEX AND ME – SENIOR PROM NITE

ANOTHER WAY OFF BASE

SHEP AND ME

Chapter 13

To Vandenberg Air Force Base

All that occurred fell within the year of 1962 through 1965.

During my duties on Base Police one Sunday stood out among all of the others.

It was on a Mother's Day that was prominent while serving as an Air Policeman driving patrol. I checked my watch and knew the day would soon be over and it would be break time. The call came over the radio that there had been a roll over accident outside the Main Gate. We knew as we turned on our emergency lights, sirens, and made a swift turn-around what had to be ahead of us. The ambulance had been requested and there were some three to four units routed to the scene.

I arrived on the scene along with one unit to see where the blue MGB Midget involved in the collision had landed. The car was launched from the gravel on the median of the roadway. It had flown off the edge of the road in mid-air for approximately some one hundred and sixty-five feet, before landing on four flattened tires. The sports car was crumpled beyond recognition.

My partner and I slid down the bank making our way to the occupants of the vehicle. Both the driver and the passenger were lodged in the front seats buckled by much more than their safety belts. We tried to administer First Aid to the driver and his passenger. We checked vital signs and saw there was little we could do for either of them. At the same time we checked their wallets and identification that revealed they were stationed at Vandenberg A.F.B. When I reached the passengers side I found the young Airmen partially hanging outside of their vehicle. He was bleeding from the mouth and was barely coherent. There wasn't any way to save him. His breathing was quite shallow, his color was jaundiced and he had a bruised look all over his face. His eyes never opened and he seemed to have no muscle control as he hung limp. I tried to rouse him, but he died in my arms. We helped to carry both of the Airmen up the side of the hill to the ambulance.

I drove my patrol vehicle to Base Police Headquarters and spent hours completing paper work related to all we had seen that afternoon. From there I returned to my barracks and burst into tears for both their souls and for their mothers, soon to receive such word on Mother's Day.

Consider this single action taken as assigned then pause while weighing all stated. All, inclusive occurred long before being able to know the total message to come later. Where in all others views I should have fallen away due to such stress, instead you'll be able to see by example I did quite the opposite. The thorough training received throughout undoubtedly had more to do with my completing this call as others within my enlistment. At the same time, there was something deep within me that I hope revealed to my fellow Airmen I had what it took and more. That being so would be the finest complement I could have ever expected. Furthermore, each and every assigned duty from the first throughout my three-and-a –half years at Vandenberg A.F.B., California, spoke loudly regarding all that I strived to accomplish.

While working between 1961-62 within the 4392nd Combat Defense Squadron, I joined others on the Funeral Detail and worked on the precision needed. At first our timing was off, but we kept drilling so we improved daily.

We received word we would be standing duty for our first funeral in the near future. This brought us to polish all commands making sure of the firing of our weapons and the folding and handling of our countries colors with its proper respect. I remember there were few attending the officer's funeral, but we were in place as we should have been. The expressions varied from graven to literal sorrow to a graying look and those shedding their needed tears in release of the situation.

Through all we were spit and polish from our brims to our boots, accented by our white cap covers, white gloves, holding our weapons ready to fire the volley that broke the silence of the wind off the California Coast. Then came the folding of the flag for the final display and our handing it to the loved ones present.

This was my introduction to all that lay ahead, while there, for three-and-a-half years until my early discharge so that I could begin my academic work toward my AA Degree at Allan Hancock College in Santa Maria, California.

The morning sun was already warming, and the whipping wind from the passing traffic required me to hang on until I would be on my way south. Even though I was a blur among all of the traffic, the sprawling cement of the roadways and overpasses above, I discovered something I would never forget.

Each time I returned home it became more glaring that this wasn't home anymore. I would realize the answer that I asked of my mother before my departure of the past. "How, and why now, when everything seems to be working so well and finally making sense in our lives?"

I enlisted in the Air Force November 1st, 1961. My fortune was with me that morning as the first car that stopped was going my way.

They knew the Base was out toward the coast. The fine people agreed they would take me directly to the front gate.

I thought at the time here was a couple doing what I knew my parents should have done. The main thing was I had the ride and didn't need to be concerned regarding that anymore. They were the nicest people. In fact they reminded me of Chuck and Betty from Louisiana from my boyhood. They didn't seem to be able to help me enough. We were cruising down Highway 101 South, passing through cities and towns I would gain deeper familiarity of in the future.

That led to Paso Robles and on down the coast to Pismo Beach and other beach towns that brought us into the outskirts of Santa Maria. They knew it was only thirty more miles out to the base. The entire trip was my first through all of the area and definitely not my last. As we approached the Main Gate, the gentleman said, "Well Airman, there's your Base and your future home." The couple waved as they rolled away. I didn't realize how profound his words were. I thanked them both for the ride and how much I had enjoyed their company all the way down the coast.

I was finally there. I looked at the outstretched sign and logo, depicting what would be my home much longer than I imagined. Then I grabbed my duffel bag and brief case, walked up to the Air Policeman at the Main Gate and told him I was just arriving and he directed me to the Visitors Control Center. They asked for my orders, which I showed them. The next thing I knew they called for my shuttle that gave me a ride to our Squadron Administration Building processing me into the unit I was to be assigned. It was a relief to have a place to set that heavy bag down. I reported back to the Administration offices and they continued to process me on board. As it turned out, I had to wait as much as two to three weeks before confirming my full assignment.

Vandenberg A.F.B. was covered with vegetation called Ice Plant. This plant was similar to a rubber plant and flowered each year. It was perfect for holding the outstretched dunes and plains of sand. I soon came to realize it was referred to as a semi-isolated Base with the closest community to the south, some ten miles, called Lompoc, California. Traveling toward highway 101 was Santa Maria, and Santa Barbara some seventy-five miles south down highway 101 leading to Los Angeles, California.

The memorable site while there or perhaps on your travels, are the sprawling magnificent fields of bountiful flowers, by the rows to gaze upon, as did the viewers during WWII. It was then the growers saw to the flowering valley being planted to reveal, "Old Faithful", regally displaying the waving stretches of the stars and stripes, signifying their support for our troops throughout the world.

Rather than spend the time pushing a lawn mower on the grounds crew, I volunteered to join the Funeral Detail. How ironic the result was while stationed at Vandenberg A.F.B. I was much the same at that semi-isolated military base where I spent three-and-one half years of my first hitch staring down "that track," a lonely hearted man. I wasn't unlike many of my fellow Airmen of whom I was stationed with or assigned. Upon arrival to the Base I was to be an Air Policeman who would grasp each and every opportunity as to all assignments in the career field.

I first worked as a Security Guard and was assigned to outlying posts and gates. The duties were to control those entering and exiting Security Clearance areas. Our Squadron was quite tight with anything related to Security throughout the Base. Here we all found that our barracks life was improved from what we had experienced at our Basic and Technical Training.

Our barracks were painted white on the outside. They were two story buildings and our rooms were up and down each side of the hallway with a floor shimmering to glow at all times. At the end of each hall that faced west and east was a stairwell. At the end of each bay was the latrine, showers, basins, with equal numbers of mirrors, so we could clean up and get ready for inspection before going on duty.

I was extremely fortunate to be tapped time after time for various assignments a part of our career field. Due to this I found myself accepting opportunities including: Security Guard, Security Clearance, Desk Sergeant, and Sentry Dog Handler, which I held for one year.

During that year I know I talked more to my dog, Shep, than I did any human being. Medical circumstances gave my dog his orders well ahead of me. Shep's condition was an ongoing goiter beneath his neck that continually filled with fluid, which required being lanced to heal temporarily, yet the condition persisted. After a time he was to be shipped; I was to be transferred to another section along with holding duties at every gate or post throughout the base working confinement work details and aiding at Visitors Control.

Before all of this transpired, I was introduced to my dog Shep; he and I took to each other from our first meeting. I never thought of him, but as a pet. I hoped with all of heart, I would be able to have or take him home with me upon being discharged.

His and my moments with each other, were more like a young boy who had the dog of his dreams. We accomplished the training phases necessary from giving him commands of "attack", to observe him do exactly that, with the fellow handler in the burlap padded suit and to recall him by saying with authority, "Shep, Out".

To this day what stood out for me were the moments of being able to tend weekend duties by being at the kennels feeding and caring for Shep, as well as the other dogs. Venus and Chip, which was part Chow, the meanest dog that attacked the suit in an unusual way, of always going after the one in the suit with a fiercest manner and without question always grabbing a hold between the legs "down and under". Consequently, wearing that suit wasn't something I relished at any time.

When you check out the photos of Shep and me, you'll be able to see all I have shared. He and I had more fun frolicking than imagined. While behind the fenced areas of the overall kennels we could take their leashes off and let them run freely, which was best for him and the other dogs as well.

The superiors never told me whether he was put to death or shipped elsewhere. My hunch has always been he long before joined all of his fellow guard dogs in the heavens above. You see they are invaluable to the Air Force, as there is the training, medical care, not to mention all other facets related to their status and the jobs they performed so well.

Adam, a fellow Handler, had to face his dog dying. The funeral detail was the very same for this deceased dog which was more than emotional for all of us assigned to the unit. They are observed as any other G.I. fallen from standing their post near harm's way.

This brought me back into guarding some of the most sophisticated missiles of that time and their installations. I was assigned to H. L. C. Head Launch Control of the Minuteman facilities. While involved at these assigned installations, there was a relationship between those guarding and protecting all therein. The site crews we saw only momentarily and the remaining time was spent via telephone. Due to the number of shifts held, the time conversing with the crews brought us to know one another. We shared our hobbies, fishing stories, and camping outings with each other.

I found quite a change from all of my previous duties. While assigned to the Security Clearance office for the Base. There were three to four of us Non Commissioned personnel assigned to our office. The boss was Master Sergeant Rye, who was one terrific NCO (Non-Commissioned Officer) to work with, as were the other two Staff Sergeants. Their instruction and patience was the best throughout. Not only did we process security clearances for Base Personnel, we issued the same for the contractors assigned to the Base.

We worked well with each other, which was due to the jokester Master Sergeant Rye. When he was getting to know us, the subject came up regarding families and he would always say, "I always carry all of my loved ones near my heart." Then he would open up his frayed leather wallet carried in his hind pocket and would proudly show his wife and kids. That light kind of environment was greatly appreciated.

Every one of the assignments became mine between 1962 into 1965.

I remember all the times being on post and having little or no traffic pass through the entire eight-hour shift. It didn't take that long before I decided I would attend college no matter what, as there was no way I could continue such mundane assignments.

Being assigned to the Security Clearance Office brought my next promotion as an Airman Second Class.

I became aware of the entire AFSC (Air Force Specialty Classification) and I heard I was being considered to join the ranks of the Sentry Dog Division. The Sergeant in charge took me on a tour. And he explained all that was involved in the assignment.

I talked this over with Master Sergeant Rye; he thought I should accept as undoubtedly there would be another stripe in such a change. He also said they would miss me, but he totally understood.

Had I known then I would have trained at Lackland A.F.B., Texas to become a "Sentry-Dog-Handler" I was now. I was able to enter the division at Vandenberg on an O.J.T., On the Job Training basis. At first, I was literally living at the kennels learning all needed, but mainly becoming familiar with my dog Shep. Looking at Shep, no one would have believed he was a Sentry Dog. He weighed out at about sixty-five pounds and was a black German Shepherd with brown markings. He and I became acquainted rapidly; there wasn't a day I didn't want to take him with me upon being discharged. His manner was considerably more timid than the other dogs.

All the guys always kidded me because they thought Shep was like his handler. Ironically, we worked nights with our dogs and trained them during the day. Our shifts and responsibilities varied, and included kennel duties, caring for all of the dogs, and our offices. .

The variables of our posts included working the warehouse areas where theft had become evident. Our being present regularly diminished the losses. Other assignments were to the Reentry Vehicle Area.

Shep and I worked together in all of the seasons including the rain and fog, which were commonplace at Vandenberg. The reason for the inclement weather was due to the Base jutting out to the Pacific on the California coastline.

This weather was Shep's favorite and we would work the fence lines. He would get the scent of a rabbit and would lunge forward and the race was on, especially if that rabbit happened to duck under the fence and came in Shep's path. Such times as these helped break up the hours during each shift. A lot of people wouldn't believe it, but such a dog is similar to students I would have in later years. The teacher is the one that learns the most, both from a Sentry Dog and from his students.

I became a member of the Base Police Section and vividly remember wondering whether or not I would find myself in dress blues, white cap cover with white gloves. My first assignments were no different as I was working various gates on the Base including the Main Gate. I knew then I was going to apply for my early discharge and attend college. Along with that decision and processing for such an end came months of gate assignments where the most exciting factor was to salute an officer upon his or her entry or exit. What came of this was not being shipped to Vietnam.

It was during 1964 through 1965, at the age of twenty-one that I was assigned to Patrol on Base. At that time our vehicles were Chevrolet pickup trucks. Our duties included raising the colors at Division and Wing Headquarters and spending our shifts patrolling within our assigned areas. We worked anything that pertained to traffic control and periodically found we were dealing with domestic disputes or brawls at the N.C.O. Club or the Airmen's Club. Our shifts were the same as before while working Security. They included working three swing shifts and three mid-night shifts and three day, shifts. What helped us to prepare for each shift change was a twenty-four hour break before making the change, to have three days off at the end of each cycle. Consider completing three of the cycles mentioned then trying to track what day or month it was. This turned out to be the challenge of all challenges for all of us.

I remember one night while on patrol the visibility was nil due to the fog that encompassed the entire Base. I had just pulled up to the corner by the hill above where the dog kennels were located when I saw this vehicle come flying by which caused me to pursue it. I immediately turned on my emergency red light to make the driver know I wanted him or her to pull over to the right side of the road. He was exceeding the speed limit considerably, steering a coarse of some eighty to ninety miles per hour down through Base proper. I was finally able to close in enough to read the plates and call them in for a check for wants and warrants. I stopped him directly across from our Base Police Headquarters and used my microphone to instruct the driver to remain in his vehicle as I approached him. Before I stepped out, the driver's door become ajar and, as I still had the microphone in my hand, I announced it again firmly but to no avail.

The driver insisted on getting out and starting back to me in a brash manner. I planted my feet solidly on the ground as he took steps toward me I slapped my holster. At that moment, I saw a grown man leap in mid air back into his vehicle.

I cautiously approached his vehicle, asked for his license and registration and told him without any hesitation to remain in his vehicle. I called in the information explaining my location along with the infractions I was citing him for on that traffic stop. All came back as an all clear, so I returned to his vehicle and heard a constant raving and ranting as I handed him the citation signifying he was driving negligently with excessive speed due to the conditions on the roadway. I handed his license and registration back to him and he snatched them out of my hand and he yelled, "Who and where is your office because I'm going to report all you've done." I informed him, "You're in luck as our headquarters are across the street."

He pulled out and turned into our parking lot. I followed him and parked. He stormed into our office raising his voice and asked, "Who is the boss of Air Policeman Bradley who just cited me moments before across from your headquarters?" He found he was about to receive his answer by meeting our OIC Warrant Officer and Senior Master Sergeant Carlson at the same time who gave him his answer: "Don't you ever come in here questioning any of my Air Policemen as to their duties and particularly in the manner you have. Now, if there is nothing else to discuss I suggest you get on your way before it becomes more serious." That was one day in court I didn't ever hear about afterwards.

Before accepting other duties, I had an appointment never to forget, while concluding my assignment in security.

When I turned twenty-one years old, I had my first opportunity to vote. I told the duty Sergeant that I definitely wanted to go and vote that night. He replied, "We'll make sure of that." We stood our inspection and were taken to our posts.

That night I anticipated their remembering that I would be able to participate as an active citizen. The hours passed, it looked like it wasn't going to happen and I became more perplexed by the minute. I looked up the road and saw headlights coming down toward my gate. I wasn't sure who it was and soon found the Sergeant and my replacement to enable me to go and vote. The Sergeant yelled, "Let's go so we can get you there before the polls close. Don't worry, I'll get you there as fast as I can."

Gerry Bradley

We sped across the base and zipped through the main gate. I couldn't understand why we were leaving the base, but soon realized we were headed for Lompoc. I thought we were going to town. Then the Sergeant turned onto the road that led to the Federal Penitentiary, south of the base before arriving in Lompoc. We pulled up at the Prison gate and the guard waved us through as if he knew we were coming.

Not only did I get to vote in 1964, I didn't have to return to my post that night. I couldn't help but remember that experience from then onward.

Later in 1973-74 when returning to law enforcement, I was in the midst of Police Academy and we toured Mc Neil Island Federal Prison, in Washington State. The experience brought me to remember that night all over again.

For a guy twenty-two years old, without wheels, it was really hard to break away from base. Occasionally, you could catch a ride with one of your buddies and go to town.

This wasn't nearly as enjoyable, as it was to break away with my finest friend Adam Campbell. He and I would hitchhike down the coast to Santa Barbara where we would change at the bus station into our civies. We locked our uniforms and gear into a bus terminal locker. From there we hit the town! Our plan usually meant we would dine at the finest restaurants and follow that with a superb evening of dancing into the night at one of the leading hotels with a dance floor for us to practice our latest steps. All that was needed was the approval of the husbands to loan us their ladies for one twirl around the floor. We stayed over and made our way back to the Base stopping on the beaches along the way northward up the coast. Those breaks were exactly what we needed.

Before us was Adam's oncoming date of discharge, so he could attend college at Claremont Men's College, in Southern California. His departure was a shock for me as we were more like brothers of complete trust and respect.

One evening ten years later in 1975, the telephone rang. I answered it and immediately realized Adam was on the end of the line. I was in a state of shock to hear from him that many years later. We talked for quite some time and I hated to hang up. From that point on I haven't heard a word from him.

The last thing I heard regarding him was the fact that he was working in Southern California, and was married and had two children. He is one I hope and pray does read this book. Oh one more thing, I tried every way possible to contact him via the Internet and was sure I saw him in the photograph of the members of the board from Claremont Men's College, but still was unable to confirm or determine a way to finally surprise him as I intended.

Adam took me under his wings in 1963, when I was twenty-two years old. He did this to help me in every way possible in settling at Vandenberg A.F.B.

When I first met him, I saw the sharpest Airman among any others within our Squadron. Adam showed confidence from the top of his head to the crowning of his boots. His entire uniform appeared to have come from having extra starch and pressing. Even, his fatigue hat for security assignments stood taller than most. As you swept your eyes down you saw an impeccably starched pressed fatigue shirt, with creases down the seams to his wrists, the same crease at the top of his buttoned blouse and a totally white pressed t-shirt. His trousers had that same flair met by perfectly tied and bloused boots. When looking at his boots they were shined so you could see the cracks of your teeth in the sheen of the toes of each boot. All of his leather, including his holster, was of the same shine. He moved with that same sharpness no matter where he was bound. He carried himself totally erect and directed his spellbound smile toward all that he met He made sure that all of his brass was always shining. Adam never had to be concerned regarding any inspection because he made sure all within his room was always standing ready. His items in the closet were precisely spaced and placed to meet Air Force standards. He left everything opened and available to be inspected. What had to confirm his being the Outstanding Airman of every inspection were his rolled underwear, t-shirts and pressed handkerchiefs. The true stand out were his seven toothbrushes all in a row for their inspection. You never saw his teeth without a similar shine as his boots. His smile was captivating as was his personality. After a short time of his schooling me in all of the areas, he took me aside and explained to me. "There won't be anything, preventing your being promoted, if you follow all I am sharing with you". Sure, enough, it was short order and I became an Airman Second Class.

Adam painstakingly taught me to use the methodology of first showing each precept, then permitting me to practice and ask any questions, related to each phase, finally letting me practice alone knowing he, the instructor, was there for questions if needed. The review and testing was on the final presentation.

While working toward my degree, we were taking the method classes and would you believe I thought of Adam and his methods he taught me years past.

The time of practicum paid off when I taught, no matter what level from fourth grade to High School, and finally the long sought opportunity to teach at the Community College level, after ten plus years.

I still remember his showing me how he washed, stretched and ironed those fatigues to stand at attention when he hung them in his closet. Adam had all kinds of hints, down right secrets, when it came to polishing brass and exactly how to keep our boots and all leather gear to gleam. Each piece rose with level on level of polish put on with a circular lighter touch.

I asked him one evening, "Why do you have seven toothbrushes?" He explained, "I have one for every day of the week, this way each brush can properly dry before using it again." Adam was that kind of a precision oriented guy.

We grew close through all of our experiences that took us up and down the California coastline between Vandenberg A.F.B., and the Los Angeles Basin.

One weekend he invited me to go with him to meet his father for a very special event he and his father had participated in since he was a boy. We were to travel and meet his father and associates for a Skeet Shoot, united with a dove shoot. I definitely remember how they had a line or boundary, and you couldn't shoot any bird until they had flown beyond the boundary. All of these men thoroughly enjoyed the sport of this event.

Adam's father was nearly the same size as Adam. He had a glowing, California tan that swept over his forehead, to his white hair, crowning his bald- head. And he had the same bright full of life eyes. I shook his hand at our introduction. The shake was firm, yet there was real kindness in his shake. That entire afternoon he treated both Adam and me royally. It was so apparent how much they loved and respected each other.

I wouldn't have missed this day for anything. When it came time for us to head north and return to the Base, I shook Adam's father's hand and thanked him and the others for such a fine time. Adam turned to his father and they gave each other a loving hug and both kissed each other on the lips. That was the heightening moment for me to see this expression of such love between a son and father. Adam knew this touched me deeply so he explained they had always kissed like that from the time he was a young boy. I told him how that touched my heart to see such love conveyed in this way

Other journeys included our making quick runs down to the beaches in 1964, south of the Base, and north of Santa Barbara. We located one beach we found called Refugio. On one of our weekends we met Shirley and, shortly afterwards, her mother and father.

It was no time at all until this family all but adopted both of us. They planned time to be at their cabin just up Highway 101 where we would meet them on our days off that summer. Shirley and her mother came to the Base to pick us up so we could spend our days off with them.

They stayed in their cabin while Adam and I had a make shift camping set up outside completely covered from the moisture and the mosquitoes. It was a great set up!

We went to Refugio Beach every moment we were there. Her parents wouldn't think of us spending our money on any meals so where wood needed to be cut or any other work in camp we pitched in and earned our way.

Shirley was all of five foot seven or eight inches tall, with long auburn hair that flowed down to her shoulders with a natural wave like quality. She had the bluest eyes, as the blue of the ocean when the sun shined and sparkled. Her features were quite petite. In fact she had much the same look as Audrey Hepburn. The three of us thoroughly enjoyed each other.

Our days off weren't the same as most civilians with weekends. Much of the time we were there during the week while Shirley's father was there only over the weekends. Consequently, all of us saw each other coming and going. As the summer continued, Shirley and I became closer. By all pretenses I believed she and I had a real something going between us.

I was nuts about her and equally loved her parents. The three of us would go to Santa Barbara for the evening to dance into the night. Shirley drove her parent's car and we enjoyed one another's company, to and from, wonderful nights of dining and dancing. She and I would dance and have flowing steps for each dance. Adam never had any difficulty finding another to dance with, as he was equally the finest of ballroom, dancers on the floor.

Afterwards, we would turn to Refugio, the cabin, and our tenting place. Once we even drove all the way down to her home outside of Los Angeles and celebrated her birthday.

The memory I have held over all of these years were the nights we went down on the beach and climbed up on the shelf, where we would light our bon fire, sit and talk, and sing songs into the morning, peering into the heavens above and sighting something very special that we would always remember.

What truly revealed how Adam and I really felt toward each other came as he and I made our last visit, with Shirley, and her, mother. He said he had to make me aware of the truth first, not to hurt me, rather to totally protect me. He went on and said that he knew I believed Shirley was my girl, but the truth was, she was more interested in him. Before I went to my room, I told him how much I respected his being so forthright with me. Our bond was even stronger from that moment on as he and I were assigned to go out on post with our Sentry Dogs.

We both had some real laughs regarding the finale of what we left at Refugio Beach. There was nothing left; it was natural to think about all those weeks and months of that memorable summer on the California beaches.

Before Adam and I realized, it was 1963; he was packing and processing for his discharge so he could continue his collegiate work. He had worked around the clock both on post and on his off hours tending bar at the Officer's Club. Our last hug brought tears to our eyes, as we must have known we wouldn't see each other for many years, if at all. I thanked him for all he had taught me and helped me to better myself. I knew how deeply I would miss his companionship and all we shared together and wished him the very best of luck!

Considerably before, I vividly recall another 'calling' moment that came by Adam's request.

Even all these years later I would appreciate hearing from him and being in contact, which I know would be to pick up where we left off that night he telephoned.

He turned and disappeared that morning into the Vandenberg mist. I thought of one story he told me about when he was on one of his weekends, which brought him down on the railroad tracks along the California coast. While there, he described what it was like to meet this hobo brewing coffee his special way. He told me, "That coffee I drank was the finest I ever tasted, much the same as that hobo." He told me how he saved his money for the necessities of attending school.

Even after arriving for his work toward his degree he had to live out of his car and do all of his studying at the neighborhood laundry mat. That best said of Adam who he was and had always been, a guy that could do so much more than survive, rather, rise to any and all opportunities presented.

Sometime before Adam departed, there were two more events that brought needed change in me. Adam made me aware of a visiting ministry that was to be on Base for the coming week at our Base Chapel. He told me some of the details pertaining to the event, but he most of all hoped I would consider attending.

The first two nights I remained away. I can't even remember what moved me to go the third night. When I arrived, Adam saw me and had saved me a seat. I soon found the main presenter was a visiting evangelist who had previously been with Billy Graham and the Crusade. I was never as moved as I was by Bob Moomaw's message that he preached. In fact, I found myself awe struck at much more than his message. At the end of the service he had what was called an altar call, where those wanting to be forgiven of their sins could openly confess before God and all present that night. I went down the aisle, which I had never done before. I knew something phenomenal had happened to me, but I asked if I could see and talk with him further the next day. So we set an appointment.

I was quite sure as to what happened the night before and he and I sat and talked about the complete experience. He asked me what I believed had happened and I told him, "I believed I had received Christ. I had become a new born Christian." The evangelist said, "You're right." Then he began to help me with the specifics of this spiritual experience that would be mine from thereon. Before leaving him that day, he gave me a Bible and pointed out verses and passages to help me gain an understanding of this happening, and how to gain daily guidance from that point forward. Needless to say, from that first evening I completed hearing the messages he had for the duration of the week. Just as our Lord has for all of us, this gift of His grace became evident to me from that point forward. What stood out was the way I treated one and all. When we reported to the various posts, I took all of my gear with me including additional materials that related to my Bible studies.

Before resuming, I know this is the moment I need to share other real moments that continued within my heart. My arrival brought me to turn to the sound of aircraft lifting off of the Base, heading to any direction or destination. I knew all that I wanted was to be aboard any of those planes leaving that very moment. The continuity that seemed to be present at Lackland A.F.B. wasn't near the same upon my arrival at Vandenberg A.F.B. Undoubtedly, the perceptions that surfaced had a lot to do with lows that took over more than expected. Highs that accompany the lows were far and few at that time.

I am more than certain, the death like swing downward, revealed deepening despondency that wouldn't seem to surface. To bring you to know the severity of such times, that when hearing the departure of planes,

I would run out on the top porch or steps and saying, "Do you happen to have any room aboard, I don't care where you're bound."

At that crucial time, I began to take a better posture. In fact, I began to drop any and all ideas of the departing planes as before. This behavior was one that brought, to the surface the fact of my mishandling all of the unknown factors that came, while trying to settle and be a part of the overall scene. An example was, when I was assigned to my first barracks. I tried to introduce myself to the other guys, but found them more than cold. As you might expect, this denial was hard to deal with for sometime.

I know you can recall, how I had given it my all "to blend" while attending my senior year at San Rafael High School, I found through sheer stepping up and addressing credibility and striving to gain the respect of my fellow students much of this and more came.

I had a brand new radio that was given to me before leaving to report at Vandenberg A.F.B. Being fool worthy I left my room unlocked to grab a shower. When I returned, my radio was gone; from this occurring I found out that a fellow Air Policeman I lived with wouldn't acknowledge having ripped me off. Matters such as these were turning points bringing me to inquire as to whether I could be reassigned to the barracks where my fellow funeral detail members were. Fortunately, this was confirmed.

After fulfilling my duty with the previous crew, future opportunities came to me to minister to the Airmen present at the Missile Sites I was assigned to each evening. They came to realize my future intentions were to complete my degree and continue on to Theological Seminary. It wasn't long until I was referred to as the "Preacher Cop" and one opportunity came on top of another.

Gerry Bradley

I wasn't on Security Posts long, as the transfer came to join the Security Clearance section at Wing Headquarters. While there, I became totally immersed in all of the following: officiating the Little League Games, teaching Sunday School for the Elementary grades, Base Sunday School Superintendent, President of the Base Cycling Club, member of the Chapel choir, and foremost, I became a true member of this my home which was Vandenberg A.F.B.

Before I received my Honorable Discharge in 1965, I began taking Law Enforcement courses. They were interesting and challenging. I knew I would do nothing, but apply for my early discharge to attend college. This work proved I was more than ready to continue at Allan Hancock College, in Santa Maria, to earn my Associate of Arts Degree.

Even though the Cuban Crisis was resolved at the end of those extremely crucial thirty-one days in 1962, we returned to previous duties. That didn't surprise any of us, as undoubtedly, all were waiting for "proof of the pudding" which came later.

All Americans were glued to their televisions and radios awaiting the prayed for result that came, allowing all of us to have the biggest sigh of relief. That same relief came for me when realizing so many honors had come after making an effort to assist a fellow Airman who was in need to care for his family and was followed by the trip accomplished on my French ten-speed bike.

Every event that happened was far beyond anything I had ever imagined. Just to think of the articles written. Then I received further word of being nominated for President Kennedy's Physical Fitness Team. This meant that I would be competing against others throughout California. Due to this, I was able to form a Base Cycling Club for interested cyclists

240

who wanted to break away from the Base, long enough to grab moments of fresh air. The membership was never over twelve, but all of us had great times sharing our rides with one another.

After Adams's departure, I slipped back into a dulling kind of feeling, ever lonely and certainly low in mood and motivation. What saved me then, was that deep seated involvement in all on base mentioned; I found a girl back home on a final visit and started writing her and welcomed every return letter from her at the same time.

Ironically, as was true while at Basic and Technical Training and at Vandenberg, there seemed to be a deluge of "Dear John letters" being received by the other guys. Such tended to make any thought of becoming overly involved with any young lady not all that plausible. Fortunately for me, those letters kept coming. A change took place and that was my taking off on the weekends riding to Solvang, Santa Maria, and a farther up the coast on my bike. Those excursions were vastly helpful while dealing with any stress brought on by the letters being less and less; that was undoubtedly due to my not being able to get away or find any other reason for I had long before realized without a doubt where my home was.

I have always believed what drew me through such times had much more to do with "just toughing it out", following the advice I had learned long before to, "Keep my head up and continue straight ahead", accepting each and every opportunity that came, and running with it. Having no knowledge of my dealing with any behaviors that would become much more pronounced had to be a great lifesaver.

One night in 1963, I was exiting the Post Office from picking up my mail and nearly knocked this female officer down as I swung the door open that she was entering at the same time. I apologized, gave her a smart salute and continued walking back toward our barracks. I took a quick look to see just who she was. She had to be about five-foot two, had blue eyes and looked smart in her two- piece blue dress uniform. Upon arriving I read my mail and continued shining, and pressing uniforms, readying for another day and weeks work.

I continued seeing this Second Lieutenant at the mailroom and about Base. I finally inquired, and found she was assigned as, an administrative officer.

It seemed appropriate to send a bouquet to her office, which proved better than nearly knocking her down at the Base Post Office. The two of us contacted each other in the future. Our doing so, meant something vital for both of us to fill a void of being away from our homes and being lonely.

I had been a part of the scene on the Base, yet I met her, and I seemed to tip the scale as never before. I continued to see the Lieutenant, and she began to take interest in our cycling club.

The next thing that happened was she asked me to help her select a new bike. Our weekend arrived, and we found a bike shop; after looking in depth, she selected one she felt more comfortable riding. Soon afterwards, she joined the cycling club, and revealed her interest to the extent of going on rides and helping haul several bikes on top of her car. Furthermore, she let the members pile in her car when we were going longer distances.

We used to quip with each other that our courtship turned out to be the two of us pedaling all over the perimeter of Vandenberg A.F.B. Our first months together were easily handled as we both worked days.

When considering the current rulings, I am certain we would have let it all go by the wayside.

She was getting flack from her OIC (Officer In Charge), and tried to assuage his concerns by introducing me to the Major. We liked each other, but there was this internal breach of behavior, with my being an Enlisted Airman, and she an Officer, that couldn't be waived. The Major made it clear were she to marry me, as we planned, she would have to secure another office in which to work.

My fellow Airmen did everything in their power to see that I did anything but continue down the path I had pursued.

All the time my best buddy, Adam Campbell, and my fellow Airmen kept trying to make me aware to drop the entire notion. I realized later how right all of them were. There wasn't anything that was going to affect me then. Our friendship grew, but I accepted the reiterated message of holding tight as they continued to say abruptly, "Don't marry her."

Still there were no letters coming from the girl back home. Had there been, I know all would have been terminated. Her father was a minister, so he and I talked quite a lot on our telephone conversations, but that ceased as well.

So much occurred on Bases throughout the world then, as we heard the announcement from President Kennedy as to the status during the Cuban Crisis. This directly affected us within our Squadron. We went on immediate alert, and remained as every military station did throughout for thirty-one days. All of us with other positions such as mine, returned to Security Details where we were needed most. We worked around the clock. At first our shifts were eighteen hours, and later twelve-hour shifts. The assignments weren't as before. Many were "out there" on Radomes, Missiles Sites, installation areas, even the areas of repair and accessories. It was the rigidity and the lack of breaks that closed on us as our free time was in making sure we hit the Chow Hall, readied our gear for the next shift, and secured the necessary sleep. It didn't take many times of finding we had been dropped at one of those far away sites or domes that we knew our mind was playing tricks on us. And my condition was overtaking my senses for the moment. A key element that repeats itself is that there is the constant imbalance or inability at all times to keep all from being distorted.

When considering the hours not only now but in the mode we found ourselves, I couldn't think about the hours of standing at the ready over these colossal missiles and their sites. When I peered at them standing there in their own halo of lights, the missiles were as cold as the night air off the Pacific Ocean. It is that coldness of which I bring to your attention. I felt the same along with a kind of stand off position from all that had been happening. I supposed each of these were warnings from the start. Needless to say, the mundane functions, the constant stress and frustration came without warning.

I tried to spend time with my Second Lieutenant, but it was futile, as the shifts were too long, requiring sheer self-discipline to be at the ready as our Commander-In-Chief had ordered of us.

My observations during that period of time revealed how every contractors comings and goings were so different. They showed us a new respect as never before. All within our nation had to take much more than a second thought as to the level of threat we were facing. We realized all of the contractors, courtesy and respect was evident throughout those thirty-one days.

I can't respond as to how many dark and long nights I was placed on duty, that I knew I was in real trouble, maybe it was literal fear; perhaps, I just wasn't cut right to keep this vigil up day and night as we had. Fortunately, I turned to the right Master Sergeant, a true friend. I didn't know until that night how well he really knew me. I ran to catch him after we were coming off duty. I said, "Sergeant, I've got to talk to you or someone." I asked whether or not he and the officer in charge could see clear to welcome my other talents, such as my typing proficiency instead of the present assignments.

The next day of reporting, I was requested into the Administration office to learn, "We hear you're quite a typist. Your assignment has been changed as of this moment."

I continued through the duration doing much more than typing daily blotters and logs. I became a Desk Sergeant, working the radio and learning the communications aspects that had direct reference to all I found myself doing.

The staff found they were right regarding my receiving this opportunity. I remember after I became relaxed, the two Chief Master Sergeants stood and gestured, "By God he can type faster than any Airman we have ever seen."

It was thirty-one days of vigilance on our Squadrons behalf that we stood ready and served, as did Military Bases throughout the world for what could have been the most devastating results for all within the Continental United States and beyond.

I definitely remember Saturday, November 22, 1963, while I was at the Base PX in the process of selecting an engagement ring to hear the announcement that the President had been shot along with Governor Connaly from Texas. The entire PX became dead still with a quiet beyond belief, much like a cavernous, hollowing sound surrounding all present. It was as though all took the deepest of breaths, awaiting the confirmation that he had been killed. Confirming word came shortly afterwards that the President was dead. What a note to become engaged under!

I can still remember finishing my purchase and running out of the PX area all the way back to our Squadron. It was probably due to all experienced before during the Cuban Crisis that I couldn't help but think this terrible loss to our country would bring another flare heard and felt throughout the world.

This shattered the spirit of our land and beyond. The events leading to that roll of the drum, which was heard by all from that earthshaking day, the selected cortege by Mrs. Kennedy carrying our President, to what would be, *The Eternal Flame* at Arlington National Cemetery, was somber for all. And yet, Mrs. Kennedy's combined stance, of her being so proud and stately, was what our nation needed coast to coast and throughout the world. Dreams of an entire generation were lost. All that lay ahead would reveal this and more.

Our seeing John Jr., standing next to his mother and sister, seeing him salute his father, has remained within our memories and spirits from thereon.

We didn't get the call for another alert until July 17, 1999 when we heard that John Jr. and his wife Carolyn Bisset-Kennedy and her sister had disappeared from their flight to Martha's Vineyard to attend his cousin Rory's wedding. The alert became the worlds as we sat, prayed and hoped, with all of our hearts on the evening of July 18th, that the mission had changed to Search and Discovery.

Before receiving my early discharge in September 1965 to make it possible for me to begin my studies toward an AA Degree, my bride, her Bridesmaid, my Best Man and a few members of the church joined together so we could be married.

Earlier that morning, as I exited the barracks for the last time, as we had already moved all our effects to what would be our first home, I was met by all from the barracks on the way down the outside stairs saying everything possible to bring me to my senses. I know I had each of their statements running through my mind as I drove into Santa Maria. Had I somehow been able to perceive they stood positively on my behalf, all would have been avoided.

I drove into Santa Maria and thought deeply regarding their reaction. They were cognizant of the true picture, which I had either missed or was standing to close to the mirror to see. I left early enough to stop and eat breakfast. That stop turned out to be a haunting element to deal with for I sat at the counter, and before me were those eyes again reflected in the mirror. As I peered into my reflection I knew the truth!

After my long visit with the truth and breakfast, I drove over to the church and was greeted by the Pastor. He piped up and said, "I'm glad you could make it, but your bride beat you to it. She left running down the street wearing her tennis shoes." In retrospect, I realized this was his way, of warning me as my fellow Airmen had tried earlier that morning. But too many tracks had been crossed since then, it seemed far too late to turn back.

I was standing there with the Pastor and my Best Man when my bride entered with her Bridesmaid. She was in a short full-skirted wedding dress, and had on her veil. The Pastor talked with us briefly and helped us to relax. He invited us to the altar along with our attendants. The wedding was small. We stood looking into each other's eyes, holding hands, lovingly repeating our vows and placed our rings on each other's fingers. The Pastor gave his smile and announced, "You can kiss your bride." When we made our turn to go down the aisle, neither her parents nor family members nor mine, were present. However, before we were married my parents had pronounced, "You don't want to marry her!"

From the start there was no parental support which was vital for us, as for all young couples.

We thanked my Best man and her Bridesmaid for standing with us on this our wedding day.

They came outside to where our TR-4 was all shined and ready for us to leave on our honeymoon.

This was my first sports car! We had made a special trip down to Santa Barbara months before in 1963 to purchase it before our wedding day.

I had mentioned in conversation, that I had wanted a red sports car since I was sixteen years old. When seeing a friend pull up in their brand new Corvette, I went for a ride and never forgot what a thrill it was.

One of our weekends in 1963, she said, "Let's go to Santa Barbara for the day." So we drove down the coast to Santa Barbara. Before we arrived she said, "Today I'm going to buy your wedding present." I responded, "What do you have in mind?" She replied, "Today you're going to pick out what you've wanted since you were sixteen." I told her, "That is entirely too much," but she insisted, so we stopped and parked at the TRIUMPH, MG, AUSTIN HEALEY dealer.

Thinking back at our earlier departure, I had thought what a nice day it would be for us to get away and shop for special gifts for our coming wedding and life together.

We saw the bright red TRIUMPH with a white soft-top, and spoke wheels. Then we sat down and began to talk with a salesman. Her plan was to trade her car toward the gift she had in mind. The salesman asked, "Would you like to test drive the car?" We agreed, and took another car out for a spin, but I found shortly afterwards she had "the red one" in mind. The reason being she knew that was the standout in my mind

All of this took the balance of our morning and finally we agreed. The usual meeting that occurs in a small office with the salesman began. An agreement was drawn and I heard, "This is his wedding present, but he'll have to pay it off." I thought that was a fair deal. We thanked the salesman for all of his help and he gave me the keys for our brand new TR-4. Before leaving, he explained the manuals, gauges, safety devices, everything under that bonnet including the equipment the spare tire, necessary equipment and how to lower and raise the soft top properly. He closed by saying, "It has been a pleasure dealing with the two of you. May you enjoy many safe miles; do come down for your regular service."

It was too much! Here we were sitting side by side with the top up and turned the ignition on to hear it purr. There were four on the floor with overdrive. I turned and we rolled off the lot, on to the main street of town and continued for several blocks, when she said, "Pull over at the curb and I'll get out and shop." She continued saying, "Take it for a spin and enjoy it." I turned and said happily, "Are you sure?" She nodded yes. We said, "Let's put the top down." I pulled over to the curb where she jumped out and was off to shop.

As I pulled away, I saw her in the rear view mirror with a grin of real pleasure. I turned those spoke wheels and entered the lane of traffic. I'm sure I wasn't unlike anyone else who had just begun driving, being attentive of the instrument panel, even sneaking a glance of the profile of my new set of wheels in the store windows. I was driving on my first real drive in this dreamed for automobile. I didn't take all that long before returning to pick up my bride to be; we began to drive north up Highway 101 to return to Vandenberg A.F.B.

The guys from my unit were really surprised as we drove up to my barracks. There we changed seats and she drove to her quarters.

I can still remember how much attention I paid her as I opened the passenger door for her to sit down, swinging her legs inside. I had a glimpse of her blue garter on her ankle and tucked her petticoats in so nothing was hanging outside. We were off for our honeymoon trip and we turned briefly to wave at everyone standing outside the church. I had made reservations up the coast.

Our honeymoon included beach combing and a Hearst Castle tour. Time came sooner than imagined for us to turn toward Santa Maria, our new home and life together.

In the fall of 1963, signs were evident in the earliest stages of our being married, in the fall of 1963, which became eventuality five years later. I snapped back into reality after being married six months! It was as though I heard all of the beck and calls of before as truth. Seldom do such findings bring both cause and effect that are so stark as to bring couples to part their ways. That was true for us as we continued fulfilling our roles just as before.

She continued until being promoted to become a First Lieutenant. Her assignment was altered as her previous Officer in Charge had promised. I resumed working in my Base Police functions, working all three shifts: swing, midnight, and day shifts. This presented an immediate hindrance.

We were passing each other either in the night or on the road, seeing each other while I periodically stood gate duty where she would pass through demanding my return salute.

My final assignment at Vandenberg A.F.B. was with Base Police. I took Law Enforcement courses at night fulfilling my duties and making way toward my early discharge, which came sooner than I could imagine.

I never forgot receiving the ride to the Main Gate with one of the Sergeants I had worked with all of those months and hearing him say, "You have always wanted out of this man's Air Force. Well you're out now so don't even think of returning later." I didn't have any trouble over this gospel and departed and definitely didn't look back.

Chapter 14

Another Way Off Base

Day 1

Even though I had been asked by my fellow airman to help him, I couldn't help wonder in the summer of 1962 whether I could complete such a journey on my ten-speed bike. My answer was, "Of course I can."

I was overwhelmed by the see-air, which surrounded me riding across the Golden Gate Bridge. I was coming off the bridge and the bridge tender announced over the P.A. "You on the bicycle, come through gate one!" Needless to say, I was really surprised at this announcement. I slowed up and asked the bridge tender, "How much?" and he said, "Where are you coming from and where are you bound?" He added, "There is no charge and the very best to you and be safe!" I knew I was in the best of hands after that happened. I continued on and connected with the tunnel taking me down bordering the Presidio toward San Francisco State College. I was moving south with a good morning wind already on my back, and soon found myself on the cliffs overlooking the scenic coast so I stopped for the first time to relieve myself.

While at the gas station, I reviewed my map and hurriedly realized how long it would be to go down Highway 1. I asked the owner of the station as to another route that would be best. He told me that if he were doing what I was in the midst of doing, the last thing he would do, would be to continue down the coast. He showed me a much better route to consider and why.

Right there, I modified my plans and made way to the hilltop route that would take me southward leading into Palo Alto and San Jose, California. To do this I would pedal a route atop of the others.

Highway 1 was below, and not only the coast, but far longer than imagined, battling constant climbing and hair-pin turns, but most of all, the wind off the ocean would be in my face the whole way. To my left and down in the valley was Highway 101, which was far too dangerous, due to the amount of traffic and speeds.

Before I realized it, I had altered my entire trip, and was I ever thankful for this decision from thereon. I had to climb the ribbon of the road.

In no time, I was plenty warm so I began to take off layers of my clothes. First, came my windbreaker, and later one of my shirts, leaving only a T-shirt on. Up I went and, unknown to me, there would be very little slope going downhill. I forgot to mention that prior to launching this voyage, I had not been near my bike for two years! This began to tell a tale all of its own as I rapidly realized I had muscles in my body I wasn't aware of, particularly in my posterior section.

The morning was passing quicker than I expected. I held a steady pace and kept my derailleur in the climbing gear to lessen the pressure on my legs. Along with wiping my brow from the dripping sweat, I reached out for my water bottle, and took only small sips. There were few stops all morning or into the afternoon. The saddle was wearing thin on my butt. I knew there was only one way to deal with this. That was to set down solid and ride it through. By afternoon, I had to veto that theory and began to take off one shirt then the other T-shirt, anything at all to gain some comfort, padding the saddle from one sore butt. As the afternoon ebbed

I finally had to take my jacket off and roll it up so I could sit on it. That helped some, but all the time I knew I would have to digress the coming days and miles to the truth of sitting into the saddle and getting tougher mile by mile.

There was new scenery which I had no familiarity with until now. I thought of all the sights and was no longer being governed by that ache in my body. The pace eased some, and the road signs were reminding me of the distance left to draw me in Palo Alto, near Stanford University. The climb seemed to be drawing to an end as I cruised downhill.

I was getting hungry and thirsty as well and took another drink from my bottle, but it had warmed from the sun throughout the day. I could see that I was nearing Palo Alto or civilization as shown on the map, so I stopped and had a hamburger with a cold drink and even found a shade tree to light beneath for awhile.

Afterwards I continued on, but wanted to check my route to be sure, so I stopped at an attorney's office. I went in and introduced myself to the attorney and said, "I started in San Rafael early this morning and am headed to Vandenberg A.F.B., which I must reach by three and no more than four days from now, to prevent my being AWOL." He listened closely and asked me, if I would like a glass of ice water and to use the restroom. After I refreshed, I asked him, "Would you mind if I sat for a bit." He was aware that I was more than fatigued and said, "You go back in my study and stretch out on my sofa." I replied, "Thank you, I sure do appreciate it." He went back to work and I did just as he had suggested. Some minutes later I sat up and clicked out due to my clips on my cycling shoes and thanked him again.

He said, "You know I think we'll have you out to our home this evening," and I told him, "I don't want to inconvenience you and your family." I expressed my thanks for his consideration and asked him how much farther it was to San Jose. I told him I'd be back in touch with him after arriving at the Base. He asked me, "Where are you going to sleep tonight?" My reply was, "Either the Police Station, the Fire Department or a neighboring church."

He stood there on the steps of his office and gave me a big wave as I pedaled out of sight on my way to San Jose.

The weather couldn't have been better for the entire day. I wasn't that familiar with San Jose, so I had to be heads up as I rolled into the outskirts of the city. I had no idea that I happened to hit the very boulevard where the Main Fire Station was located. I rolled up in front of the Fire Station, leaned and locked my bike outside, and entered inquiring as to who was the Chief. The Fireman told me where to find him. I walked right into his office and introduced myself. Just as with the attorney earlier, I explained all including the purpose of my cycling trip. I asked him whether or not I might be able to stay over that night. In fact I didn't mean to quip, but told him, "I'm not proud; I'd be happy to sleep under the Fire engine. If only you will wake me if there is a fire." By now he was laughing and grinning from ear to ear. He said, "Hold on a minute," and shortly afterwards he said, "We have a perfect place for you." All I had to do was follow another Fireman over to the Annex, Station House. I thanked him, and went back to my bike, unlocked the lock and followed as arranged. When we arrived at the Annex, and the fireman introduced the Battalion Chief, who introduced me to the entire staff and said, "Come on back and

I'll show you where you can drop your gear and store your bike so it'll be safe." He added, "You can share my room for the night."

Needless to say, I was blown out at this arrangement and just couldn't thank them enough. He said, "Anyone willing to make such a journey in three days should have our thanks."

I was all set for the night and took time to shave and grab a shower so I could go out and have dinner before turning in for the night.

Afterwards, I walked into the Chief's room and got out of my clothes and crawled under the clean smelling sheets and that was all I remembered as I went fast to sleep. I am sure that night there were no dreams including the days' activities or for that matter the ones that lay ahead,

Day 2

Morning came earlier than I would have liked. I showered and got dressed, then, I found the Chief and thanked him and the staff for all they had done the night before. He said, "We hope you weren't awakened as we had to cover three blazing house fires and saw how you slept through every one of them."

I told him, "Well I had better be on my way in order to get as far down the coast as possible and ease the pressure on my final days travel to the Base." As I pulled away, I gave the entire staff one big salute of thanks, and they turned up the sirens on the Fire trucks, and I rolled south, down through the groves of Eucalyptus trees bound for Salinas, and King City, California.

It was a typical summer morning, with the fog and mist clinging to the valleys and the trees about me. I knew the morning sun would burn this off. I was well on my way down Highway 101, which would take me into Salinas, and King City, California where I met the finest people only a few days before. My bike was clicking right along. I couldn't help but think of those I had met the day and evening before. I had a long ways to go so I drifted in thought as I pedaled.

I noticed were the big twelve wheelers would swerve around me, rather than remain flush with me as we moved southward. That fact had been true ever since leaving the Golden Gate Bridge and the Bridge Tender. They not only gave me this courtesy, but many of them waved to give a signal of their own kind of foghorns as they passed. I sure appreciated their gestures because the wind factor with the other traffic flying by was more than enough. I was more than certain Henrietta and I were being looked out for throughout that trip; I really knew we were on our way. I had a name for my bike, which had long before called her, Henrietta, and I had no idea where this name came from, but I knew it fit.

Even though there was the company of the passersby, I could have been seen talking out loud to Henrietta for company to be sure. I remarked to her, "Well Old Girl, we're definitely on our way. To think we pedaled one-hundred and twelve miles yesterday and I haven't been near you for two years."

I thanked her for such a ride, as when we used to pedal to Bolinas, California west of San Rafael, in 1961. Then turned north and continued until reaching the Russian River on to Guernesville, California and returned on Highway 101, considerably north of our mark for the moment. Once on Highway 101, I kept her in cruising gear pedaling a pace of thirty miles per hour all the way back into San Rafael for what had been a fine day of cycling.

Such outings as these would have prepared me even more for the ride I was in the midst of on this morning. Earlier, before leaving the Fire Station, I thanked God for this wonderful opportunity He had given me; all of His care each and every mile. Now I thought of that prayer, and realized how God was in every moment of this trip. I knew I was in His care when a California Highway Patrolman passed me and gave me a big wave, no stop or anything pertaining to my being on that busy thoroughfare. In fact, the same behavior throughout that morning pedaling southward was evident. the California sun was breaking through and all that was left was much like droplets on the blades of grass.

That made me remember the first time I saw Amy as she arrived in her little car, which I had seen before, but not quite as clearly as that morning. I was sitting across the campus lawn and watched her begin to walk up the slope on to the lawn where I was sitting. I was drawn to her tall frame, of what had to be some six foot one inches or more in height, as she walked toward me. She was wearing a light top and what was called a midi-length skirt, a soft brown with small pink patterned flowers, as she carried her books casually. The closer she got, I was able to recognize her brown eyes. I nicknamed her right there on the spot and I told my buddy Stan, sitting with me, "That has to be the one I've been searching for." Then I said, "good morning" to her as she passed by us. It wasn't long afterwards that I realized we were in one class together.

I thought what a break that was even though the class was Geology I, which I found was anything but where I belonged. It enabled us to become acquainted with each other though I remained coy until I couldn't hold it anymore. I found that Stan, and another co-ed he was becoming aware of, happened to know her. That was a relief as we began to talk about our going out after a game.

Beep-Beep. The swirling winds brought me to know to pay closer attention to hanging on to Henrietta. Traffic was building and morning was moving right along just as we were. I settled into the saddle by sitting down into the narrow grooves of the leather. I found this to be the best policy and stayed with it for the entire morning into mid-day.

Amy and I began to date, and most of our time was spent with others we attended college with, going to movies, meeting for pizza with the entire gang, and having fun as we better got to know each other. My work had turned more serious in 1962 as I was able to get Grace Line Inc. to accept my change of hours allowing me to attend school in the mornings and work in the afternoons.

That proved to be even more of a race than I was involved in currently. I completed my last class for the morning, and gave Amy a brief kiss as I burst across the campus to catch my bus in time in order to meet the trolley at the top of California and Van Ness Avenue in San Francisco. I rode down to the bottom of the Cable Car run to Pine Street, and leapt off, ran with my books around the corner to #2 Pine into our corporate headquarters where I raced through the doors and down the aisles waving to my fellow employees. I took my seat and reached for the bills-of-lading, which needed typing that afternoon.

At the end of the day, I made my way down to the Embarcadero where I joined all of the familiar faces I had grown to know commuting back and forth to Marin County. From there I walked and picked my car and headed for home.

I pulled over and leaned Henrietta up next to a tree beside the road. Then I unzipped my jacket and felt more comfortable back in a T-shirt and my riding shorts and took a drink of cool water from my water bottle, stretched my legs and body to remain in flex and not to get knotted from the ride.

I suppose that date from the night before had my mind reeling. I remembered in 1961 when I was twenty years old, how Amy and our friends enjoyed all of the activities, especially when we went out for the evenings to find ourselves at Samuel Taylor Park for a barbeque.

What all of us enjoyed most during those Saturday evenings in the summer was dancing under the stars in Larkspur where the "Rose Garden" The sponsor was the Larkspur Fire Department. Couples came from miles around including San Francisco, to dance into the night beneath the oak grove, strung with colored lights, and a wonderful dance floor beneath our feet, with some of the finest dance bands around. After we had danced and held each other, we made a quick stop for coffee and dessert, then, drove with the top down beneath the stars of Northern California.

All of us were working and progressing in our lives. We spent days in the sun, especially during the weekends, swimming and enjoying each others' company before heading in the unheard directions none of us would have anticipated as we had already thrown our graduation robes away.

Honk, Honk, Again my attention was back to where it needed to be. The day was warm by now; I was getting hungry beyond the snack I brought for this moment. It was about 1:30 that afternoon when I heard a "Shh…" and looked down to my rear tire and saw I had a flat tire.

The terrain I was in was barren in comparison to where I came from yesterday. Fortunately, I saw a sign that read "Bradley, California", just ahead. So I stopped to take the weight off the tire and took a look at the situation. At first I pushed Henrietta, and later lifted her up over my right shoulder and walked her into town for that was the least I could do in return for all the generous miles she had given me. It seemed to be quite a walk, but it came to an end as I saw this tiny little town ahead.

I knew what I needed most was the companionship of one in the town while I patched the tire as I walked into town to find four to five garages or gas stations; I know I was a sore sight. I walked up to the first garage and introduced myself to have the old attendant turn away from me and not say one word. I thought this wasn't my last name, so I plodded over to the next station and introduced myself to another owner. After assuring him…and he replied, "I'm busy and don't have any time to talk or help for that matter." I hadn't been through the whole metropolis of Bradley, so I approached a third attendant and I could have sworn by now, they were communicating with each other before I arrived. I said before any other comment was blurted out, "All I want is a little bit of moral support while I fix the tire and I will be on my way."

The owner said, "I've got to hand it to you, you're a sticker. How about a cold drink while you change your tire?" He said, "I see you became acquainted with one and all in our fine town." I replied, "All I hoped for was common decency which you're showing me." He sat with me, wiping his brow and I went right to work on the tire. Before I could believe it I was done and I thanked him for taking a few minutes from his day. I gathered some snack food and cold drinks before mounting and pushing off, first to extend my gloved hand to one from the town of Bradley, California who said, "Any time you're coming through, stop and say Hi."

It hit me many years after, that in Bradley, California I had both practiced and learned what would be an invaluable lesson which would apply from then on in my life to "Keep On, Keep On", no matter what.

Now I had something to talk to Henrietta about as we cruised into the afternoon. All signs that were posted kept reminding me I was closing in on Salinas, California. It was after lunch, around 1:30 or 2:00 p.m., when I saw the Desert Sands Motel off to my right so I turned into the grounds. I parked Henrietta next to the building so she could have a breather from the heat of the road while I went into the office to introduce myself. I asked the Motel Manager, "May I stretch out on the chaise lounge?" She replied, "You go ahead and take a swim if you'd like to." I responded, "I'm not spending the night so I don't think it's right to swim." She went on and said, "You go ahead and stretch out and rest as long as you want."

I must have slept awfully deep for I awoke to two brown eyed wonders; two of the cutest little girls you would ever wish for, sitting there giggling at me as I was snoring away. I awoke and opened one eye to blink away the light of the afternoon sun to laugh with them, at the position I had been caught in at that moment. I immediately looked to see what time it was when I realized it was well into the afternoon, and I jumped up and went over to the office and told the manager, "I've got to be on my way, since I need to make as many miles down the coast as possible before the end of the day."

I wouldn't have believed that all whom I met would be friends of mine for years to come. I had the afternoon wind on my back so I took my shirt and turned it inside out to make a sail and geared up to my highest gear to be able to extend and really go. And go I did for the entire afternoon!

Had you passed me then you would have seen how my legs were fully in the pedals pulling with ease, thanks to my clip pedals referred to as "rat-trap" pedals. As I approached King City, California, I came upon a long grove of Eucalyptis trees off on the right side of the highway. There were some branches and debris from the fallen limbs that I tried to evade, yet keep the same pace into town. I cruised into town and saw a familiar spot I knew I would be visiting, Keeper's Restaurant.

I had stopped there three days before to eat and met the Keeper sisters while there. I wanted them to know I would be coming through again, but I would be on my ten-speed bicycle bound to Vandenberg A.F.B. I shared more of the particulars with them and thanked them for a wonderful meal and made my way north to deliver the car and effects at the Oakland Army Terminal.

I had made it this far and had an excellent start toward my final mark taking me to Vandenberg A.F.B. I slowed up and lifted both feet out of the clip pedals and pulled up to Keeper's, to find a safe place where I could watch my bike while I ate dinner. I was a sight, as I had forgotten what that wind on my back did to me all afternoon. I was dirty from the road, in fact I was bronzed, just plain Indian red.

Before sitting down I went into the restroom to scrub up and cool down in the same sweep. When I reentered the restaurant, I saw the Keeper sisters so I asked my waitress to ask them to come to my table hello. There I was, in the midst of eating the biggest meal I had since starting the trip. Both of them came over and they asked if I was enjoying my meal and sat for a while to visit. The sisters remembered my first stop only days before;

I wanted them to know how pleased I had been with the fine food and had planned to stop and see them on my return trip. After our visit, the waitress came over to my table and announced, "The meal is on the house care of the Keeper sisters."

I started to thank them and they said, "Where are you planning to stay tonight?" I replied, "I stayed at the Fire Station in San Jose last night, so I'm pretty sure I can do that here or perhaps at the Police Department or a neighborhood church." They responded, "Go out and check your bike and equipment, and take a brief walk around town and come back to see us." I followed their suggestion and a bit later I returned to see them. They amazed me by saying "We have a fine surprise for you. All you have to do is go to the Motel across the street, go in and introduce yourself to the Manager and she'll show you your room for the night." I replied, "That's way to much; you didn't need to do that." They piped up and said, "You need a place so you can rest for the last day of your journey. Besides, you don't really have any other place to go for the night."

I went down to the motel. This time I unwound by pushing my bike across the main street and down the walkway. When I arrived, the Manager was awaiting my arrival. She said she was expecting me per the instructions from the Keeper sisters.

I said to her the only way I could accept to stay was the following: I said, "The sisters have done too much already." I went on and explained, "I'll have my payroll check upon arrival and I'll send money in the mail to pay for my room." She agreed. Then she had me sign in leaving everything, but my vehicle information and said, "I know you'll want to keep your bike in your room for safe keeping during the night." I thanked her for her warm welcome.

After entering the room, I unpacked and showered, then went out to the pool, stepped down the stairs at the shallow end and sat down in the water to relax. I had no idea until I took my shower that I had burned so badly that afternoon coming down the highway with all that wind and the beaming sun on my back. I don't know how long I sat there, but it felt wonderful. Afterwards, I dressed and took a stroll before calling it an evening. I stepped across the street to Keeper's, for a cup of coffee and dessert before bedding down until morning.

After I finished and was relaxed, the headed back to the Motel, did a check of my equipment and bent over to look at the tires and noticed something sticking out that I had no awareness of until then. Two of my spokes were broken out. I got my tool kit out knowing I couldn't go anywhere without this being fixed. I found I didn't have the right part to pull the socket on the wheel and knew there wasn't anything I could do that night. I tried to relax and turned the T.V. off and drifted into a deep sleep.

Day 3

Early the next morning I found a bicycle shop and explained that I had the wrong part to fix the spokes. I thanked him for his trying and asked where the Bus Station was.

Then I stopped at the Bus Station and inquired about shipping my bike to the Base. They told me the only way I could ship the bike, would be to have it in a wooden crate. I asked them where I could locate such, and the agent shrugged his shoulders to infer, "I guess that's your problem. "Next."

I had tried everything I could come up with and I didn't have an answer. It was breakfast time so I thought I might as well go and grab another bit at Keeper's and one of the Keeper sisters came over and said, " I thought you would be on your way by now." I told her, "That would have been true, but I, " then I told her the spot I was in.

She said, "Go ahead and enjoy your breakfast, I've got an idea that I know you'll like." As she walked away she added, "Give us one hour and I'm sure all of this will be taken care of in quick order."

Not only were the Keeper sisters timely, they had a terrific way to kill two birds at the same time. What they related to me revealed that they were so excited they could hardly hold it in and give the surprise away. Both said, "You have helped us to make up our minds because we've been planning a shopping trip to Salinas for sometime. They continued, "This will be the perfect time for us to shop up a storm. You can put Henrietta in the trunk and go with us and while there, you can get the bike worked on."

Here I had met two Birds who long before learned the importance of giving it away and who undoubtedly had been showered with an equal number of blessings.

Shortly, afterwards, they pulled up to the curb in their car. We unlocked the trunk and found there was ample room for my bike. They sat in the front seat and I sat in the back seat. Both of them were more like two young high school girls getting to go to town so they could get their hair done and spend the entire afternoon shopping for the latest in fashion. I thoroughly enjoyed them the entire way and it gave us even more free time to be acquainted with each other.

From the first time I met them, I saw how smart they dressed and carried themselves, and at the same time they were genuinely pleased that this would help me meet my deadline of reporting back to the Base. The radio was off the whole way. We really enjoyed the ride and I couldn't express my thanks enough for all they had done. What got me, was that trip back to Salinas, was in exactly half the time! They knew Salinas well having lived in the region all of their lives. In fact they knew exactly where they were going to shop. The next thing was to locate a bike shop that could do the work needed that afternoon. She turned around a corner and we saw a bike shop. She pulled up and parked. I told them, "Hang tight, until I am certain they can do the work." I uncurled from where I was sitting so comfortably, excused myself and went into the shop. I asked the owner whether he could work on import bicycles. He said, "Bring your bike in and I'll get on it immediately, so you can be on your way to Vandenberg." I wondered how he knew that much about my trip, as I had just met him.

I went back and told them the good news and got my Henrietta and while the owner began the work, I selected a cold pop and a snack and read every magazine they had in their shop while I waited.

I would always remember how the Keeper sisters had reached out and at the same time had helped lift my overall attitude. One additional train of thought I recalled was that none of the adversity faced seemed to bring me to the lows to be described later. Admittedly, all of the generosity of the Keeper sisters was beyond anything I would have ever expected, but I couldn't help but think, isn't that the way, when our Lord said, "Ask and it shall be given unto you."

All of their wonderful ways would be something I would reflect on for years afterwards. My greatest thanks even this many years later has to include them along with many others, for all they did for me then as true Birds.

"Your bike is done, and it wasn't as bad as you may have thought it was. I did a total tuning so you'll not have any other problems." He told me how much all of this cost. Fortunately, I had played it right, holding back on my dollars, as this just about wiped me out. I thanked him for the way he had altered his work schedule to get me rolling again.

Then I pushed my bike out the front door and saw the sisters pulling up to meet me as we had planned. They looked stunning with their uplifted hairstyles, and the car was full of packages from their shopping spree. They had to get back to the restaurant for the evening crowd, so I loaded Henrietta in the trunk and squeezed into the back seat. They asked me about the work, and both of them were pleased I was able to get everything repaired. Then they began laughing and telling all about their shopping. We thoroughly enjoyed the return trip. As we approached King City, they didn't give me a chance to respond before saying, "Gerry, you come for dinner with us and go ahead and stay at the Motel tonight, that way you'll be fully rested for launching into your final day which will be your longest." I accepted all as a marvelous gift from them to help an Airman to his Base. The truth was, I was colliding with that place on those tracks long ago.

We all sat and laughed and talked over the wonderful dinner. Afterwards, I said the biggest thanks I could for everything they had done. Mostly, I thanked them for becoming my friends. I said, "Goodnight," and headed back to the Motel. Before bedding down, I said all of my prayers and read from my Bible. I crashed that night! Before I left the next morning, I wrote a brief note for the Manager to remind her I would send the price for the two nights of lodging when I arrived on Base as previously mentioned.

Day 4

The Final Day

I rose earlier than usual because I knew every hour on the road on this, the fourth day, was the day I would complete the journey. By pedaling for thirteen hours, for a total of one hundred and thirty-four miles, equaling three hundred and forty miles in nearly three days, would take me to the finish line. And the same courtesies from the truckers passing were evident. The weather was superb for the whole trip. I was as fresh and vigorous as the bite of the morning air I pedaled through. It was down right crisp; in fact my windbreaker, riding gloves and added layer of tops were needed, as the sun had not risen, so the fog in the bogs I pedaled by made my teeth chatter. What I would have done for a cup of the Keeper's coffee and a plate of hot breakfast.

Wait a minute. The very thought of that fog was exactly what we faced years before on our double date on New Year's Eve two years after graduating from San Rafael High School. Stan and I had made plans to drive up to the Flamingo Hotel in Santa Rosa to spend our New Years Eve. The drive from San Rafael to Santa Rosa was anticipated that evening. We entered the ballroom, and were greeted by a throng, of men and women there, for the same festivity. The mid-night hour was about to turn. I know you'll be able to relate to the humorous fact that we didn't know any of those people, nor did they know us, but the real lark was we had a great time throughout among all of those strangers we sat and dined and danced among.

First came the planned for dinner with all of the treats, whistles, horns and ridiculous paper hats that led to the turn of the clock into the New Year. Even though none of us knew any of those about, we had the best evening we had for a long time. The exclamation of the evening came with a blast of the champagne cork and a rousing "Happy New Year" followed by hugging and kissing that was perfect.

Ahead of us was the longest thirty-five mile return trip we would have ever imagined. You see, that was the problem; the fog was so thick we practically needed to have one of us get out of the car and lead the rest of us down 101 all the way back to San Rafael. Those mile were so encumbered we nearly took ten times that these miles usually took to make that return drive home that evening. In fact it was so dangerous, we couldn't even kiss or neck sitting there in the back seat. That kind of fog is something you can't forget. Believe me, I won't forget what fog is all about after that experience.

I had all of those fine meals, conversation and aids to kick up, to be as bright and empowered as I was this the final morning on the highway moving south. I had long before realized I had been touched, "tapped on the shoulder," as I was to find I would never be the person I had been, rather what God knew I could and would be, no matter where I was on the road or the track.

My pace was about as perfect as I could have hoped for and the traffic revealed the time was in sync, including some trucks, semi's as before, a toot or blast of their horns as they swerved around me to pass. They were good companions the entire trip which was more than appreciated when they winked at me with their tail lights to signal they were clear, mostly to affirm we were traveling buddies to my final destination.

There was little wind so I kept all at the same rhythm throughout the morning. As the hour swiftly caught up with me, the welcome sight of old man sun began to creep over the eastern horizon. I could see that this was going to be a scorching day.

I reached out over the handlebars to pull my water bottle free of its holder and took the cap off, and tilted the lip against mine for a good drink. I had some incline in this section of the roadway so I grabbed the grips and knew the riding gloves were perfect for a secure grip on the road. I reached down and made the necessary gear changes to have an even smoother ride through this portion of the highway.

Now more traffic seemed to be waking up, showing its face as it passed me. The oncoming increased. Many passing vehicles had continued to wave even yell "Good Luck", as they passed on their way to their special destinations. Granted, there were those that exercised hand signals that were anything but helpful as I stretched my legs on the down swing and pulled upwards on the crank.

I didn't have any trouble knowing why the state of California had been given the motto of being "The Golden State," as this was mostly parched terrain that I was looking at on each side of the highway.

No wonder I was hungry, but at the same time my budget was limited due to the costs of repairs the day before. It was wonderful to think of the Keeper sisters and the fine qualities they shared with me even though we had known one another for such a short period of time. The timing couldn't have been more perfect as all within our world seemed to be holding tight to being able to trust others so much more freely. That made it a perfect time indeed to start and push with all Henrietta and I had to finish the mission. That factor became evident every mile I pedaled down the coast.

It hit me as to why my traveling companion had been given that name as our family had long before named our first car with the blowing, torn off top that still had a bit of the black paint on it, Henrietta. Why, back in those days I could still recall how dad with his fine tenor voice brought T.J. and me to sing right along with harmony cruising down those two lane roads no matter where we were bound.

When you're out there as I was, all becomes so apparent that God was present in every portion of the trip, from start to finish: the loving assurance of mother's apprehension felt the morning I departed, the welcome message from the gate keeper at the Golden Gate Bridge, the attorney outside of Palo Alto, the great group so willing to see that I had a fine place to sleep after those first 112 miles, to the garage owner in Bradley, California. All aiding me in every way possible for this journey I was in the midst of taking to the end of my originally planned trip to reach Vandenberg A.F.B. and not to be AWOL.

Ahead was Paso Robles, California, appearing sooner than I had anticipated. I located a drive-inn off to the right side that was surrounded by shade cast from the towering cottonwood trees. The place was so tidy I couldn't help but flash back to my summer of 1958 cooking at Gil's Drive-Inn Restaurant in San Rafael, where I continued to attend my senior year of high school and graduate with the class of 1959.

The menu seemed much the same as Gil's. I ordered to keep my budget flowing all the way, not only to Vandenberg, but leading me to the mailbox where my check would be waiting to carry me to the next paycheck. I enjoyed every bite and took my time for the afternoon of riding and closing on my final miles. I was in the throng of their rush so to "people watch" was perfect. I had selected another favorite "Chit-Chat" spot. I went to the restroom and refreshed with a sponge bath to get as cool as I could. And I didn't bother toweling down so I looked like I had either come from the shower or the neighborhood swimming pool as I was dripping wet.

As it turned out, even when sitting in the saddle, I felt how my butt soaked into the leather. We continued ahead in this the worst condition I had experienced since starting the trip. What was occurring was a kind of adversity not experienced previously. Henrietta and I were one entity bound and determined to fulfill the overall aim and objective yet, I knew I was dehydrated for I had been taking small sips of water from my water bottle and had drunk the last of it. Even my sun block was being beat in the process and I was soaking wet with the sweat from my body; doing all possible to pace myself for the road that lay ahead.

This was the approach to San Luis Obispo. Not only was I suffering, Henrietta was experiencing the same heat from her tires to the ball bearings in the hubs of both wheels. She seemed to be creaking and I knew I was and had the thought to throw in the trip, or the towel, and end it all right there in the Paso Robles Flats as they were appropriately called. Not knowing what to do, I threw out a Charles Lindberg prayer to God and it was like yelling it out with the strength I had left. I bellowed, "God Help Me!" No more had I prayed this, the shortest prayer I had ever enunciated, than did a small English Wren appear like a flash directly from the thicket on the right of the highway. It flew straight out as though to broadside me; instead, it was a bit out in front of me; he flew a course where he remained directly in front of the direction of my front wheel. As tiny birds do, he rolled his shoulder back at me with his beak open. Even as I sit this many years later, I know he was chuckling or laughing at me, saying so clearly, "Come on boy, you can do it." Before I knew it, I was smiling and laughing with my new traveling companion, if only for this brief moment, and I was picking up my pace and posture and beginning to feel strong again. I knew Henrietta and I were definitely bound to meet our original goal.

All of these thoughts had overcome me; I looked one more time for my wonderful new friend. He outstretched his wings and was gone from sight. I would never have imagined what was cast deeply in my soul because of this one tiny little bird that appeared from the thicket to guide, encourage and reveal his love for me, would do in my life from that moment forward.

I looked to one side and the other and realized I was climbing the grade that would take me to the pinnacle that would never be forgotten. I dropped the derailleur in my mountain climbing gear, taking all of the work out of such a climb. Having Henrietta geared this way meant sitting down firmly in the saddle, pushing down and pulling on the magnificent rattrap pedals, knowing I was on top. I pulled over, coasted to a stop and wiped my brow, face and arms. I wanted all to be in perfect working order for the descent and checked all of the equipment and knew we were ready.

I waited after letting several cars come up the grade to pass and make their way downward. It was so much cooler up in the pines. Here the breeze from the nearby Pacific Ocean was evident.

We pushed off the top of the steep grade awaiting the falling slope ahead. I leaned out over the handlebars and crouched as low as I could get and thought of the summer of 1960 and how my friend Stan and I had cycled up and down Mount Tamalpais in Marin County in Northern California.

Here I was in 1964, in my high gear, pulling with all of my might, much like the speed of my friend that flicked in front of me, for such a sacred moment. I was flying down and around each and every turn. The way was clear, and I remained on the shoulder, but I knew I had just passed that car! I couldn't look, as there were more turns ahead, and the descent was more than steep. The wind was blowing in my face and it was refreshing me from my plight from before. I became joyous, as though to feel how terrific it would have been to yell with sheer joy at the experience and lift my arms far into the air. All of these emotions would be held in check as I could see the valley and San Luis Obispo was ahead. I slipped downward back into civilization and looked to the right to see the familiar rocklike structure well known by all travelers. I began to catch up with myself, and Henrietta's jet stream from moments before, and pulled into the parking lot of the Madonna Inn.

I was a sight, but I needed to use the restroom and refresh myself, particularly to request from the bar tender tumblers of ice water. I know he was miffed with my appearance and the clicking of my bike shoes on the stone floor. Nevertheless, I asked him for ice water. I should have known he wanted me to order a drink or lunch. So, I told him the story that others had heard the day before. He was anything but interested and I didn't think he was going to oblige me until a gentleman at the bar said, "For God sake man, give him all the water he needs. I just saw him on top of the grade as he passed me. I looked at my speedometer and he was going sixty-five miles an hour. Anyone that can do that and has completed the miles he has, deserves even more than a glass of ice water. You should line up glasses of ice-water for him to refresh before he continues."

At that, the bar tender smiled big and turned on the tap until there were twelve tall tumblers in front of me. I picked up each, lifting them as from a cistern, and held the glasses one by one to soak up the cold from the outside, as I slowly drank with a fitting, "Ahh," after each. I explained, "I'd order more, but my cash is really thin and I need all of it to get to my final destination."

The bar tender was totally different now from my first meeting him. He offered me the menu and my choice on the house! I thanked him for his hospitality, and replied, "I'll eat here on my very next return." As I clicked across those rocks poured into the floor, I heard the bartender and the fellow traveler say, "There is a young Airman we must lift our glass to." I walked through the huge heavy door to reunite with Henrietta. She and I had our last chat. I threw my right leg up and over the cross bar and coasted off the parking lot back out on the highway moving down the coast. Ahead was Pismo Beach. I knew we were on the coast as the wind was in my face making the pumping a steady pull.

To think I had broken the record when it came to coming off that grade! The salt air was so refreshing and more than welcomed.

I remembered back in 1962, on that very corner, I was hitching a ride in one awful rainstorm; I finally received the ride I needed to get home to attend my friends wedding in Marin County. There was no way I could forget that trip. I so wanted to be home with my family and friends. The truth was annunciated that I ate too much and was in the way. Then I heard the same message as before, "Go ahead and get on back to your base." If that wasn't bad enough, I perceived a similar message from friends of the past, who made me know I was in their way. You know when you come to reckon with such is when you realize where your home is, or was, and in my case, Vandenberg A.F.B. had become mine.

The traffic had been building. I knew how much further it was. I decided to stop along the coast and have a bowl of soup. I knew I had enough cash for that and a cup of coffee. The waitress asked me what I would like and I told her.

I enjoyed that bowl of clam chowder and my coffee and another tumbler of ice water. The view out on the ocean and the sprawling beach was such a relief. I thanked the waitress for her service and went outside to catch a gust of the sea air before climbing on my bike.

There was time to pray thanks to God for everything this day and all the days before. I pushed off and we were on our way to Santa Maria, California, our last town before heading for the final miles to the Base. It had seemed farther when thinking back to Pismo Beach, where the clam chowder had tasted so good.

Before realizing it, I was starting to approach the outskirts of Santa Maria, where I would live in the years of 1965 thru 1967 with my friends from the college. There was this Mexican restaurant, that served the best soft tacos and beans that fit our budget while going to college together. We went there periodically and had our lunch.

Other sights were on both sides of the main boulevard as I cruised into Santa Maria.

The hour was getting late so I just kept pedaling westward toward Vandenberg .

Gerry Bradley

These last thirty some miles were the same ones I traveled time after time, as we went into town to get off Base. I came to the moment of truth that I never prepared for by insuring I had a front and rear light, if needed. That time was now as the day's light was slipping from the sky into the west. I kept coaxing Henrietta onward and forgot everything but getting to the Main Gate before we were caught in the nightfall out on that desolate highway, where you could confront raccoons, possums, coyotes, owls screeching from the surrounding Oak trees, deer pouncing out in front of your path and dealing with the traffic coming and going. I kept climbing off and adjusting the frame; after doing this several times I praised her. I pulled up and together we proclaimed, we had nearly made it, but this was too much for her. We continued on, as the light of day was gone, and we were wrapped in the dark.

Passing motorists, headlights gave us refractory light to continue farther. We were nearing the Base when this car and driver pulled over and the driver said, "Come on Airman, let's throw your bike in the trunk and I'll help you get on out to the Base. We can't leave you out here with no light; it just isn't safe." He not only gave us the lift to the front gate, he took us right to my Squadron and my barracks. As we pulled into the parking lot he stopped and came back to the trunk, and helped me lift Henrietta out of the trunk of his car. I never saw him again, but he became on that dark night out on the road leading us to the finish line, another bona fide *Bird From the Thicket*. Three of my fellow Airmen coming from the Day Room were pleased to see me and know I had made it back safely and on time. They wanted to hear all about my trip. Honestly, I was way too tired to take them through any of the details that evening. One of my buddies helped me with the doors as I carried Henrietta up the stairs into my room so we could both rest and be ready for the coming day of duty.

Before calling it a night, I shaved and showered to feel presentable. Then I took a walk over to the Day Room to say hi to all of the guys. Afterwards, I walked over to the Mail Room and collected my mail, particularly my check. Then I felt secure and knew I could meet all of my promises in King City, California. I saw a couple of the guys on our floor and told them I had better get some sleep before time to report. I closed the door of my room, and sat down on the side of my bed and said, "I sincerely thank you Henrietta for the ride of a life time. You performed remarkably well throughout our journey. I wanted you to know how grateful I am for the way you carried me across all of those miles. After I get you into a bike shop, you'll be as good as new. Then we'll be ready for even more ventures with each other." I sat there and stared at what had been my companion as we made our way down the coast of California completing this feat of pedaling from San Rafael, California to Vandenberg A.F.B., California. There wasn't a way I could be any prouder at that moment. My prayers were longer and considerably more detailed. That night I took time to read my Bible before going to bed.

The next morning came ever so fast. When I reported to our Security Clearance Offices at Wing Headquarters, I knew without a doubt I was a much better Airman and person than before, affirming I would help my Sergeant due to his emergency condition. Master Sergeant Rye and our staff were glad to have me back on board. All of them wanted to hear all about the entire trip and all of my ventures along the way. As you might imagine, there wasn't much time to share a lot as the doors opened and our daily clientele began to arrive.

After days and moments of free time, I was able to share a lot of the trip with them. They were interested in the entire account. Later that week, I got one of my buddies to help me get my bike into a shop. Shortly after, we went back and picked up Henrietta in top form. We were ready to strike out for many more miles of riding and enjoyment.

One morning directly afterward, two journalists came from the Base newspaper asking Master Sergeant Rye if they could have a moment of my time to interview me regarding this trip that I had completed. He more than agreed by saying, "We don't have a celebrity in our office all that often!" I went out into the hallway as we looked for the coffee room and sat down, as they began to ask me all about my trip. They wanted to know how it came about so I shared the story. After they had enough to write, they said they would appreciate my arranging a time in the near future where I could go to the Main Gate so they could take a photo of me entering as I had that night. I confirmed this with Master Sergeant Rye. He more than agreed and added, "We can't stop the press; whatever we do." So I met with the press. They, got their photograph and, unknown to me, this became quite a story. It was in the Base Newspaper and I later found it had been in the San Rafael edition and papers up and down the coast. It wasn't long afterwards, that a new member, who was transferred to our Sentry Dog Unit from England, mentioned while we were working together, "You mean you're the bloke we saw in the Stars and Stripes that made that bike trip?"

Shortly after that, I was notified that I had been nominated to be on President John Fitzgerald Kennedy's Physical Fitness Team, which meant I was competing within the state of California. What an honor this was and certainly not even considered. From there I was able to form a

Base Cycling Club for other interested riders who wanted to get clear of the Base on their days off. Our membership wasn't that large, but it was a great time for a group of guys to strike out and see new sights.

While all of this was going on, I was entrenched singing in the Chapel Choir and teaching Sunday school. Afterwards, I was asked to be Superintendent of the Sunday school and, at the same time, I coached Little League and officiated at their games. All of these activities brought me to know many more within the citizenry throughout the Base than before and I realized, more than ever before, this was my home.

I am more than certain throughout this journey, none of whom I had met would have believed of my having an unknown condition that I would come to know as Bi-Polar-Mood-Swing Disorder, that would become something I would have to face and live with from that time onward.

Chapter 15

Early Discharge to Allan Hancock College

I missed being shipped to Vietnam in September 1965 and began my undergraduate work at Allan Hancock College. While there, I became Vice President of the A Cappella Choir, Associated Men's Student President and a Feature Year Book Writer.

I had the superb opportunity to interview the other parties who knew the founder of Allan Hancock College. The more I gathered the facts, the more intense I became writing about his being a great man who had accomplished so much within his lifetime. Imagine how he rowed his little row- boat on the surface of, believe it or not, the La Brea Tar Pits of the greater Los Angeles Basin. He grew to accept each and every opportunity before him. I found by having chats with his wife, his chief cook, friend, and bottle washer, he had been a member of the Los Angeles Philharmonic Orchestra; his instrument was the cello. And if that wasn't enough, he became an aviator, a railroad engineer, philanthropist, husband and father. What I gained was much more than that of this mans life, rather, that all of that and more could be mine, or any persons, by merely accepting all doors of opportunity waiting for them to reopen a second time.

Consequently, my assignment brought the piece for others to read and glean the facts regarding the man Allan Hancock.

While in Summer school of 1967, I was tagged as a future Union Labor Delegate attending my classes at Cal Polytechnic College in San Luis Obispo, California. There we dealt with Labor Law oriented cases.

I took more classes dealing with the art of discussion and the History of Speech toward my major. I was able to grasp opportunities as a guest speaker, as well as storyteller, and attained insight and practice in the art of interpretative work of literature. All of this was the true sign that signified my major discipline, that I would pursue concluding my BA Degree while at Seattle Pacific College in Seattle, Washington.

Before beginning my work in college and exiting Vandenberg A.F.B. with my discharge in hand, we settled in our first home out on the west side of Santa Maria, where the roadside produce stands were located. There was evidence of the sprawl throughout town, as it grew overnight due to all of the contractors assigned to Vandenberg A.F.B.

Our paths coincided as so many young married couples do. My wife was working the day shifts; I continued working the three split shifts completing my assignment with Base Police and my enlistment. At first we would wave at each other as we passed going or coming. Later, we passed without any acknowledgement whatsoever, due to the aggravation this posed. I teamed up to car pool with other Airmen who were married and lived in Santa Maria.

Coarse behavior rose due to the lack of seeing each other as I knew we should have, it was deep seated, and festered more and more.

Where so many couples weather such altered paths, the old behaviors came to the surface. You'll see them intervene as you continue the rest of the story. Each and every time a wrongful choice was made, it was merely an amount of time before similar rifts were present. More time passed and had I known, I would have been able to deal with all of the upheaval more effectively. Furthermore, when I, or anyone suffering the unknown behaviors where it seemed all others were quite aware of my wavering up and down on a scale, still was not revealed to me. All of this affects others and their staying powers only so long. Then the inevitable occurs. It came in many facets as conveyed throughout the story.

Another, distorted belief was acted upon by me, when I was standing my post and I had to return my wife's salute, followed by her wink, that, brought me, to become more angered than I could have believed. I told her to leave the Air Force and teach school in Santa Maria. She had her degree and was trained to do so.

One example was the realization that perhaps the desired home wasn't there at all. This seemed to always plague me, no matter when, where or why.

Everyone has their breaking point and, as expected, that same person or persons I lived with would leave. In each case, I was once again peering down that track over and over, in search of all lost so many years before, when I faced more changes than I would have imagined.

As years passed and continued, few knew the hours I spent shedding tears, searching my soul for so many unheard of moments, places, people, ways of life deep seated within my spirit calling down the track, for a better understanding within self. All of this came even during the confusion, distortion of fact, times of raving about others supposedly, in fact the truth was, I was doing all of this trying to make some sense of everything occurring.

Granted, I couldn't see or perceive what should have been done then. If she reads this story now, she will come to know, I fully admit all should have been left alone. That included her keeping her commission in the United States Air Force. The decision should have been hers, not mine, or any other persons!

While all this was going on, we found our lives considerably different, more settled, drawn to each other and our involvements within the community. The remaining time that I referred to as being a "short timer," prior to my discharge, passed quickly after we were married.

My approval for an early discharge made it possible for me to attend Allan Hancock College where I worked toward my AA degree. Along with fulfilling my final days on duty, I was preparing for my future classes coming in the Fall Quarter of 1965.

I was twenty-three and it was 1965. In the meantime I chose my classes, got the books I needed; and readied for my discharge.

While all of this was going on, I was becoming even more entrenched at the college. As is expected, the venture included getting to know new professors who taught me subjects such as my Speech classes, from Mr. Burke, who challenged us to the hilt with all possible avenues so we could see all of the possibilities leading to our future. He appeared interesting from the start. He came into our class with a weathered brief case that had the contents of our class work for each session. He wore a tweed sport coat and plain colored pants. He was a bit gimpy in one leg and had a glass eye, not to be taken for his not seeing all about him, as he gained this fighting in WWII. What I appreciated most from him was the way he saw to our having every opportunity possible.

After speaking for the hour, I always looked forward to my class in the Introduction of Art taught by Joe Lowell. He turned out to be one of the most fascinating Profs. His mastery of the subject was astounding and captivating, both to the subject at hand and to his gregarious personality, which he shared with all of his students. He was always in his smock like jacket and you couldn't miss him. He was short in stature, but made up for it in every other way, mostly the way he would reach out to us even to offer to me, "Anytime you decide to return, I'm here to teach you to paint." This is one promise I still look forward to claim in the future. His daily lectures always included one question for us to probe. One of those questions left was pertaining to the high-rise buildings being build across the country. He finally shared that one of the perturbing factors not considered engineers or architects alike was how to drop mail down all those stories via the mail chute and still be intact. The result was seeing all of the mail in cinders.

There always was a break between classes, so I could better get to know Arthur Jones, who revealed by his powerful form he had played football in his day. He was the Dean of Men Students. He understood the position we took in the setting, where there was a constant complaint of the campus being nothing, but "a higher level school that had ash trays".

Such a transition forward was more like taking steps backwards, having to adapt to the younger set of students about me. I found the success of this came the same way as before, while preparing to graduate from high school, by attending the classes with one and all and becoming as involved in the activities as possible.

My friendship with Arthur Jones led me to become the Men's Student President, which enabled me to draw on opportunities in student government.

I never forgot the Professor I had while taking my introductory psychology class. He was about the same size as Joe Lowell, only of slighter build, and where Joe Lowell had a bald, head this man had wavy hair, that would be hard to hold down in a good California wind. Seldom would I have another instructor that would come the first day of our class, take the chalk in hand, stand at the blackboard and draw one big circle on the board. None of us knew then that this circle would remain throughout our class to its end. He used this as his medium to teach the overall subject to us each day. I found this stuck, and found myself using it in future years of teaching my classes as well.

I learned more regarding teaching directly after the lunch hour.

The class was A Cappella Choir, taught by what came to be the finest teacher to date, Ben Montinni. He gained our attention through the music he selected that we would perform in the future. Our class sessions were captivating and it always seemed as though the end of each session came far too soon. A personal lesson he advocated was to always remember, "opportunity may only knock once." Where this concept touched me most was during our second year of studies with each other as we were readying to leave on our year's choir tour.

I had turned out for the track team and was preparing for the events with my fellow members of the team. Mr. Montinni called me in after one of our class sessions and voiced, "If you want to turn out for track that's fine, but if you're going to remain as a member of A Cappella Choir, and be among those about to leave on tour, you will have to choose one or the other."

At first it seemed absurd, but after further thought, I left the team and remained as Vice-President of our choir and united in the effort that lay ahead. That decision didn't make sense until we packed all of our effects, including our risers on the bus, and we pulled away from the college for all points directing us toward that very "opportunity" that none of us could have imagined.

It was a certainty, I could continue the daily workouts and preparing for the events for the track team. None of them, including running the hurdles or even the 200 meter run, would have touched all that lay ahead. In the end, I could say my thanks to Ben Montinni for his wisdom.

That tour included our traveling together on the bus as one unit bound more by the miles as we closed on our route of Southern California, on to Las Vegas, then to Southern Utah, working our way north toward Provo, Utah. We were able to sing for the student body at Brigham Young University via televising our appearance on their campus.

What was more significant was how we sang three and four concerts each day along the entire route. Heightened moments throughout included, gathering at the base of the Sequoia Giants in King's Canyon National Park where we sang for the travelers passing through.

Our choir came to sing as if one voice. We had been told that would be our goal from the very first day we joined each other, taking hold of solid selections of Brahms, Bach and other classical composers. The audiences were as varied as the schools, churches, and civic organizations.

We found ourselves standing before the Mormon Tabernacle Choir after listening to them in their rehearsal. They asked us to sing for them afterwards even though we were the number we were, in contrast of the size of the Tabernacle Choir. Their complements afterwards were uplifting for all of us.

Where the tour prominently marked me, was back in King's Canyon and Bryce Canyon National Park, where we couldn't help but share "Master of Human Destiny", which soared into the heavens above us.

When we left Salt Lake City, we turned north and continued on to Northern California and began our southern leg back to Santa Maria, where we began ten days before.

The only time there was any tentative problem was in hearing Mr. Montinni instruct us not to be late for the bus or they would leave without looking back.

This happened only once, when two were late and we held tight, finally to hear our Director say, "We'll have to leave without them." One of the members was looking back, sure enough they came scurrying and we weren't sure whether he would have the driver slow up or not. This time, he stopped and the two members of our choir boarded, saying their thanks and apologizing at the same time. There were no more episodes such as this! We knew who our Director was and came to respect his being the taskmaster he was. I found I drew on his teaching ability in every way possible, especially when teaching on the Junior High and High School levels later.

Another phenomenal instructor was Scott Bailey, who taught U. S. History. He drew on the previous years sabbatical when he had visited every President's place of birth and death. His intent was to construct all that he taught regarding our country's history around all of his findings. Our class sat mesmerized as he shared his accounts gathered mile by mile. Needless to say, this methodology brought history off the page of our text. He wasn't very tall, and had the sharp chiseled look in his face of one that would set out as he did, to gather such factual data and incorporate it for all of his students in the future. I found that the subject was hard to recall, yet proved to be more than inspiring and drew me deeper into our country's history.

So I found the help I needed from Mrs. Swanson, who accepted my request to teach me to learn how to study more effectively. She proved her willingness by taking me on increment by increment; I came to learn the effective ways to study. I had no idea as to the significance this would take in my future. I improved regarding all I was studying working toward my Associated Arts Degree, finding and practicing these newly learned skills that made the learning and studying more enjoyable to say the least. Such skills brought a transformation for me as a student. I became a true achiever for the first time!

Coach Bill Woods was both our Cross Country and Track coach. He coached for years and was excellent. He took team after team to the State finals year after year. His ability was superb when it came to recruiting. We had members on the team from points overseas to Washington D.C.

It was the daily workouts and how I became good friends with the guys that patiently helped bring me along to get in shape to begin running our Cross Country events. Our jaunts took us on roadways bordering the strawberry fields surrounding the campus. It was the scent of those berries that undoubtedly helped pull me along mile by mile, along with each of the fellow members that gave me a hint that I carried down the track as a future Track Coach later in my teaching/coaching experiences. The hint was to keep my eyes on the heels of the runner in front, and not lose sight of those heels, and I would find how magnetic they would prove for me when, training or competing.

Our workout for the track team was a regimented daily course we followed. Two aspects of those workouts included, running interval training with flak jackets with sand in the pockets of the jacket. Each day we ran a said number at three-quarter speed for distances that insured our stride would be lengthened. Just as we concluded this, Coach Woods would drive out on the track in his beat up old jeep. It didn't take long for us to know the reason. He would literally hitch us up as if we were plow horses. At first he started out easy with us running behind, but in no time we were on the straightaway and had lengthened our strides, in order to keep up with the increased speed. It sure worked!

Before all of this happened, there was the last of the summer months and I spent considerable time at the pool where we lived. It was there that I met various families and visitors during the summer.

One day this lithe, long legged, pearly blond appeared who was, visiting relatives at the apartments for a portion of the vacation. I knew from the start that here was another much like my girl of the past. Getting to know her was something I treated delicately.

I told her the truth from the start that I was married.

Later finds revealed I didn't fill the void of gambling, committing acts such as taking our car out and driving down the roadway and pushing car upon car up on the curbing, or any other behaviors that would seem outright questionable.

Getting to know her at the pool was a natural as we both loved to swim and that was our perfect meeting place. All the time she remained with her relatives and I would return to our apartment. This occurred before I began my work at Allan Hancock College.

Some would have the wanderlust of others or drank or spent wildly or behaved out of control as they dealt with the similar condition I still wasn't aware I had.

Consequently, I persuaded Ellen to come down to the pool with me occasionally. One dive was more than enough for me; to come to the surface and see the woman I was married to sitting there on the side of the pool in her wool skirt draped over her knees, with a wool sweater and white blouse during the warmest months of the year, knitting.

I knew from that moment on, I was way too young to be in this position or place in life. Strangely, such behavior wasn't evident while attending classes as I worked to attain my Associated Arts Degree.

Our talks brought her to say, "You can go all you want, but know you can come home when you decide to." I retorted, "This is anything, but what I needed to hear from you." This remained her stance for the total time we were together.

All became more and more damaged as the months ensued. We separated; I found a wonderful couple that provided me a fine room in the second story of their home in Santa Maria.

I was running track daily. Afterwards, I returned to my room, bushed. The last thing I wanted was to eat dinner, but a shower was perfect. Shortly afterwards I would drop off for a nap, wakened later and studied into the night. That was the regimen during that time period of searching and trying to find myself,

I remained there with this family for the duration of the Spring Semester. Admittedly, I was being nudged by the fact we had our own home before all of this took place. Finally, I returned and we began to work out the areas that had been giving us fitful times prior to this.

Shortly afterwards, I located an advertisement on the school bulletin board that caught my attention. It was regarding the possibility to take individual voice lessons. As it turned out, the teacher had performed on Broadway stages for seven years. Working with her was very uplifting and a great help to more effectively develop my voice.

I noted the Christian Scientist church was in need of a soloist. I paid them a visit, applied and, before I knew it, I was singing for their membership each week. Unknown to me, I found they paid their soloist so I accepted this and turned it directly back into my lesson money.

Both of us realized we got along famously when we were traveling, but it was quite different living together. Arriving home brought a big surprise to say the least! I found out that she had discontinued taking the pill while we were apart. There was one hitch however, and that was her not advising me of this. Strange thing, she became pregnant!

Events were unfolding before our eyes faster than either of us could imagine. That was a good time when we would go over to Guadalupe or Cashmere in the evenings and had the best steak dinners in the overall area.

We entertained in our front lawn where we had lemon trees and big looming avocado trees. Those we invited were her faculty members, my buddies from the Base and periodically those from the church.

We sold our TR-4, as she hated that car from the start. I said, "Why didn't you say so." She said, "It always embarrassed me due to the color and the attention it brought to me when driving it." So we traded it in and picked out a racing green MGB GT, with a swept back trunk. This seemed to be more to her liking.

The assignments that came during my Speech class included, being able to read and tell stories to primary age children at their schools. I found real delight in sharing prose and literature with neighboring ladies of auxiliary clubs, bringing the needed rounding out as to that we practiced daily in our classroom sessions. Such assured: exposure with impromptu, extemporaneous, entertainment, comical format, and finally came our test on our manuscript speech. Our work included devouring our textbook and staying abreast of *"Vital Speech."*

Gerry Bradley

Now was the time I had strived for, to transfer and gain furthering opportunities in search of my BA degree.

Toward the end of my freshman year at Allan Hancock College came a question from one of my fellow students. He shared with me that he was preparing to go for the summer to tour Europe. He wanted to know if that would be something I would consider.

Somehow the topic came up between us at home one evening and her reply was, "You should go, after all you missed going after your senior year in high school." She went further by saying, "We have the money in the bank, so go ahead and take one half of the total deposit for your trip." I took some time to talk all of the details over with her before going down to the bank. I asked, "What will you do while I am sojourning?" She said, "I want to take some classes and it will be a perfect time to do this. Afterwards, I'll more than likely go home to be with my parents and then we can meet back here come fall." I thought it was entirely too simple. We discussed it more; I finally went and withdrew the money and determined all of the details. Before I knew it, I would be on my way for the summer.

Chapter 16

European Disaster

My fellow traveling companion made the claim he spoke French so we had that much going for us.

I learned through my wife one of her fellow staff members was driving to the east coast immediately after the school year.

We met with him and asked if he would appreciate having us along as companions. He agreed and it was only a few days until he would be pulling up out front of our home to make way to New York City, New York.

The desired trip was before the end of my freshman year 1965-1966.

The morning we were to leave, we embraced and kissed each other. I walked down the driveway to meet the teacher we were to travel with to the east coast. I turned and waved as she did to me.

Shortly afterwards, we picked up my buddy and were off in this two door, reddish orange Mustang for points east. The car was a two door and it brought the one resting in the back seat cramped, have to roll back and forth side-to-side. Finally came our turn south, leading us into the Los Angeles Basin where we turned east and headed for Scottsdale, Arizona.

One would drive for a stint, another would remain in the passenger seat as the navigator and the third was in the back seat grabbing all the rest possible. Each time we made a round robin shift to keep moving at all times toward our destination.

Before arriving in Oklahoma, we kept shifting from seat to seat on a regular basis. Finally, it was my buddy's turn to drive. That was short lived to his chagrin. Climbing into the mountains of Arizona, he scared the two of us to the point the teacher had to ask him to pull over to the side. He explained, "We just want to get there on time, but most of all we want to get there." That came after we saw and felt the edge of the cliff as he sped kicking up more than gravel. From that time forward, we adjusted so the teacher and I did the driving all the way to New York City.

The first real stop did not occur until we were in Ada, Oklahoma where we found the community swimming pool. It was there we took our first shower, and totally cleaned up before jumping in the pool to be refreshed. None of us had any inclination to get out of that pool and the restful state we were in, there in my home state, not that far from my home town. This time I would have to forego going on to Enid, Oklahoma to see my relatives. Our schedule was far to pressing. While there, all three of us were able to take full advantage of the time before loading up and pushing eastward.

When we arrived in New York City, we pulled up to where Mayor Lindsey's office was. We checked the time frame realizing we had made the entire journey across the country in a total of fifty-two hours. All of us exchanged our thanks to each other and we got out of the car and immediately knew we were beyond spent. In fact, we felt down right sick. Our ride and driver pulled away and we were left standing in the heart of New York City.

Having been there before, knowing the Avenue Of The America's and that The Sheraton Hotel was located nearby, we caught a bus headed that way, but made certain we would be able to get where we were destined.

Our hold over was due to our flight leaving in twenty-four hours. What we needed most was a shower, shave and some good sleep. The myth regarding those in the Big Apple became just that. There wasn't one we asked help from that didn't aid us in every way.

I told my buddy, "The Sheraton is just up the walk." We walked through the rotating door in our casual attire carrying our brief cases. I walked up to the main desk to determine whether or not we could book a room for one night. The reply was anything but what we wanted to hear, "There aren't any vacancies due to the city being full of conventions."

When I went over to inform my traveling companion, I found him to be anything but indulgent at this news. Some words were exchanged between the two of us there in this regal setting in the Sheraton Hotel off of 37th Avenue in greater Manhattan.

I put some space between us in seeking some help. I found myself down on the lower level where the barber and shoeshine man were. I talked to the two of them and the barber piped up and said, "Do you need all of this finery?" And my reply was, "All we need is a clean room where we can rest and get ready for our coming flight." The more he talked the more I listened. He said, "There is a fine hotel just up the street that will meet your needs." I asked him "What's the name of the hotel?" He and the shoeshine man were laughing and winking at the same time when he replied, "The name of the hotel is the YMCA."

At that, all three of us had a good- hearted laugh and I returned and told my friend, "I found a nearby room for us tonight." He asked me, "What's the name of the hotel and how far is it."

We left the lobby, walked out on the sidewalk among the masses, crossed at the boulevard and found our hotel only paces away, from where we had found ourselves in such a predicament. As it turned out there were rooms available, so we checked in and made way to our room. It didn't take long for us to undress and crawl under the clean sheets and sleep deeply until the next morning.

When I woke up I began to see a pattern of behavior that would repeat itself over and over by my traveling companion. He was not to be found. I looked for him throughout the YMCA and the adjacent café. I went ahead and stopped to have breakfast; shortly afterwards, I returned to the room and arranged all of my gear and in walked you know who.

Years later, you would have heard: "He had a real attitude," that was a mouthful. I tried to talk with him and make him realize that I was concerned and had been looking for him, but there was no note to explain that he was out walking and sight seeing. I asked him if he had breakfast and he said, "I'm on my way to do just that." So we went downstairs to order breakfast while I had another cup of coffee. We made plans for the afternoon to walk over to the United Nations Building. The attitude was extended to that stroll where he first walked dragging his feet along. It was apparent he was in a real mood toward me, which ended by his walking on the opposite side of the boulevard.

I was determined to see the UN Building and the grounds. There wasn't much time remaining before making way via subway to Kennedy International. We were able to complete the walk, but the sulking continued and so did the distance as we made our way back to the room at the YMCA.

Part of our research before leaving, included reading *How to Save and Travel Europe on $5.00 a day*. Key hints included the most efficient way to get to the airport was, to take the subway down to the very tunnel that would take us to Kennedy International Airport.

I can still remember what it was like for me riding my first subway train, sitting there anticipating we would be certain to get the exact stop for our connection. Upon arrival at the terminal, I located Air France and made certain as to the departure time and gate. I turned around to explain the details to him and you may have guessed he wasn't anywhere around.

I spent the entire time while waiting to board our aircraft searching every possible area for him. It wasn't until right before our call to board, that I finally found him on the observation deck viewing the planes coming and leaving. By now, I was exasperated at his immature behavior and lacking thought, as to anyone else in his plan of events. I walked back to the area where all of the college students were waiting to board.

It was very clear to me that the trip wasn't going to be anywhere near what he and I had originally planned.

If everyone was nervous, down to the sweaty palms that I had, we were in true form for the venture we were about to take. In my case, I had been air sick all too many times, flying hops while in the Air Force, back and forth across the country. I was doing everything to remain as cool as I possibly could. I couldn't help but think as to the whirlwind of events that transpired bringing me to this moment, seated aboard the flight that would take us first to Paris, France. I am more than sure that few got much sleep. We began to roll down the airstrip to take our place in line to take off for our summer in Europe.

While we were waiting our turn on the runway, I thought back on two thoughts. The first was, how surprised my finest friend Alex, would have been to know that after all of this time, I was completing what he and

I had planned after graduating from high school. One other mental image that nearly knocked me down on the sidewalks, of New York City, occurred on the morning we were walking over to the UN Building. We walked outside of the YMCA, turned and I walked right into two fellow students that I graduated with from San Rafael High, in San Rafael, California. The three of us were on the same track team together. They were just as amazed as I was, and we exchanged greetings with each other. As it turned out, they were just returning from having been in Europe; I was on my way. That made me know how small this planet is!

We could feel the plane lunge forward, as it rolled down the runway, and before we could take a breath, we were air bound on our way at long last.

I found much the same constant of being "an old man," George, mentioned in *It's A Wonderful Life,* among all on board.

Where everyone was in the midst of their own "chit-chat" as to their plans, I sat there in deep thought of my wife and our marriage. I couldn't help but wonder if this decision on my behalf was a wise one in the long run. At the same time, four of the cutest co-eds were sitting across from us. They were passing their enthusiasm back and forth, regarding all they intended to do upon their arrival in Paris.

I didn't know at that very moment that our craft was merging to cross the Atlantic Ocean. Charles Lindberg had traversed years before. I felt that same awe, he had to feel when considering the distance ahead of him, and vast unknowns ahead in that historical flight, that none throughout the world would ever forget. I peered out into that dark night through the window, where the deep-seated thought was, of those tracks all over again. All of us were discussing the number of hours our flight would take before landing in Paris, France. Many of us were embarking on much more than a summer vacation, rather an altered state that would prove worthy of the gift we were receiving.

"What did she say?" I inquired, and realized the stewardess was attempting to serve us drinks and appetizers before serving our meal. I knew through the entire venture that there was definitely something amiss. I could remember when I would find myself crying for no reason, yet, continued as I was swallowed up, literally gazing out the window into the darkness, not only of the night, but vastly more important, into the recesses of my mind. I was able to regain my composure, among all of the loose chatter and frivolous behavior from those about me.

I knew as I sat there, I had done this all wrong. The first thing that was needed was to have read and prepared for such a journey. Time didn't allow this. There was barely time to read the volume on *How to Save or Get by in Europe on $5.00 a Day*. I knew this fell short of what we really needed.

The tour was set up so our first stop was Paris; then four days before catching our plane and flying across the channel into London, where we would have another four days for travel. Afterwards, we would fly directly to Belgium, then on to Copenhagen to spend our remaining four there. From there we were on our own, and had to be back in Paris at the end of our tour, to catch the return flight to New York City.

My partner and I had already sent for our Euro rail tickets and knew we would leave Copenhagen and be bound for Vienna, then continue on rail to Italy. We had planned to bicycle back after touring the Riviera and return to Paris. All of this was enthralling, but at the same time, it was entirely too much to fathom. In retrospect, our plans were far too much even for this short time.

The serving of our dinner that night was with elegance at some thirty-seven thousand feet above the Atlantic Ocean. The early morning hours dragged by, at least for me. Toward the end of our flight, one and all were becoming more than nervous at the thought of our landing. Some drank way too much, including, you know whom without my elaborating.

I remember watching the movie presented while aboard. I always enjoyed Paul Newman, as an actor. The film was *Harper,* which had a good plot that kept the interest. The flick came to an end, directly before hearing the Captain announce our approach to Oreille International Airport in Paris, France.

All of us were fussing and gathering our effects as we began our descent our ears were popping, clearing for all ahead of us. We knew we were on approach as we were able to see the City of Lights, into the early morning hour. As we strolled down the aisle waiting our turn to step back into the terminal we thanked the crew for our flight.

I immediately realized we were in a foreign country to be sure. What continued to ring constantly was, the hollow sounding clock that rang on the hour reverberating throughout the airport. We made our way to where we could collect our luggage. It was there, that I found another abrupt result that nearly terminated his and my traveling together, from that moment forward.

While on board, we got to know the four young women and were becoming friends with them. Everyone was excited and clawing to grab individual bags. When it was all said and done, one of the four found her luggage was missing. Apparently, they had not loaded it on the flight. Her girl friends were calloused and didn't reveal that they cared one way or another. She was rightfully upset, for she had nothing except her purse and the clothes on her back. The situation worsened, as her girl friends and my fellow traveler, who had teamed up with them were walking away. At that, I asked all of them, "What if this had been you or me?" This at least made them realize how selfish and self centered their action was toward her. I really don't think this made a dent in him and all that transpired from that moment forward.

I left them to help their traveling mate. She and I went to inquire as to the status of her luggage and found it had missed being sent on our aircraft. The trace revealed they had sent it on the very next plane to arrive the next morning. This helped her, so all of us regrouped and hailed our first Parisian taxi cab taking us to the Left Bank, to stay those four days. None of us had made any previous arrangements.

After the harrowing ride with that taxi driver, who did all possible to chisel us for the fee of the cab, we arrived to look across the Seine and view the Cathedral of Notre Dame.

The girls left us and we found Le Hotel. Now was my buddy's turn to draw on his French, by helping us to attain our room while staying there. I found immediately he couldn't even do that, as he stated. I knew we had to have a room to be off the street and gain the needed rest for our days of touring Paris. So I walked up to the manager and said, "Bonjour Madam/Mademoiselle, Parlevous' Francais?" That exhausted my lengthy knowledge of French. I asked her if she spoke English and for a room in Le Hotel.

Admittedly, I used every source I could draw on including my Scotch- Irish, French and even Cherokee Indian blood to get that room.

303

Gerry Bradley

The main objective was to kill her with all kindness and gentlemanlike behavior. You're right I got the room!

After we entered, she showed us our room. In short order, the companion who had done so much to enable us to have the accommodations, was the first to try to understand what that extra bowl was all about in the lavatory. It was later that he came to know what a douche bowl was.

We had made arrangements to meet the girls and go out for something to eat. Our gathering spot turned out to be one sidewalk café between Le Hotel and the bank looking across to the Cathedral. It was there that I realized I was in cultural shock. I wasn't skilled in exchanging the currency and probably had been shortened when transferring currency at the airport. I felt like such a dope and didn't know what to do.

Here I want to flash ahead considerably, as to another awkward occurrence that affected me, and my loved ones much the same way as I was facing there in Paris, France. What surfaced in both cases was the inadequacy I felt in both experiences, of not being knowledgeable enough to cope with the situation at hand. That altered state that I found myself in, had a great deal to do with my having something deeply within, that I still knew nothing of, at least while in Paris.

It was horrendous to realize how helpless I felt. However, the conflicting behavior of my travel partner certainly didn't help. But, in truth, it was my deepest fall in that lost state, where I became paralyzed within the overall scene. Later, as you read further in the story line, you'll see real similarity of the two times and events that brought me to question, there had to be something that brought this on; to recognize a weak link with a certainty.

304

Another factor was how the Parisian men displayed such obnoxious antics toward us Yanks.

I didn't eat after that experience, of not knowing what in the world I was ordering or eating. From there, I returned to our hotel room and the others were off on the excursion. I slept so deep that night and woke during the early morning to find my roommate hadn't returned.

Here we were in Paris and he was pulling one of his absurd moves that I had become familiar with by then. He came sauntering in the next morning and I asked where he had been. He informed me that he had walked to the Eiffel Tower. From that point forward I didn't see any more of him, as if that was any loss.

I knew we only had four days and we would rejoin all on our flight to London, England. I became a recluse literally, to that of the deepest fear and anxieties, unknown to me before that time. That state became very serious and the panic over took me.

On the fourth day, I heard a still voice speaking English up the stairs in our hotel. I ran up the stairs to determine who this was. There she stood, a pretty, blond woman with the bluest eyes, and what turned out to be the most generous spirit, I could have ever hoped for at that moment.

I explained all to her, and asked her if she could help me. She more than understood and said, "Get your gear, and meet me in the lobby." I followed her as she was a quick stepper leading us to the subway, which I knew I would have been lost on had I not found her, one wonderful Bird willing to help me every way possible. We got off the subway at the precise stop, that she had inquired about before we left. This way she could take me directly back to the corporate offices of Air France. She remained with me and helped with the interpretation needed. We found that the original program of the tour was locked. I decided to return to New York and then on to Los Angeles. I added additional funds for ticketing on TWA. My aid said, "You'll be all right now, because they will take you to Oreille where you'll be able to depart homeward." I gave her a loving hug and I just couldn't hold the tears from my eyes. She had saved me from God only knows what!

I watched her trot across the boulevard and I was certain she was on her way back to Le Hotel. The proof of the matter was, how I remembered her willing spirit. I thought briefly, how that roommate of mine would return to not find me for a change.

The staff dispatched me back to the airport, which was exactly what I needed. It was actually the best to hear the familiar ring of the clock on the hour for twenty-nine hours, while I connected with my flight to return home. All of those hours were perfect to read and "people watch" those coming and going.

When panic, and pressing fear took hold, I was battling something not even diagnosed, all eroded before my eyes. That is what happened to me on my first trip to Europe. Due to this, I was anything but equipped to handle any aspect within the tour.

I was dealing with my shame of having come in the first place, spending the savings to learn as I did, and not fulfilling my obligation as a husband to my wife.

There wasn't one corner in all of Oreille International Airport, where I was freed from the resounding chime of that clock, while waiting to board my flight and return on the route taken days before. Not only did I, "people watch", I took extensive walks throughout the airport, and located the observation deck, where I watched planes land and take off. While there, an airline attendant (stewardess) walked up, but her appearance was more of a surprise, as I turned, and there she was standing beside me and we began talking with each other.

All of this vacillation definitely reveals, more than can be explained, any other way than the way all transpired. My actions weren't so different than a well- known movie director, who would walk away from the set, and catch the first train and returned to his home in the south, to be found by his wife and friends later, and returned to their home. When they found him, he would be ambling the streets of what had been home many years before.

What comes to the forefront for me, when pondering his behavior or mine, has to be that same place and time, where I have looked down those tracks in search of so much lost along the way of the entire journey within my lifetime.

I found out her name was Sharon. She was striking in her uniform of Navy Blue, with red trim on the sleeves, and her British Airways lapel pin shining the bright daylight. I was drawn to her dark brown hair with a cute perk haircut, with deep blue eyes to match the isles she was from in England, and that best revealed her red burgundy lipstick. She told me she had several hours to wait before her assigned flight that was bound for London near her home.

What struck me from the very first moment was how she didn't portray "coffee, tea, or..." Instead she conveyed a compassionate caring spirit. We stood there for some time talking. A bit later, we went inside out of the wind and away from the noise of the jet engines blasting. We found a comfortable area where there was less turmoil and continued to talk awhile. I asked her to join me for a bite to eat; she said all she wanted was a drink. I walked with her carrying my brief and she had her light bag and raincoat draped over one arm. We walked and talked until arriving at the bar where I opened the door for her, then, I asked for a table. We sat down and ordered two lemonades. Our conversation seemed to include anything and everything.

It was so apparent that we didn't meet by chance as our topics became more and more serious. After we had our drink, we walked back into the terminal. She said, before I was able to get it out of my mouth, "It's a shame that we didn't meet long before this." At that I reached out gently to hold her hand, and I turned and said, "Why don't we catch a taxi and you can show me the 'City of Lights,' that I have seen none of during my brief stay?"

Both of us considered taking a room in the nearby hotel. We decided against this and remained together through the hours awaiting our departures. I know now that I have never forgotten Sharon from Great Britain, due to such wonderful moments of sharing the chimes throughout the airport together.

We heard the announcement regarding my TWA flight about to board passengers. I never forgot how she went with me to the boarding area and we paused, and I reached out and hugged her and we kissed for much more than a parting kiss. I knew it would be another hour before she would be flying homeward, and even though our passages were separated, she would be rejoining her boyfriend upon arrival. I wasn't certain as to what I would find upon arriving back to be with my wife and my home in Santa Maria, California.

I knew what had happened to bring me to arrive at the plan I was taking, but I wasn't sure anyone else would be as understanding. Here, I had waited all of twenty-nine hours for this return flight and I was boarding and stashing my brief above my seat. There was another woman in the seat next to me. I said, "Hello", to her and she replied.

All of the passengers were aboard and situated buckling up their seat belts. The plane began to roll away from the terminal and took its place in line for takeoff.

I don't know what it is about me, but something happens to me when I fly, when taking off and landing many times the tears well up in my eyes. Sure enough, the same occurred when rolling down the runway feeling the lift as we rose above Paris. The lady next to me became concerned as she saw what a state I was in and overheard me saying, "I'll be back again Paris, I promise you." I continued, "When I return I'll be ready for you." At that she said, "I don't want to interfere, but I hate seeing you so upset and am willing to listen if you care to share the story with me."

Ironically, this very good looking blond haired woman, Patty, with lovely legs, and shoulder length hair tied back, draping over the collar, of her two piece mint suit with accessories to match, was the sweetest person I could have hoped to be seated next to me all the way to Los Angeles.

Our first stop over would be at Kennedy International in New York City. Then we'd be on our way across this great country of ours to Los Angeles International Airport. This being so, we would have ample time to visit and get to know each other.

The first thing was to find out about her trip and how extensive it had been for her. She told me she had been in Europe traveling, tending to her business, now she was on her way home after several weeks away.

What I appreciated most was she didn't probe. She waited for me to feel comfortable enough before starting to open up. When I did,

I brought her to understand where and what I had been dealing with the entire trip. As I unwrapped and rolled out the details involved, in what had been and what may or may not be ahead, she came to perceive the position that caused me to crumble there, in that seat as we left the ground and were leaving the continent of Europe, beginning the flight of return across the Atlantic Ocean.

What needs to be reiterated is this was considerably before knowing the truth that was to come out there in the blue that lay ahead in time and events to follow. My behaviors depicted this and more, but in not having knowledge, all that indicated was the severity of the events and how I dealt with each, that seemed to be around another corner ahead. Undoubtedly, others were able to see and know that there was definitely something not quite right.

We talked, selected our snacks, and drinks and specified what we would prefer for our dinner. I found her to be most interesting and appreciated her charm and finesse as we became acquainted with each other. Our being with each other was uplifting. After hours of talking and enjoying the symphony on our headsets, we decided to catch the film being shown to be surprised, the movie didn't hold our interest as we thought it would, so we continued conversing. She told me all about her business enterprise and where she lived in Southern California, in the vicinity of Orange County. I told her I lived in Santa Maria, due north up Highway 101. Our talk became chatter with each other.

The hours of the flight passed quickly. The pilot announced our timetable and that we would be arriving in New York, which was much sooner than we could believe. Sure enough, it was short order and we were looking out on all of New York City to hear, "Fasten your seatbelts as we're approaching Kennedy International. Those continuing on, please check the list of various connecting flights and gates. The crew hopes you have enjoyed the flight, and will fly again with us in the future. Do have a wonderful day in 'The Big Apple.'"

When we finally rolled to a full stop, we were able to gather our packages and I helped her with her effects from above our seats. As we waited for the passengers to exit, we kept visiting. I asked her to join me for a brief lunch while we waited to connect with our flight to Los Angeles. She accepted and we began to edge our way down the aisle. By the time we passed the lovely attendants, we both thanked them for all they did to make our trip so comfortable.

Here I was, in the familiar setting of the terminal, I had already become quite familiar with only days before. We stopped in one of the airport dining rooms. I held the door for her and requested a table for us. We sat more relaxed and ordered a light meal as we knew we would be eating later aboard our second leg of the flight to our home base, the state of California. The time together was an excellent way to carry us to the gate and connect with TWA leaving for Los Angeles. Those moments also gave us a chance to better get to know each other.

Afterwards, we had time to stroll to our assigned gate and I was sure I had left my emotions hours before in Paris, France. The call for us to board came, which we did as, we were extended passengers. That was helpful since we had ample time to stretch; I could help her take her jacket off, and mine as well, then place all in the hatch above us. I said to her, "Well, here we are again." Both of us were well acquainted as though we had known each other for a good part of our lives. Consequently, the entire flight was one of ease and we were listening, when the Captain announced,

"Below is the biggest ditch in the U.S., the Grand Canyon," which made us know, this trip we had been sharing was coming to an end.

Before we approached Los Angeles International Airport, she looked at me and said, "Why don't you join me at my home for a few days before you go north." This was like that wind I felt back in Paris, while standing and taking all of the coming and going flights, and the surprise of Sharon just appearing at my side.

I sincerely replied, "That is more than I would even have imagined." I added, "Are you sure my appearing won't interfere with your home life?" She said, "Don't you worry one bit." I mulled the invitation over the whole way that remained and I know she knew that was what I was doing. I held tight from responding until we had landed and were well off the plane.

I accompanied her to the baggage claim area; we located her bags and I hefted them off the turnstile for her. We started to exit the air terminal and I paused and set her bags down. I thanked her for her offer and told her, "I have to pass, as I'd better get on home." I finally said, "How wonderful it has been to have met and had the opportunity to know you." I wished her the best, we hugged and I helped her catch a taxi and loaded her luggage. As I stood, I watched her pull away into the flowing traffic.

Then I headed for the car rental area. I selected what vehicle I wanted to drive on to Santa Maria; I decided I might as well wrap up the entire venture right so I selected a convertible. My path took me on to the freeway headed north up Highway 101.

I knew I was home, and didn't have to deal with another culture, currency exchange, lack of foreign languages and so much more behind me now. Were I to share with anyone all that had transpired within these last few days, no one would have believed it.

It had taken all that I began with plus the cost for driving the last miles homeward. I knew there was wrongness in all of it, yet I knew I could make up the deficit by working hard as I had before. I saw the signs that were more than familiar such as Anaheim, where Disneyland is located, and it was no time, before I was taking in the beaches up the coast. I knew it wouldn't be all that long and I would merge with Santa Barbara, one of my favorite towns, that Adam and I frequented many evenings in the past while dining and dancing before returning back to the Base. What came to mind was Refugio Beach, where we had spent that wonderful summer.

The feelings that overcome us called home are like being able to turn corner after corner and say to your self, "I know that place, and want to turn other corners for the same reason." Such places leave us with a kind of warmth on our shoulders that glow through our bodies to the level of our souls. Such was how I felt mile by mile. I thought I had just passed the sign that we had taken to divert on out to the Base so many times. Now, I was cruising right along and the sun glasses were perfect, what with the wind blowing through my hair, as I thoroughly enjoyed the feel of this convertible, a bigger car than my TR-4 of yesterday. I looked out on the rolling hills covered with looming Oak trees, on both sides of the highway that, would soon converge with the oil wells south of Santa Maria. Sure enough, there were the derricks doing their work in the Central Coastal California terrain. Now I was feeling somewhat tense not knowing what I might find upon my arrival.

I passed Allan Hancock College. I would resume classes shortly after spending the rest of the summer months working to regain the loss. I turned off at the exit that would take me to our street. It was important to look for the rental location, where I would return the car that evening

313

or the next morning. When I pulled up to our home, I was surprised to find our car parked in the driveway. Everything looked all closed up and secure. Fortunately, I had kept my keys, so I could open the door and go right in the house. When I entered all looked as it did when I left, but my wife wasn't anywhere to be found. I wasn't expecting any kind of a note or welcome, as she had told me she had some course work she was going to pursue. I stayed home and found I was suffering true jet lag, so I fixed myself something to eat, showered, and put on my summer pajamas. I watched some T.V. then went right to bed.

The next morning I awoke, when I heard a car pull up in the driveway, and I heard my wife quietly open the front door. I was about half awake when she came in the bedroom and stood looking at me and said, "I thought you were in Europe." I expected either alarm or the simmering heat she was exhuming at the moment. I replied, "Give me a moment to wake up and brush my teeth, and I'll join you and try to explain the situation to you."

I tried, but at the same time, I know I didn't do a very good job of it. She remained in a state for the day from hot to heated, just plain simmering which began to cool throughout the day. I didn't push it one bit during that day.

She was beginning to cool into the evening, so we could converse some while reading the newspapers and watching some T.V. That night we went to bed and slept. I rose the next morning to smell breakfast cooking and the coffee was ready for our first cup to start the new day. Later she came over to me and said, "Well, I don't know what you're going to do for the rest of the summer, but I'm going to go east and be with my parents for a portion of it. I've just completed the seminar classes I intended so I'm clear to make this trip."

Before I could intervene with my comments, she said, "By the way, I'm going to need a chauffeur, do you happen to know of anyone that might want the job?"

Chapter 17

A Last Trip Together

We both smiled and began packing for leaving the next day for our trip to be with Ellen's parents on the east coast just outside of Baltimore, Maryland. She already had gathered the maps that would be needed from AAA, so we spread all of them out and considered the route we would take.

There was newness in the air from then on. As already mentioned, we traveled well together. It had been that way from the start. We got everything packed and ready following our checklist. I was able to load some of our luggage that evening and tied the sleeping bags and other essentials on our luggage rack the next morning.

We made our way up the California coastline, and our first stop was in San Francisco to visit my brother. His rudeness toward my wife brought us to quickly depart.

From there, we left for Marin County, in San Rafael to stay briefly with my mother before making our way eastward. She was pleased, but nervous the whole time, especially when thinking of the distance we were about to take going east to be with Ellen's parents. Our stay in San Rafael was brief, but at least we cared enough to stop and spend time with her before repacking and leaving for the Eastern shoreline.

The morning of our departure came sooner than we might have wanted, but the rising sun was aglow and we were ready to face all of those miles that lay ahead of us. We decided to surprise her parents and loved ones rather than bring them to fuss while we were on our way.

We hugged and kissed mother and thanked her for all of the good company, fine meals, and time of stretching out by the pool before leaving. I checked to make sure all of our bags and effects were in place.

Mother said, "Your trip is like the morning you left on Henrietta to ride your bike to Vandenberg A.F.B."

We pulled away from the front of the house, threw her a big kiss and cruised back out on the freeway turning eastward.

I had the top down for the entire trip, until later, when it became necessary to put it up due to the weather. Our TR-4 was cruising right along, but concerning sounds and warning lights were enough to bring me to stop at a garage in Sacramento, California to have the car checked. That took a good portion of the day. The wait was anything but pleasant, as it had warmed up earlier; we just had to wait to be repaired. Not only was it timely and aggravating for both of us, the costs were more than we had intended. In fact, we nearly ended the entire voyage there in that shop.

I knew it would be better to get away, where we could get something to eat and drink to cool our thoughts. We decided to continue with hopes of no more troubles.

The mechanic had completed the work by late afternoon. I took care of the damage and we continued on into the dusk and night. Even though the evening air was getting cool, we took the Air Force blanket as we did many times before and wrapped it around our shoulders and I kept driving into the night. Ahead was Reno, and "Glitter Gulch". First, would come Squaw Valley, fortunately without the drifts found there in the skiing season. We were worn out and made the decision to throw our sleeping bags beneath the ski lift that crowned above us. Both of us were far too weary to question whether we could be eaten alive there by some wild animal. We were cared for as we awakened to the magnificent dew on the surrounding meadow about us. I rolled out and began to roll our sleeping bags up and retie all, then cleaned the windshield from the fog during the night. Neither she, nor I, could believe how soundly we slept.

I started the car and turned the defroster on for some warmth; we grabbed our coats, bundled up, and were on our way to Reno, Nevada.

It was there I saw something in her eyes I'd never seen before, but we were safe, as we had set our limit and no more. My God, she did like those one-arm bandits! I know we made enough to pay for our gas and food for a few days from that stop.

As we were departing Reno, on the way to Salt Lake City, I was driving and I wound our speed up to one hundred plus miles per hour and sat on it out there on the desert floor. The time came for us to change seats and Ellen had been driving or awhile, when I looked up the road and saw how a piggy-back trailer swerved at the crest of the down side of the hill ahead. That moment we had a blowout and I didn't want to reveal panic to her, rather, did everything to convey total trust and help on how to control the car preventing it from rolling. She hung on tightly, slowed up and finally was able to pull over on the median. The adrenaline and sweat was rolling off our faces and afterwards the driver of the rig said, "Had I not seen the very first swerve I never would have been signaled to begin stopping all of this tonnage."

We knew after fixing the flat and slowly, cautiously, continuing on to Salt Lake City, that we had been protected that afternoon without question. What had occurred was, the heat and the friction from the roadway on the desert deflated our tire leaving us in jeopardy. This brought us to pause for some time while praying our thanks with tears slipping down our cheeks. Our pause brought us to more than hug it, brought us to cling to each other, fully realizing what the outcome could have been there on the Salt Flats taking us on to Salt Lake City, Utah.

After that came Salt Lake City, which was the first time I had been in that city since my junior year in high school. We did anything but look anyone up while there.

From Salt Lake City, I turned north and proceeded on to Logan, Utah. This definitely became significant later. I pulled to the shore side of Bear Lake which was pristine in its setting. The one piece of equipment we didn't have and would from then on was a tent. This idea of sleeping under the blanket of the heavens and stars was very romantic, except by morning, we knew we had the company of the biggest, flying birds in the state of Utah. Those mosquitoes literally carried us from place to place. They had eaten us alive in our sleep and the original beauty of this wonderful spot had another image to be sure.

It was time to be on our way into the Rockies, as our next stop was going to be Cody, Wyoming. Our route was the northern route that would take us all the way to Chicago and then to the Eastern Seaboard. Just outside of Logan, Utah we found we were traversing where the Utah, Idaho and Wyoming state lines merge together.

As I approached the valley below, we were catching scents of what had to be the best food in the land. The restaurant was connected to a cheese factory. Of all the breakfasts we had ever had, this was the very finest. They fed us as though we were miners from the looming rock like cliffs surrounding us, or at least like we were lumberjacks. In fact, all was piled on our platters to resemble the same cliffs. There was no way either of us could eat half of that breakfast. I said then, "This is one place we have to return to someday."

That morning was memorable and we talked about this for some time afterwards. I pulled out on the two lane highway headed for Cody, when out of the fields came this huge herd of sheep being driven directly across the road in our path. As I pulled up we found ourselves surrounded by the entire herd and saw the Basque shepherds with their walking sticks talking to the sheep dogs moving the herd on across the road. We were sure we would have a lamb or sheep in our laps or in the back seat before this was over. I looked at her, and she looked at me with astonishment, we were laughing at the same time through the entire ordeal. There seemed to be no hurry on the part of either of the two shepherds, but there was a definite plan to get all of the sheep safely beyond the road. We watched the two dogs barking and nipping at the stragglers to get them to move clear off the road. The shepherds turned and waved at us with the biggest smiles, then returned talking in their gentle way to their dogs hard at work. We talked about that experience the entire trip.

Throughout the day we saw some of God's country. I kept our compass in an eastward setting bringing us to pull into Cody, Wyoming before dark. We were able to locate a nice motel where we cleaned up and went out to dinner that evening. It was there that we both had our first buffalo steak dinners. We found this delicious and bid the innkeeper a goodnight, knowing we would be up early the next morning bound for Chicago.

After Cody, we drove down into the canyon leading us to take in Mt. Rushmore, with time to gaze upon those magnificent figures of our famous Presidents, chiseled into the rock above us. We had lunch in that very dining hall that Cary Grant and Eve Marie Saint were in while playing their part in *North by Northwest*.

Next would be Rapid City, leading to the canyon roadway down in the city below. From there we continued into the lake country and the rolling hills of Minnesota. What stood out for us was stopping at one market to replenish our food and drinks. While there we met the friendliest people we had met on the entire trip thus far. That was true all the way across Minnesota.

We pulled into Madison, Wisconsin and had to take our buggy into the shop for more work. It seemed we were heating up and had gained a new noise that needed to be checked, which turned out to be wheel bearings. Even though it was a blue-sky day it was a lot hotter now than where we had come from. We spent the day milling about the university setting while they were working to put us back on the road. It was late that afternoon before we were able to continue east.

The radio had been off all day, so we were anything but aware of what lay ahead of us in La Crosse, Wisconsin. It became extremely black with the boiling clouds that made us know we would have to put the top up immediately. I pulled into a service station unannounced, and heard the attendant yell, "What are you two doing out in this weather? We're about to be hit by a tornado; didn't you know it?" We didn't, but no sooner had he said this and a boisterous wind hit across the street from where we were and we heard and saw cars slamming into each other. We screamed, "Where can we go to get out of the fury of this storm?" He yelled with all of his might, "There is a motel down the road where you might be able to get into for the night."

We hustled down to the motel and felt welcomed by its dim lights from the road. I pulled up, and ran in to determine whether we could have a room for the night. We were very fortunate, as we were being looked out for with a certainty. I went back out to get our luggage and put the top up. It started to rain unlike any rain I had ever seen in my lifetime! The interior was literally catching the water. I went back in and asked my wife to bring a bucket, or anything that we could use to bail water out of the car. She bailed and I scrambled to get the top raised. It took both of us bailing the water out of the car that saturated the entire interior. We knew with some beaming sunshine the car would quickly dry out tomorrow. What was most important was we were out of the path of the tornado and safe for the night. After we got into our room, it was time to shower and warm up. The howling storm outside concerned us throughout the night, at least until we drifted off into a deep sleep.

The next morning, we arose and were amazed at the apparent damage with downed limbs, telephone poles and wires, wrecked buildings, homes and automobiles; the sirens heard from the night were quiet. There was no argument that we would pack and be on our way. I can assure you we never forgot that night in La Crosse, Wisconsin.

Now our compass heading would take us to Chicago. All of this country was completely new for me. What helped me was the agreement that she and I long before agreed to, her relieving me every day for a couple of hours from driving. That turned out to be my time of rest.

We knew after fixing the flat and slowly, cautiously, continuing on to Salt Lake City, that we had been protected that afternoon without question. What had occurred was the heat and the friction from the roadway on the desert floor, deflated our tire, leaving us in jeopardy. This brought us to pause for some time while praying our thanks with tears slipping down our cheeks. Our pause brought us to more than hug, it brought us to cling to each other, fully realizing what the outcome could have been there on the Salt Flats taking us on to Salt Lake City, Utah.

We looked at each other and spontaneously remembered another trip we had made together before being married.

We caught a flight at Hamilton A.F.B. near my home in San Rafael. She was a Second Lieutenant and I had just made my Airman Second class. We had driven up to visit my family before continuing from Hamilton A.F.B., California on a C119 with the duel fuselage. Such aircrafts were for the purpose of carrying paratroopers. Neither of us could believe our ears when we boarded and the crew threw us a parachute, and the Captain yelled, "Keep that close. In fact, it would be a good idea to put it on, because these planes are known to go down." We looked at each other as if to say, what have we got ourselves into this time? That was a hill and dale flight above the hedges up the coast to San Point Naval Station into Seattle, Washington.

Doing this enabled me to introduce my new bride to my grandparents. I called ahead so my grandfather would meet us upon our arrival. Our stay with them was as generous as when I lived with them during my junior year in High School.

After our stay we lined up to board our flight on a C-124 flying to Birmingham, Alabama hauling an aircraft engine mounted in it's casing between where we sat and the cockpit for the crew. As we began to board, we heard there was a Skylifter about to depart across the pole into Andrews A.F.B., to think we just missed it. Once again we were sitting in these paratrooper seats. All went all the way across the state of Washington.

323

We were invited up into the cockpit where we could see all the lights of the towns and cities below out into the dark night. Had the remainder of that flight been that smooth, we would have had it made. But, that aircraft engine was mounted to take the ride, and that it did. Every time I looked forward, that engine swung left and right, then with the air pockets it would shift up and down. You're right; became very ill and remained that way on into Birmingham. I was so glad to take off the oxygen mask that I sucked on the entire way, after using any and all receptacles to debrief my inner linings and run out onto the tarmac of that runway to get all the fresh air I could in my body.

Then we made our way to the railway station where we were to catch the Eastern Seaboard Railway north toward Washington D.C. and Baltimore, Maryland.

We entered the terminal; I was feeling considerably better than before our arrival. We took a break on the hard wooden pew like benches, I pulled a novel out that I had been reading and sat there enjoying the unfolding of the plot. Ellen was "people watching," and we kept hearing this young white woman and her companion, a smaller, slender black girl, giggling and pointing to me. My wife turned to me and asked, "Do you know why they're carrying on as they are?" I said, "I sure don't," and she added, "It's something for them to see someone such as you sitting there and laughing as you read. They can't read!"

We heard the first call over the loudspeaker that it was time to board our train, and as we stepped up on the coach, I looked back to see both of the young women behind us. Apparently they were traveling with us.

Before going to dinner, I told Ellen, I was going to introduce myself to them and see if I could begin to teach them how to read. So I went over and introduced myself to them. Furthermore, I visited with them to ease any tension that they might feel meeting me as they were. Finally, I came to the point by asking one of them whether they could read or not. As it turned out neither of them was able to read. This was a perfect time to ask them whether or not they would like me to begin to teach them how to read. Time was against us, but I began by working with them on the basic sounds of letters and some words. I could tell they really enjoyed it. There just wasn't enough time as they were to get off at the first stop up the track. They gathered their packages, as they were traveling light. I tried to encourage them to find someone in their town to continue teaching them to read. I added, "Don't stop, learn to read, and your lives will definitely become much different, I assure you." Then the conductor called out their stop and they thanked me again for offering them a lesson in learning to read. They were so ready to continue and learn as they stepped down from the coach. I waved to them as they walked off the landing at the Railroad Depot down the dusty road to I didn't know where.

Then I returned to sit with my fiancée before going to dinner. I couldn't help but think, I really hoped they were able to find that special Bird in their surrounding community, and resume where I left off with them in gaining the privilege to read and enjoy the pleasures that would come from their readings over the years ahead.

There have been many times and circumstances that brought me to know I wanted to become a teacher. This was one of those times that led me to my doing exactly that, teach and coach.

As it turned out my Second Lieutenant had made arrangements to surprise me on the eve of my birthday. She ordered me a Sole fish dinner. When they brought it to our table and set it down before me I was staring into the eye of that fish. When only hours before, I was contending with airsickness, now the train was weaving up the track to the Capitol and this God awful fish was staring at me. I jumped up and was running down through the car looking for any kind of a paper bag again.

She felt terrible over this incident thinking I was much improved after we were away from such a flight. Our journeys together from the start to the finish were full of variables and that alone made it ideal for both of us. Some married people just can't take the humdrum of daily existing together and we were such a couple.

The final days of that leave were spent meeting her parents and family members, getting out and about in the region, seeing the Capitol grounds to include one very romantic evening listening to "Bolero" by the symphony orchestra while seated on the back lawn overlooking the Potomac River and taking one final look at Abraham Lincoln up the long steps into the memorial.

Seeing the Smithsoneon Museum was awesome. It previewed a view of the past to the very present and above was The Spirit of St. Louis, bringing us to wonder how any one person could have achieved what he did in such a little plane, compared to what we were flying in now. Then, to compare that to the capsule of Friendship VII that John Glenn had orbited the Earth in, was a fitting contrast for this my first visit there.

We took in the Naval Academy down the road from her parents home. We also went to Arlington Cemetery in Arlington, Virginia and outlying areas leading to Mount Vernon and then to Williamsburg, where we could have been lost for sometime.

We ate Blue Crab for my first time with her family. Soft Crab made wonderful sandwiches. Why, we even went crabbing before it was time to return from our leave. I found that unique. All that was needed was a long line with metal nuts and washers tied to weight the line to the bottom, with a chicken wing tied to the line and dropped over the side of our boat. We felt the tug and pulled up more crabs. Then all of the crabs were dumped into this big pot that we filled while there in the beaming sunshine on the Susquahanna River. This was one fishing expedition where all caught something. That last tug, was the same as cinching up our luggage and readying to catch the return flight from Andrews A.F.B. to SAC Headquarters, Offut A.F.B. in Nebraska, then to make the final leg to Vandenberg A.F.B.

Ahead of us was the megalopolis of Chicago. I thought how harried traffic was in the Los Angeles basin that didn't even come close to what I was now seeing. I became so nervous, all I wanted to do was remain beyond all of this massive inter winding on and off the ramps, leading to who knows where. There the battle erupted, as she wanted to stay and see some of the city; in fact, she wanted to swing north into Detroit, Michigan. I vetoed this and we continued eastward. The heat of this intense argument subsided as we were passing through Ohio, on our way to Pennsylvania, and turnpikes that I had no knowledge of until I found we were in an armada of eighteen-wheelers on the descent toward Maryland.

Coming from the west coast, now to find how we were, dwarfed by such colossal vehicles, was overwhelming. One leg of a turnpike literally merged into another and before we knew it, we were nearing her parent's home. She was rightfully excited at the thought of seeing her family. When we pulled up in their driveway, all of us were hugging, shaking hands and I began to untie and unpack to stay for our visit.

Weekends, her brother and his wife took us out to see as much of the surrounding sites as they could. One memorable site was Niagra Falls. We even went over to the Canadian side, and looked down into the mist rising from the cascading water from above. It was a must to accept the available yellow raincoats, while peering at the tiny sightseeing boat cruising through what resembled the fiords in Norway.

As is true for all visits, the time came for us to leave and make way to our home in California. Even though I had just met her family, I had come to love each of them. Here her dad had insured we had the best time possible. Her mother had reached out to me in grand ways, such as shopping daily at the neighborhood bakery, bringing us fresh bread, rolls, even pastries, but the best were the moments she and I would sit and talk and better get to know each other and laugh together. I found both of parents to be so loving, "salt of the earth" kind of parents. Due to this, it was very hard to leave early the next morning and see both her dad and mother stand with tears in their eyes; both of us gave them one more hug and I shook hands firmly with her dad. Ellen was crying as we backed up out of their driveway making our way southward to Virginia.

Before we had taken the northern route; now we were going to continue down the Eastern Seaboard through Shenandoah National Park in Virginia and on into North and South Carolina, leading us to the Gulf of Mexico.

Mississippi was a world of its own. To see the sharecroppers were still living in such shacks with so little was an education of it's own. Here we were on the Gulf, thoroughly enjoying the weather and the umbrella of huge old Magnolia trees above us as we drove on to New Orleans. I had already seen so many sights, yet everything I was taking in was that which she had seen before. Now I had my own travel guide for much of the south.

Our arrival in New Orleans was toward dusk. We checked into our motel, then, we cleaned up with plans to go down to Bourbon Street and have a fine dinner. When we arrived, we were enveloped in the wonderful strains of jazz throughout. We selected a superb restaurant where we could dine outside on the veranda and continue to enjoy the ongoing trumpeting, string bass and drums with other groups intermingled in the background.

It was beyond warm and we were downright hot, but thoroughly enjoying the cuisine and service along with all of the sights. I am sure that after dinner, we weren't the first to stare over the swinging bar doors or, in her case, below the gates to see a sight indeed. Nude or near nude women were atop the bar dancing, swinging in every way possible, with the clientele seated on the bar stools below. I pulled her away and she grinned at me; then we found a great bar where the action was less nervous and served the finest Mint Juleps. Our evening was spent strolling the streets and "people watching"; then we turned in, as there "were miles to go before we could sleep" or continue homeward.

Well, we had been to New Orleans, and now were bound north through the bayous of Louisiana toward Arkansas. As it got to be toward the latter part of the day, we saw the most unusual spot called Lake Pleasant Village, on the other side of the Louisiana-Arkansas border. If there ever was a more spectacular place to camp and fish, this had to be it.

I pulled in and parked to let our buggy cool into the night. We set up camp with our bedding on the ground near our car. My word, it was so marvelous seeing the days end reveal its peace upon the waters. I turned to her and said one more time, "Would you ever have imagined we would have seen or experienced as much on this trip?" Night seemed to occur much like the blinking of our eyes. So we crawled into our sleeping bags and snuggled in for the night. No sooner had the sun disappeared and we were shifting to find that place for real comfort, when it happened. I heard the attackers aiming for us! At first I swatted them away and then the avengers came at us full force. I took the tent like covering, and tried in every way possible to shut them outside. It seemed there was going to be peace, and a night of sleep and then I heard another that had somehow penetrated and was sharing the warning of his buzz and we both realized they weren't about to leave us alone. This went on for some time and we finally said, "That 's it!" We scurried out of the sleeping bags, hurried to repack and get far from that so called heavenly place. I remember hearing her say as I pulled back up on the highway north to Little Rock, Arkansas, "No wonder we saw everyone leave as they did when we were settling in for the night."

I drove the entire night and arrived in the capital of Arkansas that morning. We were really beat from swatting those bombers from the sky. This time we decided to stay at the finest hotel in downtown Little Rock. Afterwards, we checked and made way to our room, showered and took full advantage of those separated beds and crawled in to sleep. I'm sure we sacked more deeply than any other time on the trip. After those hours of sleep and regaining our strength, we were bound for Fayetteville, Arkansas where we met with friends of ours who taught at the University. They took us to a prime lake setting, minus the outdoor elements, to have the biggest Catfish dinner since I was a boy at those neighborhood fish fries.

We hated to leave them as soon as we did, but ahead was my return to my hometown in Enid, Oklahoma. Our arrival brought us the warmest welcome from one and all. Everyone in my family us constantly and wanted to make sure we saw all possible, as it had been some time since my return. It was so important to share the main sights with her while we were there. They included: the Old Railway Station, my schools, our old house we had lived in, the movie theatres, the City Square and the site where the Chit-Chat Café was. When I had done that and visited into the late evening hours with my relatives, it was time to be on our way. All cried and hated to see us leave, but knew it was vital that we return timely and safely.

From Enid, I turned southwest to El Paso, Texas and that was due to our wanting to include seeing Carlsbad Cavern National Park. That drive from El Paso to the caves was an enchanting portrait before our eyes driving into the afternoon. We arrived there on time to take the last tour of the evening down into the caves and take in all of the sites. After we surfaced, we were like those we had toured with, squinting and looking across the desert floor that lay ahead of us. Time was of essence in order to see the desert's beauty. The panoramic view was encompassing to the point of permeating our spirits.

Now we were directed toward the Grand Canyon. Before arriving at the South Rim, there was some civilization that led to the Rim. Neither of us had any idea as to what was ahead of us until I pulled up to the parking lot. We looked up and felt that we were immediately swept away, across the Rim to all of the other Rims of the expansive walls of the Canyon reaching far below. We got out of our car and held hands as we walked over to the edge, hesitated and were totally silent, being swept into the depths of the canyon below. Even after all we had seen and shared throughout this trip and others previously taken, nothing touched what we were now observing. We heard of the tours available including: riding the burros to the base of the Canyon, which we thought we would pass on after looking at the escarpment called the trail downward. It was extremely difficult to leave when the time came. We agreed the Grand Canyon had to be the most colossal cathedral either of us had ever worshipped in throughout our lives.

We left a large part of our souls there out on the Salt Flat Desert after the near catastrophe that would have ended the entire journey. Instead, we now had memories of the following: being in the boat on the Susquehanna River in Maryland crabbing; touring at our Nation's Capitol; taking in the George Washington Monument, and still being able to descend via the stair case to the ground level, walking the entire length of the Mirroring Pool between both monuments to the expansive staircase to see the Lincoln Memorial Monument, reading the inscription for all to ponder; even being turned around on the circular boulevards there in Washington D. C.; standing in the mist overlooking Niagra Falls, strolling through all of Williamsburg, Virginia, and Mount Vernon; touring Gettysburg, Pennsylvania, walking in the memorable fields where so many gave their lives; having the spiritual heightened moment of taking the steps into the very pulpit where Peter Marshall, had ministered and delivered his sermons of sheer eloquence while serving at the New York Presbyterian Church; baling out our car and being protected by God by having missed the direct impact of the tornado in La Crosse, Wisconsin;

and penetrating the hollows of Shenandoah National Forest, which led us to find all on the Gulf Coast.

Now we were on our way to Flagstaff, Arizona in the higher mountainous country. That stop was important for just around the corner it would be one of nine Universities that would accept me after completing my work at Allan Hancock College.

Our respite would be: Disneyland, the Wax Museum, seeing all of the sites at Marine Land below the UCLA campus, taking the walks throughout Knott's Berry Farm, and, while there, being sure to have their famous fried chicken dinners, completing our time as tourists. There were key spots for us while at Disneyland, and would you believe the big one for us was, "It's A Small World," which left us ready to turn for our last stint of our journey to head for home.

As we rolled into Santa Maria, we looked at each other and felt a sense of accomplishment unfounded before making such an expedition. Our little house with the Avocado trees bordering the driveway and the lemon trees looked so good to us. We were beyond glad to be home!

Shortly after returning, I was able to secure work for the rest of the summer working for moving and van storage companies. The work was heavy, downright hard, but had daily gratification. The drivers paid us for our work at the end of each job. Each night I walked in I laid down more of the money spent frivolously earlier in the summer.

Ahead was my second year of college work and vast opportunities that led to my being accepted by every College and University I applied to attend, taking me toward my degree. I wouldn't have believed I would be having to decide between Northern Arizona State, Utah State University,

Gerry Bradley

Seattle Pacific College, San Jose State, San Francisco State College and lastly, Cal Poly Technical College in San Luis Obispo, California.

I had come to love the pursuit of higher learning, and every opportunity presented to me and for us as a couple, as we prepared for our future together.

Chapter 18

Transfer to Seattle Pacific College

Admittedly, the decision of deciding which College or University I would attend was included in my final quarter's work before graduating from Allan Hancock College.

All of the grads were making plans for the coming summer sessions, jobs and vacation, all to prepare for charging ahead for their degrees. It seemed much the same as graduation from High School. We were already feeling how all of us would be apart and not to see each other for many years in the future.

I had researched the piece now written, published and distributed for the college's yearbook. My assignment was to write about the founder of the college, Allan Hancock.

While I confirmed where I would attend the fall quarter of 1967, I purposefully completed additional credits for the summer session at Cal Polytechnic College in San Luis Obispo. The reason for this was my wife had enrolled and had been taking classes toward her Master's Degree at Cal Poly. Consequently, she believed it sound for us to remain in the area, so she could continue her work and I could complete my BA while there. As I write in this portion of events, I find it is so much like "True Confessions" as I can say now and have been able to say since her thoughts would have been best.

At first, I was denied entrance at Seattle Pacific College.

Once again, such brought me to rear up and fight, making sure this institution knew whom they were turning down. Indeed, this was a manic phase of behavior (or a high) to resubmit all of my original papers, including drawing more effective letters of testimony from the community, submitting them for more than being accepted, but to win and not be rejected. You will see time after time the same set of behavior. And this time I was accepted! Through it all I'm able to pronounce the entire decision was a wrongful one.

Such behavior played out during different times and circumstances through the years. As I peer back and down the tracks, I fully remember the reasons in each case, at the same time to see how the results were seemingly the exact opposite of what my perception happened to be.

One example was a teaching experience that is long past, yet depicts a similar kind of action I took. This overall experience was to gain insight as to the actual day of working in the classroom with the kids. At first, I was assigned with an older, much more experienced teacher. I thought another teacher, from what I could tell, was more suitable as she was a younger, progressive teacher. Consequently, I was transferred to her class. The end result was I rapidly came to realize the former assignment would have worked much better overall. However, it was too late to shift gears. What I did was to leave a much deeper experienced professional and trade it for a more youthful approach. There was daily evidence of a teacher that had to reinforce for herself, via the children in the class, her excellence; however she was a good teacher. And I realized this change was wrong from the start.

The same took place over the choice of the college I wanted most to attend which will be detailed as you read further.

My finding while attending the summer session of 1967, at California Polytechnic College, revealed there was no Speech major.

Furthermore, I couldn't be promised this would be implemented for the coming school year. So, I confirmed with Seattle Pacific College. The trade turned out to be that the Speech Department had only one Ph.D., where we received word afterwards that Cal Poly implemented the Speech major that fall. The department had eleven PhD's. It also proved to have an extensive library for the future research needed.

Another factor was how I wanted to transfer with my friends that would be attending Seattle Pacific College that fall.

We were no longer just a couple as Ellen was pregnant. We had packed and advised her Principal of her not returning to teach for the coming year.

This time our journey north was much more relaxed. We had ample time so we turned toward the coast up Highway 1 to take in all of the sights along the way, such as the Sea Lion Caves. Neither of us had ever stopped there so we thought the walk down into the caves would prove worthwhile. If you've done this, then you would be alarmed as we were when lighting at the viewing area of literally hundreds of Sea Lions on the rocks below revealed something strange. At the same time, we realized there was an infestation of strange shaped flying insects that permeated the Sea Lions, the rocks, in fact the entire area. We could have sworn we were going to end up with a mouth full!

Both of us said, "Thank God we didn't park with the top down for the car would have been invaded."

We exited and headed up the coast welcoming the wind freed of those flying creatures left on the backs of the Sea Lions. The weather was splendid the whole trip. We thoroughly enjoyed every mile. There was time to walk along the beaches, enjoy all of the seafood and not to forget the finest Crab Louie's on Monterey's Fisherman's Wharf.

As we got closer, we were on Washington's coast beginning to turn inland, which took us to I-5 north into Seattle. This was my first time on the new freeway system. I knew my way into Seattle and to Queen Anne Hill.

We stopped at my grandparents, and reported at the college and picked up our keys for student housing. I remember driving on the campus' front loop with the backdrop of the older buildings on campus. The area gave us the feeling of Ivy League, with all of the towering old maple trees around the loop and the multi-storied brick buildings in the background. In the near future I became acquainted with the chapel hall where above the doors it read, "Valiant Truth". Those words became even more prominent as the years continued. Upon our arrival, the intent was to pursue the classes that would enable me to graduate in two more years. More than the seasons hampered this progress. Neither of us, or for that matter our son who was born during the month of November of that year, were accustomed to the seasons prominent in the Pacific Northwest.

I had been in class all day during the fall quarter of 1967, keeping the same pace we were more than accustomed to and my wife abruptly said, "If you want your degree so bad, then you can just work for it and pay for it yourself." She added, "Don't count on me anymore." So I leveled the playing field that very moment by replying, "Don't you worry, I'll do just that." Who would believe such an evening could change the total scene on the spot?

Up to this time, I had my G.I. Bill to count on for the tuition and the balance toward our living costs. As already touched on, she had taught before while we were in Santa Maria. I found her decision was as solid as she was with her ancestry or blood. Oh, she agreed she would work on campus, but in comparison it would be minute compared to what we had been accustomed to before. Rather than argue or fight, we became more and more estranged.

This was a precise time where all the old behaviors I battled, that led to the knowledge that would come later, with no way to medicate or remain stable, the old behaviors began to show themselves. I was working out across from where we resided and a really cute little co-ed runner came across my path.

The park was the perfect place to continue my training, as I had, while on the Cross Country and Track Teams before. I set my schedule so I rose early every morning.

At the same time Ellen's rigidity remained the same.

Our son was born and both were perfectly healthy. We knew we were blessed and dearly loved him. There was this underlying current that swirled, boiled and finally erupted. Even though I didn't know all of it, or for that matter even part of it, I knew when such areas within our lives had real effect on me.

I wasn't over-spending our funds, gambling, involved in drugs of any kind, using plastic charge cards to the hilt, nor was I encumbered by alcohol, no I would just walk astray on a running path or otherwise be attracted to another woman. I knew enough, however, to realize it was much more than having to do with future encounters. So much of what happened was to try to deal with all of the unraveled pieces of the threads of fragments of yarn, as a ball of multi-colors on the floor had rolled and fallen totally apart. I wasn't walking away from all familiar by returning to where something called home had been. That was in truth not possible to track.

That find all these years later, now medicated and diagnosed for some twenty plus years in which I realized all that had occurred was just like that ball of yarn that strung beneath my feet, was evidence of all of the variables of differing sizes, lengths, colors of the pieces of yarn. What all of this meant was how I had been seeking two elemental, but vital, factors wrongly in so many cases for the family and the home that was lost so many years before.

I don't know if you can appreciate how much this means to me now. All you have to do is return to the preface or foreword and you'll find that my goal was to gain complete healing for the first time after telling this story. There never was one encounter along the way from that moment on that this shared wasn't true.

It's a wonder that all of the time before, more didn't occur before it did.

There were moments of being a family working toward the same goal. When that subsided so did the overall Mission Statement. All began while pedaling together and led us now to peer out on the snow- covered streets that drew us into a hold for a bit longer.

While all of this continued, relations were being built on campus between 1967-1973 among Professors, all the way to the President of the college and with fellow students. I asserted my total efforts to gain much more than a degree. I was determined to insure when the placement phase took place, I would at least have to be considered seriously. To do this brought me to attain my BA Degree in Education that would be extended to K—12, with major emphasis in Speech Communication

Skills and English, along with Minors in Music, Physical Education and Developmental Reading. The total effort proved its worth and more.

Even though I was a, registered transfer student, I remembered, while, on leave visiting my grandparents, walking on campus I found such a sincere greeting from all throughout the campus, which drew me back.

While there I spent ample time soul searching after we parted and went our ways from being a couple, to being single, with exception of her having our son which was best all the way around.

I continued my voice training during 1967-73. At the same time I continued singing with the Seattle Pacific Men's Glee, which was a great opportunity. Friendships were being gained on and off campus.

Off campus, I returned to Bethany Presbyterian Church, where all of the old gang of years ago had attended Sunday school class. While there I became a member of the church choir and a very good friend of the Pastor and his family. He realized my serious intent after meeting all requirements for my degree. I had planned to attend Theological Seminary. Consequently, the groundwork was laid with my Pastor's help. What proved to be the most vivid was how he asked me to accompany him while out on calls to parishioners.

All of the stress and frustration along with carrying a full load of classes, working my part time jobs, caught up with me one morning while on the top floor of the Speech Building. It was there on the back staircase I found myself thinking, as I would in later years, of considering plunging from that height to the sidewalk below. Fortunately, in every case, such was only for a moment. Call it the power of God or otherwise, but I also thought, you don't want to do that for all that would happen would be I would end up being crippled the rest of my days, causing more grief for all of my loved ones. From there I reentered the building and continued my grueling schedule for the day and remained away from that site never to return.

It was fitting afterwards that I was present when hearing our own organizer of the Falcon Club, later Olympic Women's Track Coach, speak on a favorite subject, that of "Champions", which he was versed about as he led team after team into the arena where they would be "Champions". What stood out in his message was the truth, that all could be "Champions", no matter where. I carried that torch from thereon!

His brother, the Dean of Instruction, provided me the needed guidance and his friendship throughout my stay. Those within the Department of Education prepared me to be a very good teacher in the future. Professors, such as the one within the Sociology-Anthropology Department, brought to the forefront his background in "Cultures of the Indians of the Northwest." An English Professor not only brought to light much more within the discipline of English, he was a fine friend. Two worked with me while studying Vocal Music who pushed me forward with my vocal training. The staff members within the Speech Department challenged me even further in my major area. Before graduation, I took one class from the Chairman of the Department of Art, which was "Art for the Elementary Teacher". It proved to be fascinating and a subject I engaged my students in regularly. I took Astronomy and found the subject matter magnetic. Here without a doubt were Birds as if they had landed on the wire above, awaiting the exact light of the day, to head for their rest so to lend the same guidance and direction to all that entered their classroom.

There wasn't a day I wouldn't have missed a class on "Ecology and The Environment". Our Tennis instructor during a summer school session smiled even bigger when she heard me say, in an intermediate tennis class, "This game is much the same as a combination of playing like a lion and a lamb." Her smile reminded me of the line in *My Fair Lady*, when we heard Professor Higgins say, "I believe she's got it."

Where before I had been a feature yearbook reporter, now I joined forces with the Business Manager and sold ads for the yearbook. Before leaving, I had additional exposure in the medium of radio, announcing news on the campus broadcast.

During the time of separation and finalizing the divorce from my wife, I know I came close to dying. Had that happened, it would have been of deepened, lonely of heart, body and soul for my, son. The marriage had never been right from the start. It was the kind of marriage, that I declared every year from the start to its end; I knew we wouldn't be together another year. During the fifth year we were finally at the end. Even though we had this marvelous son, there wasn't enough strength in our union to go any further.

Before the end of my junior year at Seattle Pacific College, she informed me her parents had sent tickets for them to come for the summer. I responded saying, "I know you want to see your family, but I don't feel it's right for you to go on their money." I told her, "We will all go, but we should pay our own way." She insisted and made their plans.

All unraveled and she prepared to go. At the same time I began searching for my new place. I located a cabin, rustic at best, up from the college on Nickerson Street. Nothing changed, except she began organizing and packing; I confirmed my place, which was unknown to her. My family was completely aware as to the consternation pertaining to all of this. My mother and grandmother told her not to do this or she would never see me again.

The morning of their departure she rose and took our son and their baggage and was waiting at the front door for their cab. I awoke and was hustling to work on campus. I told her not to expect me to be there upon their return.

I heard later, that she defiantly retorted to my mother and grandmother, "I know he'll be there when we return." They told her not to bet on it.

She said in haste at that last moment, like a flick of a match being lighted and handed him over to me. "You take him and care for him for he will need you much more in his later years than me." We both were crying our eyes out over this abrupt change. I replied, "He should be with you, after all what would I do with him."

This may have been preplanned; as it was as all of the shockwaves throughout my life. We kissed and I held my son in my arms and gingerly, lovingly, placed him back in her arms. I felt then had I held him as she stated, she would have died on the spot or, his not being in her life; would surely have killed her. She loved him so. I turned and walked away into the morning to report to work.

My work that summer of 1969, was toiling on my knees doing the landscape work about the college dorms. Had it not been for my loving, caring God and turning over the worms in the wet rich soil where I weeded, I would have been completely lost those weeks into the summer. How fortunate I was to hear the toot of the horn as both my mother and grandmother brought my lunch every day along with a fresh cold drink.

I returned to our apartment at night to be aghast at his empty crib and remaining toys lying about and no partner to shower with each morning.

During the school year, I rose at three a.m. each morning and hit the track and the hills getting my daily workout. Upon return, I did my studying for all of my class work with real dedication for two hours. Then I went into the bathroom and turned the shower on to insure the perfect temperature. I turned to see my boy already waking for the day. Sometime before, I introduced him to perhaps the earliest shower for any growing baby. Then I reached down in his crib and gently said, "Good Morning" to him. I lifted him up and held him in my arms and stepped into the shower with the water gently falling to make sure he enjoyed it each morning. I immediately found him to be like a tadpole when it came to water. I took his baby soap gingerly sudsing his body. The best part was when I held him in the air and let the gentle flowing water sprinkle over his little body with a quick rinse of his head and we were all set for the day.

What was the very best was seeing him smile and share that charming little laugh of his. After all, what could be a better daily start for a dad and his son? I have never forgotten such moments, to see what a happy baby he was.

I enjoyed bundling him up and propping him to slowly and safely pull him in his Red Ryder wagon to his grandparents. They both loved him so much.

I was destined for that cabin from the start. I couldn't handle the empty apartment. My work swung to my becoming the campus' first Policeman-Security Guard; I painted and continued landscape work. Finally, I packed and left to move to the cabin. The dynamics included it's setting down off the roadway, down a bit of a cliff with no walkway that was paved or cleared. It sat on a steppe overlooking barges on the canal bound for Alaska.

Activity was bustling on the barges during the week.

The cabin was a rustic, shingled brown, with a picket fence and a gate to enter on each return. As you entered the front door, the bathroom shower was to your left. Keeping everything cleaned, the ear- wigs remained away. An abrupt right face turn and you were staring at where my bed sat, leaving space from the kitchen and the dining room for my kitchen table and chairs. This was where I studied and was able to take glances north across the canal or down the canal. Usually, the view was distorted by the towering loads on the barges and the immense cranes swinging with a rhythm of their own loading more vans. There never was a dull moment, especially during the week.

The seasons were always with me while there from 1969-70. During the rainy season, you could, with caution and balance, slide as they did in *"The Christmas Carol"*. The only difference was it was on a muddy, slick path with fallen leaves, but there was a catch to it that was to grab a picket at the gate which would slow your slide and jerk you into position to enter the cabin. That time became "Mudslide Hill"! When the snow fell the wonderment of winter brought me to "Rocky Mountain Gulch"!

I continued attending classes as fall quarter resumed and parked out front. My daily slide and climb up and out became common. The quiet and lack of contact with others, especially my son G.P., nearly killed me piece by piece. I became acclimated due to the weather about me. My saving grace was my invitations to be with my grandparents for fine dinners I had grown up with all the years before and mostly to have the wonderful times we had always enjoyed back to when I was growing up and to the moment. They continually tried everything possible to reunite Ellen and me at their home. She and G.P. would just happen to drop in while I was there. There isn't a way I could describe this. Of course I loved my son and the moments were precious.

Our divorce became final and I was granted visitation privileges, a total of three hours every six weeks. All I could do within such structured limits was collect him and take him with me. We seemed to always find ourselves at the Woodland Park Zoo. One day after having him on a snowy day by the miniature train ride, all tucked in for the season as he and I were, I held him and wept with my complete love. I told him then, "I just can't do this any more as you and your mother will be leaving soon for your home back east." We returned and I handed him to her and wept tears that have never really subsided since. I told her, "I just can't handle it anymore; it's too hard."

I continued living in the cabin, going to school, working three to five part time jobs, and progressing as best as I could toward completing my degree.

In the meantime we were hit with a dreadful winter in 1970. Snow was nearly waist deep on the gulch and it made it tough to get up and down daily. I continued cooking gourmet meals baking wonderful carrot cakes to lift my spirits. Every Saturday I had my comparable G.I. party, consisting of scrubbing down the bathroom, sweeping, mopping, waxing the floors, dusting and cleaning the kitchen, including the oven and refrigerator. Afterwards, I would back off and stretch out on the bed while the entire place dried and shined to perfection, just as an artist would ponder his final strokes on the canvas.

Gerry Bradley

I became very ill and finally my mother and my grandfather came down one night and gathered me, and my effects and carried me out of that frigid condition they found me in that night. While I was with my grandparents, I convalesced from an illness not so unknown to many, that of being a lonely hearted man; it nearly killed me.

Along with being a transfer student to Seattle Pacific College, I became the Assistant Business Manager for the college's yearbook in 1972. While completing my BA requirements, other names and experiences included my being Recreation Leader-Coach-Referee, and Night Supervisor in neighboring grocery stores.

I never forgot the men I worked with every afternoon. They were the backbone of the college even though they were seen in dirty overalls, climbing into spaces unheard of by most; they were the custodians, pipe fitters, plumbers, and maintenance men that kept the entire place in running condition. My background being what it had become, seeing the "Black Gang" working in the caverns beneath the steel plates of the decks above, gave me an appreciation for those that worked on ships or kept any plants in full working order and always brought me to appreciate their contribution.

I was aware of all of them as I collected my messages and keys to be the turnkey each evening. History would prove I had been the first security guard on campus, the founding of the future campus Police at Seattle Pacific University. The time had finally drawn for me in 1973, winter quarter to fulfill my full Student Teaching experience. This assignment would be cause for reflection not imagined.

(Coach) G., my first basketball coach in the fifth grade at Lake City Elementary upon arrival during the winter of 1951, said he saw talent

348

in me. He was sure I would be a good one leading me to the University of Washington Huskies. The same promise was more evident years later while assigned at Magnolia Elementary for my student teaching assignment on the sixth grade level.

The Coach was the Principal, but he and I didn't recognize our earlier meeting until toward the end of my assignment. He was the same sharp, chiseled chinned, in shape man, I had known. The only difference was he was all gray-haired now.

Not only did I meet all requirements related to teaching, I introduced a mid-day intramural Physical Education program for all students.

I never forgot how at the end of the quarter Coach G. asked me to stop and see him. I had no idea as to the reason for this meeting. I stopped at his secretary's office and she said, "He will see you shortly." Only moments later she said, "You may go right in."

When I walked into his office, he offered me a chair. He sat down behind his desk with that same organized look that was always his. Our time together reminded me of those days while on our fifth grade basketball team in 1951, when he would say, "Gather around boys." Years had passed and I was on the verge of graduating from Seattle Pacific College, where I had prepared to do as he did, to teach and hopefully coach. Now he said, "I've got one huge problem due to your leaving us." I asked him, "What is the problem?" He said without a pause, "You won't be on my staff, that's what! Do you have any idea what you've accomplished these past weeks?" I started to say and he interrupted me by saying, "You've earned a superior recommendation from me and sixteen credit hours of A. More important, is the wonderful work you've done with our kids and staff while here at Magnolia Elementary." I thanked him for everything. He wrapped up our meeting sharing, "I told you in the fifth grade on our basketball team you'd be a good one someday." I replied to him, "I would like nothing more than to remain a member of your staff for the coming school year."

I never told him or anyone on the staff that during those ten weeks I had worked there at the school, I rushed home and changed, grabbed my lunch and rushed to work for a full shift at my position with the neighboring colleges' Police Department from 1970-73.

The final weeks after leaving the department I transferred to the Custodial Service Department for my duties each evening.

This meant I would prepare lesson plans on coffee breaks during my lunch period.

Upon returning home, I would finalize my preparations before another day of teaching and interrelated work. During that quarter which brought me to graduate with the Class of 1973, I slept two to three hours per night. Weekends were spent grabbing all the shut-eye I could to carry me into another week of sharing with my students all of the creative innovative spirit I could to ignite their desire to learn all possible.

How fortunate I was to have this fulfilling experience preparing me to be the best teacher and coach possible.

Chapter 19

Anything but Splendor in the Grass

How many years did it take for me to recognize what that bedraggled ball of yarn with its numerous colors and pieces stood for in my life?

The grass became parched as the seasons of 1970-1974, for I was no longer able to see my son, due to his mother having departed long before. A credit or mention that I have always exhibited has and will continue to be how I kept accepting any and all challenges before me. Had I summarized any one reason why we as a couple parted it would have come under the heading that she was unwilling to enter the arena of change, or at least modify her behavior, so to enhance us as a couple; I was equally to blame in my own case as well. Consequently, both of us didn't or wouldn't enter the arena of change. The end came more abruptly than she would have imagined. When she and our son returned from their summer vacation, I had long before departed and moved on to my cabin life.

Now, the truth of the matter is out; it not only wasn't her fault in totality. Instead it had much more to do with my having behaviors that would have driven any other person beyond crazy. It had been put so well in one of my classes that I could never forget when the Professor stated, "People don't change, rather they only modify." And without the knowledge or diagnosis I was unable to deal positively with anything related.

The reason began when we lived in Santa Maria and struggled to keep all together. Then with her pregnancy our bond definitely improved.

Do you know, I can still see her in her cute red dress with the outstretched baby flowers, in the pattern of her delicate maternity clothes. There was newness in her appearance, as she blossomed during those months before our departure leading us to Seattle, Washington.

Our positive results were announced by her doctor when he emphasized saying, "After all you two don't want to wait for another nickel before you have your child, do you."

As mentioned before, our goal was similar as we were working to complete our college work, but in the midst of my mailing materials for matriculation one of the colleges said "NO". Wouldn't you know it was Seattle Pacific College, not yet a University, which would come later.

At the same time, I made my choice with hope that we could agree for us to live in Flagstaff, Arizona and enter my degree work at Northern Arizona State University. From everything I had researched there was a great opportunity for me to obtain a strong major in Speech while there.

I soon found Ellen thought the best direction was for us to remain in our home, and for me to commute back and forth to Cal Poly in San Luis Obispo and she would resume her teaching at the local high school and attend classes at night. She wanted to complete her Master's Degree, already begun.

The cost was way too high, but not known at the time. This behavior seemed to follow me as I dragged that ball of yarn from one experience to another.

I want to refer back to Ellen's and my divorce, that came months later in 1969, by signifying what occurred while I was working nights in Seattle as a supervisor of a night stocking crew, along with carrying twelve to fourteen credit hours of work toward my degree.

I told the judge what finished me, was to reach in for my lunch and find a can of soup and a can opener. His laughter at this was resounding. He raised his gavel and slammed it down on the bench and said, "Divorce granted." He gathered his papers and commented through his ongoing laughter, "Don't let it be said of this judge that I can't see what straits this young man is in not to grant the petition. Now I can be on my way for my vacation." As he exited the bench, he continued laughing all the way into his chambers.

My attorney stood up and shook my hand and congratulated me. Considering he hadn't even uttered a word and had I remained silent, I know the divorce would never have happened. I asserted myself by asking him, "Why did I ever need your services as you did nothing in my behalf." He walked away from me stunned carrying his attaché case. I sat there for a short time trying to make sense of the moment. I left the courtroom vividly remembering walking with the same granite like expression on my face as the cold walls of the King County Courthouse in Seattle, Washington.

You know, when we are there for the moment, if only we would dwell just a bit longer; the time and all therein would be the ticket to getting us underway as never before. It was during that moment and time, when I couldn't help but think of Sara, back at the poolside in Santa Maria, who I met and clicked so perfectly with, to the extent I would have left with her, when she returned to her home state of New York.

Such trains of thought led me even further back in time. I knew back in 1959, in my senior year at San Rafael, California there was much more with Abbey, who had worn that fragile pony- tail, which I couldn't take my eyes off of. Truthfully, it was her that had drawn my attention and kept it the whole time.

I have already mentioned so many true Birds through the years that were present at the precise moments when it did more than give me the "up" way of life. Their presence kept me intact. Even though all of this is true and we think we have taken enough time between those of the past before moving on, perhaps, we still need even more time. I know I did with a certainty.

I began to meet and have friends from the campus. One that I met in the fall of 1970 proved to be anything but some of that splendor. Our eventually finding each other alone in the warmth of the summer sun, lazily rowing a scanty boat and later to find a secluded spot where we could be together, surrounded by the crowns of the weeds about us, became so much more than she or I would have imagined.

We married, knowing there was no said secret in that she was pregnant. This wasn't the way any couple would want to begin their union with each other. There really isn't reason or intent to be detailed regarding our being together with the exception of both of us realizing we should not have been together in the first place.

This came to the forefront after checking her into the hospital one evening and, seeing how her delivery was going so long, completely unlike what any woman or couple would have imagined. I had always wanted to have a little girl. Finally we knew this was true; however, there were unheard of complications with her delivery.

Remember when Ellen and I were nearly run over in 1965 by the eighteen-wheeler out on the desert, realizing we were nearly as the dust and the grit in the desert.

The same nothingness was felt by both of us. And the doctor asked that I leave the delivery room. Our little girl was born dead that night. The doctor assigned shared the news with her mother and came out and told me. I found myself crumbling like a handful of the sand clasped in a closed fist there in the hallway. I asked whether or not I could go and be with my wife. The doctor said, "That would be fine." Attempting to reach out to her with love was the hardest thing I had to do. We spent time with each other, but she was so worn from the ordeal in the delivery room, I didn't want to stay too long. I left her to rest that night.

It was when I reentered the hallways, on my way out of the hospital, that I felt nothing. It was as though I was walking down through a tunnel or a complete void. There was movement about me, conversation, telephones ringing, patients being pushed on stretchers and wheel chairs, yet I heard none of it.

It was the swish of the electric door that threw me out into the black of the night shrouded by the lights at the entrance. My weakened steps took me further and I found myself leaning against the side of the building weeping, with the same drops of the rainfall coming down the side of the building, dripping down my face, blending with my tears and broken spirit. Had anyone seen me that night and moment, they would have seen me in a heap, unable to stop crying tears regarding the loss of our baby while making my way back to the our car. Upon finally making it, I sat for quite awhile with the rainfall patting the top of our car.

From there I went to my office and shared with the Lieutenant what had happened and he said, "You go home and don't worry about anything here."

Moments had passed; I made my way to my parent's home on the rain soaked streets. I was mesmerized by the rhythm of the wiper blades and all the time wiping the tears from my eyes. When I reached my parents' home, mother turned the light on the porch and opened the door to see me unlike any other time in the past. She knew precisely what had happened and I collapsed in her arms. She said, "You come in out of the rain and stay here for the night." There are times when that of home and family are so vital and this night was one of those nights. I was all but incoherent, yet able to explain to her what had happened. After I stayed there that night she said, "There were only two nights that she heard that of 'death rattles'" My entire body rattled in that bed for the entire night.

The next day I called my friend and Pastor, and he asked if there was anything that would be helpful at all. I asked him if he could remove the crib that was all set up for our little girl and he did just that.

When I went to pick up my wife to take her home, we returned and the crib had been taken down so not to make our reentry back into our home that much harder.

I never forgot the service, but didn't realize it was then, that all therein had died along with her, leaving her to reach up and grasp the hand of the angels taking her home at long last.

More time passed, but never enough somehow.

It was much later that I learned how vital it was spending every available moment researching, doing self- query and relearning skills of attending a movie or a restaurant alone without another beside me.

By now I was closing on the final quarters of work in 1972.

I realized my tendency was to marry entirely too quickly. Furthermore, this revealed my having Bi-Polar Mood Swing Disorder more loudly than I had any idea of to see how all surfaced later.

I began my teaching career on the substitute level. Next came the process of sending packets for consideration to school districts all over the west coast. It became a prayerful answer to being considered positively by several school districts.

This gave me time to establish myself into my coming year of teaching.

Later, I resumed all that was vital, particularly following all that came from the diagnosis and taking my medication as prescribed. Equally powerful was the way I remained in search of separating loneliness and aloneness. The more I searched, the more I saw the latter take hold, no longer to be governed or controlled by my inability to live with the constant threat of being so lonely.

While there, I never forgot my weekly walk and return to my chalet on Sunday afternoon when I prayed to God, "If I am going to be here another year, I'll remain a bachelor." I had no idea at that moment how He heard my prayer as it was short order when events took a new posture.

Chapter 20

A Return to Law Enforcement

I followed the suggestion of a friend I had dated previously for a period of time during the summer of 1974, who worked for a neighboring college who said, "Due to your background, why don't you apply with the college Police Department and become a Police Officer?"

I received the position and it couldn't have come at a better time as my funding had run out from my G.I. Bill. Once again I was putting on the holster, handcuffs, mace, baton, portable radio, rain gear and the eight-cornered hat.

My duties at first included rattling doors as a Security Guard while waiting for my commission to come through. They believed it would take weeks or possibly months. All of us were surprised as I came ready to walk the beat the second week and the officers in charge informed me, "You won't need that set of keys as your commission has arrived." The Captain and Lieutenant congratulated me. The dispatcher had already requested the unit to return and pick me up as his new partner. Before we could believe it our first call came.

None of my fellow Air Policeman would have believed it had they been told that this first call was to pursue an escaped primate from the lab. We pulled over to the side of the road and got out of our patrol car, a new Plymouth, a white four-door with the college Police insignia on the front doors. We walked over to the highest tree to see the culprit was on the farthest limb for us to recover. We had our dispatcher contact the Primate

Lab so they sent their staff with a cage to be placed at the base of the tree with ample supply of bananas and assorted foods to entice his recovery.

It was exactly three months later and we found ourselves in the throng of key Weatherman and sympathizers in support of what we came to know as the Cambodian Riots.

All related to another war ground, anti-war push, on campuses across the country.

How ironic to have been out that night chasing one loose primate, now to be in full riot gear at the ready, constantly in the midst of crowd wearing our coveralls, and black gloves, baton, high top boots, sunglasses and gas masks with a case on our hips.

While there, another select duty occurred during football seasons. I worked with an entourage of V.I.P.'s working traffic detail duties, as all fans stood and yelled for the teams playing.

When citizens consider those on their neighboring Police Department, they think for the most part of one unit represented. What became evident to me was the "fish bowl" effect, of always being in view, positive or negative, no matter where we were.

In no time I realized the profession on the whole was so much more diversified than the experience I had while serving as an Air Policeman, years before at Vandenberg, A.F.B. California.

After joining the force, the Lieutenant assigned me to the Narcotics Division, where we found ourselves prowling the dingy corners of public restrooms and the like on campus. Our vigil included looking for needles, and other paraphernalia, such as their pipes, etc., and busts of addicts we found trying to hide the fact of their actions.

From there I worked on Patrol during all three shifts. Later came a walking beat through the Hospital Science Wings. During that time I didn't need any additional exercise as I came off the beat where I had walked miles every night on duty.

That beat encompassed basement level to the top of the roof overlooking the entire area with a perfect view of the entire campus.

The perspective was a real vantage point, looking down on the parking areas and through the main part of the campus. After a full viewing and hanging on to my hat, I made my way down the floors through the entire facility.

It was no time and I became acquainted with the staff on each floor. This was an assignment I thoroughly enjoyed because it was so people oriented from start to finish of each shift.

There were areas that I frequented during the shift that were standout; the first was where the sweetest children patients were about to, or already had, shunts to decrease the amount of water on their brains. I always tried to stop and help bring a smile to one of their faces each evening and I thoroughly appreciated the bond these children had with their doctors and nurses.

Another area I covered briskly was the room where the cadavers had been donated for research, specifically, for the medical students to learn and practice their gained skills. The bodies were bound in wraps, sometimes one or more not so bound.

Intermingled among assignments, we had some blasts or bombings on campus during what was called the Cambodian Riots, as other campuses did throughout the country. This included our being extremely vigilant throughout the campus from that time onward. It wasn't enough that we received bomb threats which heightened the work on assigned shifts. Those bomb threats were as alarming as receiving reports of alarms going off in the hospital or other locations.

I won't ever forget what it felt like to receive such calls even on a quiet Sunday shift. We rolled in and set our precautionary blockades on the roadway.

Nor have I forgotten how it felt to dismount my vehicle carrying a shotgun, running cautiously down the hallways with the keys jangling on my gun belt and receiving instructions over our radio at the same time. Needless to say the adrenalin was flowing and sweat was pouring from the band of my hat. Fortunately this time it was a false alarm!

Through all of this activity, none would have imagined I was able to perform as I did, what with all of the other samplings of my behavior that surely would have conflicted in every way possible. There wasn't any way I would have admitted any questionable actions because I didn't have any foundational data or results to tell me otherwise.

I don't think there was any rhyme or reason to it, but alarms and bomb threats seemed to fall on the quietest times or shifts of the weekends. It didn't matter, but looking for some pipe bomb on a parking lot at night was anything but fun. All we had as guides were outside building lights peering down on the parking areas, the beams of our flashlights, our knowledge, skills and faith that would insure we were safe.

One day the activists followed their plan and crashed into a building. This turned out to be the largest group yet and required our entire force to break it up entirely.

Our officers had already entered the building and were controlling the destruction and illegal entry, when I received a command from the

Sergeant I was assigned with to return to our vehicle. We had parked near the building. I saw the size of the crowd so averted them by running around their perimeter to get to the car. While I worked my way through the periphery of the crowd to get to the parked vehicle, I found three other officers on the inside in a state of shock. They wouldn't let me get in the vehicle. There I was standing outside staring at the key Weatherman and followers. I heard a slight snicker and turned my head slightly left to catch sight of one ready to throw a two by four across the car, which would have struck me either in the side of my head or glanced across my upper torso bringing me to fall. That's what that crowd needed.

I didn't know the other members were staring down to see me, not knowing who it could have been. I didn't telegraph any moves, rather took a stance that brought disbelief from all of them. By now I had my club in both hands and a solid grip with my black leather gloves. I stood at a parade rest position yet kept total eye contact with all in front of me. The one that was going to instigate my falling, by throwing the timber had dropped the assault item to the ground. Those in front said, "Look out because he's going to be a mean one."

Needless to say none in front of me knew whether or not I had or hadn't attended Police Academy or not, or for that matter was trained in such a way that the damage they implied would have been as they anticipated.

At that the fellow officers cracked the door, and made me aware that I was able to get in so we could make our get-a-way. Before climbing inside the patrol car, they had already begun to rock the car, with those inside.

I can vividly remember thinking two thoughts as I took my stance. First, I thought I could turn and run out of this crowd and make my way across campus, but what won out, was to stand firm and do whatever became necessary.

I know so prominently how God was ever present, among all within that crowd, as they stared, and I returned the favor toward them. Then the door flew open; I leapt in and we sped away. Those, of whom I had been facing, yelled and threw torn up bricks from the courtyard at us as we left the scene in a streak for safety.

What occurred wasn't any different than the happening at colleges and universities across the country. They had zeroed in on our names and it wasn't our imagination, for sometime after that, we found we were in the midst of groups all over campus.

As the political fervor calmed, our work regained its usual routine.

I welcomed the next assignment of guarding the President of the college, his family and mansion. This was the swing shift so when reporting, it was still daylight. I always greeted the staff at the President's mansion and after they became acquainted with me, the cook always saw to my having a nice sandwich, coffee and periodically the dessert of the evening. The duty included being on the inside of their quarters and once per hour I made my rounds around the grounds outside.

The assignment came to an end one evening while I was driving to report for duty. I was bound for the mansion and felt as if an axe handle slammed across my chest. Granted, I should have stopped and called for "Officer in need of help," but the smashing feeling eased; I continued driving on to the mansion for the evening's shift. I didn't even advise the office or our radio operator as to my status. Deep inside my spirit I was quaking.

After the shift I drove back to the office as I had night after night. Then I drove home and upon arriving, I began to have the same pains, but much worse. I was able to get help to go to the hospital and processed in that night. Four days afterward they determined the condition was due to my having bodily muscles spasms. The cause was due to the shock of having lost our child.

It was short order and my wife and I went our own ways.

In my case, I began by researching, learning it was possible to live alone effectively, not as in the past a lonely hearted man. Time certainly proved to be the best for me in the end.

Considering all that occurred then, I knew all would have been considerably the opposite had I been medicated.

Afterwards, it was short order before I resigned my commission and completed my final work toward my degree.

Chapter 21

On to Professional Scouting

All of my degree requirements were met, including my student teaching, which left me only to wait until the end of the year to participate in my commencement exercise for the class of 1973. This long sought goal took a total of eight years.

I am sure I gained your attention as to the ball of yarn, and all of the lengths, colors and how all was strewn through the years. The inability on my behalf to deal with daily life was evident from the record already mentioned.

Have you ever really stopped in your tracks and looked up in the trees about you and squinted, if necessary, because you knew you heard the trill of the sweet song coming from one sweet little bird? Your view was of its plumage, of a scarlet red crested head, intermingled red, grayish feathers that trailed to its tail feathers. I am certain by your doing this, as I have, you will always be drawn to such a melodious song. It never fails, for the little bird seems to be at the very highest limb and branch. It might make you wonder why she would insist on bobbing in the gust of wind and what takes precedence seems to be for it to sing its heart out for the listener.

I can't point to a specific time, as to realizing you were there all the time, *Birds From the Thicket*, as you were loving, caring hearers of all the segments of the journey down the track I have traveled. It had been true from the very moment I was given life that I became aware of all of you. What is definite is the fact that I saw all of you from that time onward.

I have and will continue to pay my humble respect to all of you. None of my endeavors could be, were it not due to all of you in such constant support, urging me as you have to "keep on, keep on" no matter what.

Through all of the staging was the waiting on the sidelines interviewing, and securing a sixth grade contract for the coming fall.

I wasn't willing to wait or grow moss on my backside for the school year to begin in the fall of 1973. This was during the time, when the advertisement per the Yellow Pages was to "let your fingers do the walking", which is exactly what I did. This journey took me to the entry of Boy Scouts of America of the Chief Seattle Council. I made contact and applied to find I had been hired to work with the Exploring Division, which provided programs for fourteen year olds through twenty-one-year old young adults.

Our counter parts, District Executives, worked with the Cub Scouting program.

We in the Exploring Division took an innovative turn, to avail high school students with career awareness on the school scene. They attended seminars planned for them during regular school hours. All could belong to Explorer Posts in the career areas of other interests at the same time. Being on the foundation of such an effort was very stimulating. I will always remember those whom I worked with from one campaign or effort to another providing positive opportunities for youth in our greater community.

The vast opportunity brought me to one true Bird who became one of my finest friends professionally and personally for years to come. Our original meeting was to present the overall concept which was accepted on the spot. That was my introduction to a leader for a major airline company.

He was caught up in the entire approach presented. He and needed staff members were all present on the first night for what we referred to as the "kickoff" meeting. They thought they were in agreement at first viewing, but they saw over two hundred students at their first meeting, revealing their interest in all related to the professions as their future careers unfolded.

I still remember the day in 1975 when I informed my colleagues I was leaving the profession. The refrain was, "You'll be standing in a soup line." I replied, "That might be true, but I have worked long and hard to become a certified teacher and that is what I intend to become."

Unknown to them, I matriculated into five neighboring school districts and two weeks later, I began teaching and remained working every day throughout the year. My days began as early as when attending classes working toward my degree. When I had no call, I called the school districts and mentioned I would be willing to work as a bus driver or custodian if there wasn't anything else available that day. You know what? I worked every day!

Finally, I was assigned to a fourth grade class in 1976, in the Kent School District, where I found some wonderful kids. I came to love them and gave my all to them. Their teacher had been gravely ill and relinquished her contract for the duration of the school year.

That was when I became educated, facing a kind of adversity not experienced, either in my preparations or afterwards. The details were hidden, but I took a determined stance that I would secure a contract the following year and not have to substitute any more. To do this, I mailed forty-seven applications packets bound for school districts throughout the west.

The truth did not become clear until the end of that summer, while interviewing and meeting one manly Superintendent that knew I wasn't aware as to the hindrance I was facing. In retrospect I knew, after following up on all of my inquiries, to receive an introductory interview in the following school districts, I would be ready when finally hired.

That summer, I was on the road interviewing school districts throughout the west and that was when I found I was being considered in what I realized would have been the Nespelem School District or the St. Mary's Indian Academy in Eastern Washington, where I had the interview of all.

The school board had invited me to join them on a Saturday and I can assure you I never forgot that meeting. Twenty-four members were on the review board. This prepared me for the confirming school districts ahead. Shortly afterwards, I found myself before a board of inquirers, who became interested and soon afterwards hired me for the coming school year.

Chapter 22

Finally to Teach and Coach

Finally, what I had trained for came the fall of 1976: Substitute Teacher, Secondary Teacher, Coach, even "Mr. B." and in a kidding way, "Sensai". The latter was due to my near appointment to teach in an English Academy in Japan. (By the way, Sensai means "Honored One").

What hurt was hearing from one and all, "we've done it, so why not you," much like a mimicking chorus.

My fellow teachers covered for each other for hall duty while the students passed from class to class. We took time during the day and afterwards talking about our days activities, students we worked with, and more importantly, getting to know each other and accepting invitations to their homes for visits and dinners.

I remember hearing the Head Coach was a versatile, knowledgeable Coach, who took time and patiently included me in our Girl's Basketball program. At half time during one of our games, he said, "Coach, they're yours as nothing I say seems to penetrate." My words proved to be the motivation they needed as we won big that day.

Later in August 1976, I stood outside the district Administration Office, with the Principal. He signified that he knew about the events following me to that interview. He pointedly said that he more than understood, as the same occurred with him when he was starting to teach. He continued and told me that he was hiring me.

I moved all of my effects and got situated and ready for my first year of certified teaching.

What saved me then and into the future was the work. And work I did as the first meeting with my students was before me. I completed all of my lesson plans to be reviewed by the Principal and realized these plans helped immensely. I developed and decorated our room to enhance the environment for the mainstay was to stimulate them to want to learn and make a path for their future years. The Principal came by several times during those days, just checking, to see if there was anything I needed or to answer any questions I might have while I was diligently working to receive each student assigned to our class.

I thought how ironic it was, to have the same room number, as "the old 217 West Republican", where our family lived years ago. I sat on my stool and took it all in and I knew I was ready for the first day of school.

All that I am reflecting on is what needed to be shared with the Executive Board, while they deliberated over my case and future with the district.

This portrays my position then and from thereon.

We had to have a special pass that students could use between classes, if excused to go to the restroom, or any other calls from the office. I asked the boys to make me a wooden block, engraved Room 217.

I know I was nervous and soon realized I had to adjust my level of teaching to reach my students. When I made this adjustment, I began to effectively teach and convey the meaning I had meant from the start. This was my first year of teaching.

All of the afternoon factors worsened and were cause of my facing the truth at last. I finally went for help at the Mental Health Center, at the end of my first year of teaching, and fulfilling my position as Head

Coach for Girl's Track and Field. My level checks continued along with my sessions of gaining more clarity regarding the diagnosis of having Bi-Polar Mood Swing Disorder.

Just as I was making headway toward being well, I made temporary arrangements to housesit for a lady from my church. She was to make a journey on The Orient Express to Nepal. Now, I was the teacher in my second year and a house sitter. I couldn't have been more pleased that I had made such arrangements to have a fine place to live until the owners returned.

This was the second year; not only had I held down the teaching, coaching, and instructing G.E.D. classes, I made an effort to take those needed units so to fulfill my requirements for my fifth year of certification

I discovered the river and began to run daily and strength came with the changing seasons. As I ran and was awe struck that first autumn, stopping and watching wing upon wing arriving with a gentle lilt, skidding before resuming their journey south. This was one eventful happening that I couldn't get enough of each season.

My returns from a day of teaching were so much more in balance. My experiences and daily dosages of lithium helped me every day; I continued to get stronger and in no time I was running six to twelve miles two to three days each week.

What kind of teacher was I really?

Each year our Principal knew I took my students outside at the first snow. The reason for this was to introduce a unit of poetry for all. We would exit clad in our winter garb and make our way across the walk into the city park so my students could gather and remain silent listening to the sounds about them. The entire lesson was to concentrate on the sensory abilities we all had. Then I saw to their having a few moments to throw a few snowballs. Somehow, they would miss their aim and made sure some to hit me. After all of that I took them back into our room to set the scene for them to compose their own poetry or Haiku. The results were as splendid as the soft falling snow. I really came to love those kids as well and heard how much they enjoyed our class from their parents at the annual parent-teachers meeting. It was gratifying to hear how their parents would complement my being their teacher and having come to teach their kids.

I never forgot how the other coaches past and present kept coming to me and warning me, I shouldn't expect much in the way of a turnout for Girl's Track, as they had never turned out for that sport before. I replied, "Don't be too surprised with the end result as only time will tell."

It always interested me how the girls were so surprised, as I gave everyone of them a long stem rose the day before the actual turnout. Prior, I continued to share all that would come by their turning out for track in the spring. What was satisfying was seeing all of the pundits disappear when they saw the turnout included fifty-five girls.

The first issue was there were only so many uniforms. They wanted to know if they would be considered as members of the team, even if they didn't earn a suit at first. It hit me in my senior year, with another coach and his decision, that it was my time to draw new blood on the team or not; I made it known that all of them were members on our track team. The majority of them stayed. After the meets I took them for ice-cream sundaes and somehow mine disappeared. Those were the fun times we all needed whether we won the meet or not.

There were two on our team that I wouldn't forget. The first was what I called my protégé, as she was right with me as I ran with our long distance members of our team each afternoon.

Toward the end of our season, she was on the final lap on the backside of the half-mile event and pulled up with a hamstring pull. She collapsed and wasn't able to continue the race. Our trainer and some of the girls on our team and I ran across the field to care for her. I still remember her main concern was she had failed our team. I made sure she knew the last thing she did was let any of us down. If anything, I told her, she made us so proud of the way she had developed into our team's long distance runner.

We were completing our final meet of the season ands our most powerful member of our team, a ninth grade girl, was running the hurdles and came very close to winning, but she clipped the last hurdle and fell and sprawled out on the track. What was admirable was seeing her rise with pride and continue by finishing the race among her competitors. It was quite upsetting to her; once again I told her, "What counted was the way she rose to the occasion and finished the race." She happened to be the prettiest girl throughout our entire school and was extremely talented so to hear how well she did in sporting events from graduation and continuing on to attend high school was no surprise. The community remained very proud in seeing how she became "Miss..." and continued on to compete in the "Miss Pageant of all Pageants". And one more time she received the honor of winning the honors for the overall competition. What was outstanding for me was to see her always finish the race no matter what or where. No coach or teacher could be more proud than I was to hear all mentioned in the future.

So when I told the board members that I loved their kids, it was just as though they had become my own kids. How could I convey this to them?

At the same time, they would have to take interest in all regarding my teaching G.E.D., where two incidents confirmed I had accomplished something worthy for my students in each class.

One Christmas Eve of 1979, the phone rang and upon answering it I found one of my previous students from the G.E.D. classes on the end of the line. I vividly remembered her as she had been for the best part of her life both a waitress and cook in a café, and who had made up her mind to return and complete the equivalent to that of her high school diploma no matter what. She was there promptly every session through our class. She exclaimed, "A Very Merry Christmas to you Mr. B., I wanted you to know the best news of all. I've been accepted and will continue my work at the community college to gain my AA Degree." She went on and said, "Had it not been for you, Mr. B., I doubt that I would be calling with such news now and I knew you would want to know this and Merry Christmas to you Mr. B.; how I thank you."

The summer of 1979, while standing in line at the Post Office I heard someone say, "Coach guess what", as I was being picked up off the floor and swung in a circle finally to feel my feet on the floor once again. It was Libby, who I had coached on both the girl's basketball and track team years before, and she was graduating from high school. She continued saying, "I've received a dual scholarship to play basketball and volleyball at the University." I was so pleased for her and before I could reply she said, "Coach do you remember that day you talked with me regarding my laziness and not taking full charge of the wonderful talent I had? Well, it took and I am able to share this with you now, for you were a big part in this happening."

At the same time, I knew there remained eight-credit hours of work to meet the requirement. I was informed I would be dismissed midyear due to this.

Such a time is when you find who your colleagues have been the whole way. Furthermore, these were the same teachers that I stood on strike with at the beginning of the school year.

I received an absolute confirmation from the State Superintendent, who said, he would stand behind me, "so go ahead and fulfill those final units." He added that my district would have to set precedence as well.

I convened with the union delegate and explained the entire matter to him. In doing so, I found there were others of whom they had taken photographs of during the strike from the top of the building, and later screened every striking member for any discrepancy. It was there that they forced the issue toward several of us from the overall district.

The meeting was set so I could convene with the Executive Board following the regular school board meeting. That was where I discovered how such a body could adamantly not be willing to consider, much less, set precedence for a professional who had been as deeply involved with the students in the school district as I had, not to mention all other duties related to the overall community.

There they sat; the Superintendent only willing to pontificate before the President of the board, much like a miserly type, who owned all in the room and wanted more, depicted so well in, *It's a Wonderful Life*, who found later, that the generosity of George, won out far beyond anything ever considered. The other members of the board and the union delegate, fully appeared as what they were a part of, *The Nation of Sheep,* unable to see the depth and qualities to warrant such a request. The President of the board took his ultra conservative, inflexible stance, revealing the power bestowed in him to say, "Well I don't see why you couldn't get your requirements; we got ours."

Here was a board granted power, in fact, too much power, when dealing with any person's life! More strength would surface from that moment forward than I would have ever imagined.

Such decisions never seem to include considering, as to the whereabouts, of one standing before an Executive Board pleading his case. It became more than evident that no matter how much research or findings had been secured nothing changed. Neither the Superintendent nor the President of the board, worse yet, the delegate attending and supporting the teachers union, did anything other than be present. Was any question asked then or in the future regarding the dismissal declared? Far from that, as it was proven that the cursory manner this was dealt with left me beseeching them to hear and listen to more than a valid request from a professional, that had served well for the time mentioned and who had come to love their kids, even though the parents were not present, nor were any of the fellow staff members.

All of the years of preparation including a total of eight years had gone for naught, before such a body of non- compassionate men, granted entirely too much power over the lives of others.

This is what is the cause of disarray, destruction of one's spirit, even to go on being stripped literally to the bone, by no longer holding the place within the community as before and without the securities to keep payments of regular bills becoming spoils. I found myself where this and more occurred. I fully know there will always be those who will say, "It's a tough world indeed."

To prevent total loss, I established a game plan differing from the usual schedule kept previously while still an educator in the community. I made a complete move from what I had called my chalet to a big old gray, many storied, rooming house on the outskirts of town. There, in that bleak room, the furnishings included: stacking all of my cases of books and materials on the perimeter of the room, the bed, one flimsy desk and a desk light. If that wasn't enough, there were kitchen privileges so the occupants could prepare their own meals. However, there was a serious matter and that was just keeping the food stores. From the moment of landing there I began to fight every minute to get up and out of that place as fast as possible.

It drew me back to what I experienced in my junior year of high school while on that brief turnaround visit to Salt Lake City, Utah. It was there that I left a huge part of my heart and soul without a doubt.

I can't leave all of these memories, much the same as treasures acquired while having the abundant opportunity to have been accepted, granted a superb time in my life to teach, coach, and hopefully lead my students in directions that would have bettered their lives as they did mine.

What came to mind was how I was able to inquire and be given an extended hand of needed expertise, to better than diagnose all that I was in the midst of at the same time. When one such as myself is told in eleven minutes precisely, "What's going on in your life?" And from there I was generously informed: "I believe I know what your trouble is, and know it can be treated. But, it will require your spending the time needed in therapy to bring you along the way while we get your level where it should be, so you can live a much more level way of life and total health."

When you're the one as I was at that time, and continued to recall what brought all of this to the surface, believe me, it is so much more than a diagnosis, **"IT WAS A MIRACLE",** never to be forgotten or taken lightly throughout the remainder of my life.

Speaking of depth, consider after the long days of teaching, followed by coaching my girl's team, preparing them for their next track meet and readying for teaching my students to step up and take their GED examinations successfully, they would more aims than ever hoped by them and their teacher.

There was a turning point every afternoon however. The kid's workouts were complete; I was making my regular drive homeward with the day's papers to be graded and taking note as to the lessons to teach that evening for the driven students who were doing all to better their lives. The bridge was ahead each afternoon, that led to the needed summer school work, vacations for all of my students, and time with their families, a brief period of time to turn to the garden and take a moment to hear the soft song of more than one Bird about me.

That traversing to and from, more specifically, the return trip home brought me to realize, the passageway was anything, but as I crossed that bridge each afternoon, I found something pulling me that had not since the incident shared before. I know you can remember when I nearly jumped from the Speech building to the cement below. Fortunately for me, such was brought to a close and I walked away from that perch. Now, on a nightly basis, I was experiencing the same draw or tug to turn the wheel abruptly to the right, pointed north, and to drive a course that would take me deep into the currents of the river below. This same impacting thought came back night after night and there was no way I could continue that drive or path any longer.

Consequently, I sought the help I needed far more than I would have ever have known. At first, I was fearful that one from the community that I worked in daily might see me; nevertheless, with God's loving concern, direction, and finally listening, I welcomed the help I needed, not only then, but more importantly, had needed all of the past years already shared.

The real impact, when thinking back in time, was in hearing the Pastor of my church continually say, "When you get over there and settle go and see Jon." That puzzled me, for every time I was in the Pastors presence, he said the same thing. I suppose he knew if I heard it enough I would do exactly that.

What bewildered me was to enter the clinic after making my appointment, to see "Jon" as he exited his office, and came up to me, I knew at that moment what had been reiterated for me each and every time before.

I learned long ago how much God was in my life, but when all of this transpired, I knew without any doubt, He had been there the entire time and would never leave me, or abandon me, because He was my helper and I wouldn't be "afraid" ever again.

One final point was how after being treated I knew I was on the road to a level path. I was able to say to my students, "If you see me acting a bit out of the ordinary, would one of you just come up to my desk and say, 'Mr. B. it's time for you to have a drink of water' seemingly, each of these loving, caring kids perceived more deeply, how their teacher was striving with all he had, to be the best for them the whole way. As you might know, from that time to this date, and through the future, I'll only think of them as the most loving Birds on this green earth.

Chapter 23

Return to Scouting

I applied to substitute teach in the surrounding school districts with the intent to continue those final eight units needed. However, the amount of assignments wouldn't warrant this plan to occur. That left me with a drastic decision to hit the streets and secure employment immediately. This is what separates any and all of us from becoming the wayward ones across the land with little or no purpose in our lives.

Admittedly, after those three-and-a-half years of teaching and coaching, the job I secured might have been questioned, but it turned out to be exactly what I needed to hold body and soul together.

I became a driver delivering pizzas on the night shift. Even though it was pasta oriented; I ate most of my meals there which led me up and out professionally. My character and spirit were tested while there in ways not really expected. The toughest was working side by side with the high school students who questioned where I had come from in the first place. The overall circumstances that none of whom I worked with daily had faced in their tender years became more than understandable. What is key when in such a place in life is to keep the focus, and absorb each opportunity, which I had realized was there back when working to earn my degrees. It was unfortunate that I had allowed this to occur; however, what counted most was that I had and continued to strive and work to regain all lost, most of all my pride in self.

There wasn't a day I wouldn't have preferred to return to my classroom and coaching as I had before. This became a larger time to perform within my self and to restore my altered ego at the same time.

Through all that came, I had a great lift in that I knew what I had to deal with daily and I remained medicated no matter what. Call it a buffer if you choose; in truth it had become the safe zone to make certain it occurred each and every day.

The manager was the prominent Bird never to be forgotten for he knew I needed that job and hired me that day.

We drove brown Chevy pickups with ovens on the rear of the bed. The reason I remember this was due to trying to light that infernal oven each afternoon in the wind. Here again I had another uniform of beige pants, a company polo shirt, and a sports car cap that we wore on our deliveries.

One night after five months while making my deliveries and keeping the product good and hot for each customer, I know without a doubt God spoke to me harshly by saying, "Go back to Scouting, dummy!"

Believe me, I got the message and began matriculating with the Boy Scout Council the very next day, leading to the summer of 1979. My confirmation came much quicker that I would have expected. The first assignment was to be the Day Camp Director for Cub Scouts. Our camp was moving smoothly and those from the council approached me saying, "You're much too qualified; we're sending you to our Scout camp." Upon arrival, I was to be the Professional Field Sports Director, but as I drove in those greeting me said, "You have an interview in Tacoma with the Mount Rainier Council to become a future District Executive." I turned a "W" and drove back to have my interview two days afterwards.

My interview with the Scout Executive and others resulted in my being hired on the spot. They told me to complete my assignment and return to take over my assigned district for the Council.

That summer while accomplishing all I was in the midst of, I kept my room locked, waiting for me to return after what had been one of the finest summers I had experienced for a long time. I had my own staff; we thoroughly enjoyed working with each other teaching the Scouts the skills they needed in each area. .

This is the land of the pines, the magnificent lakes surrounding the impeding cliffs above for the climber to view what can only be called, "Little Switzerland". It was really hard to leave on that last day even though I had a full time position waiting for me.

The finest gift received that summer was being selected to be the Camp Chaplain. We held services outside where the pulpit was on top of a huge rock in the grove of the Ponderosa Pine trees. All sat on slab benches while worshipping, saying their individual thanks for this immense opportunity given to each of us.

It was there I perceived I had gained more of the originally intended ministry of years past than any other place to date. Our bidding each other goodbye was much the same as after Basic Training at Lackland Air Force Base, Texas long ago in 1961.

I found our Scout Executive to be more than a fair man to work with as the staff was. From the start, I emphasized that I could do more for the council were I to be the council's first Exploring Executive, rather than a District Executive. My professional training had been oriented toward the former rather than the latter.

This truth became more evident as I continued, and finally that led me to a collision coarse due to my not having the basal training to be effective in key areas of gaining membership, manpower and the finance campaign as related to the assignment of being a District Executive. Such campaigns are approached in an obtuse manner when compared to that of an Exploring Executive's assignment. The Scout Executive finally revealed what I had tried to convey all along. I knew it was time to move on and leave the profession from that time onward.

Chapter 24

The Finest Moment Yet

When thinking of those three at the top of the Empire State Building during the winter in the year of 1979, there was a linking song that tied the story together, *In The Wee Hours of the Morning.*

This brought me to recall my walks at two to three a.m. years before. It was the time of living the single life, when I walked at the Seattle Center by the International Fountain and Flag Pavilion; I recall the Fun Center was shut down for the season of winter of 1971, but I enjoyed the mosaic and the pools at the Science Center where I remember being awestruck at the parabolas above and the intermingled falling flakes of the snow during the early morning hour.

The time of searching always seemed to take me beneath the Space Needle looking up, seeing the swirling blizzard-like snow flakes, sifting downward and covering all beneath. Even though my glasses were covered with melting flakes, all about me was getting deeper, moment, by moment. I paused one more time as I stood there in my winter cap, warm layered coat, with the collar turned up, scarf around my neck and I clapped my gloves together, causing some of the snow to fall off my arms and shoulders. Before leaving, I knew how alone I was in the wintering scene, the quiet of the moment and the entire area with no other people present or walkers about, not even one couple sitting, standing, holding hands or sharing a kiss in the falling snow.

Walks and time away from the books, preparing research papers, and working around the clock, progressing and closing on my pursued degree were all part of my schedule. But dealing with being alone and lonely, unlike ever before in my life was devastating.

I returned and parked above Rocky Mountain Gulch. After I got out of the car I locked it up, frozen tight until morning. Then I walked pushed and slid to where I would reach out at the precise moment, to catch hold of the picket of the fence where the gate was. I pushed the gate causing it to shovel an opening entrance on the ground to the front door. Even as I slid, I looked up and about me to see what could have been, a Currier and Ives scene with the branches, grass and ground covered in its winter blanket.

If ever there was a time where my life meshed in the seasons, one colliding with the other that was the time.

Spring and summer would approach and I would drive to the beaches such as Golden Gardens. While there, all I saw or heard was the lapping waves on shore and the same companion of the tracks that I entered Seattle on years before, on **The Empire Builder** in 1951, arriving at our new home.

I have reflected in my mind and perceptions as to that Sunday afternoon, while completing my daily walk around the perimeter of the shopping plaza which I took each day, especially weekends. Those walks were for much more than the physical exercise, they gave me a connection with all of the shopkeepers and to see and greet others from the community.

My residence was only across the street, one-half of a block south of Bloomington Boulevard. I had always referred to my place as my chalet.

It was the site where not only did I develop professionally, as an educator, I checked in when needed as an outpatient at the Mental Health Clinic to receive therapy and gain the fullest total health I had in all the years of my life. It was there I accepted the original diagnosis and began taking lithium for the first time. Once this was achieved they released me, but I knew if a need arose, I could check in at Emergency any time. I walked over and stayed long enough to do what I termed then to, "blow it all out of me," then turned and made my way home knowing I was making evident progress.

The snow was flying; I kept walking all bundled up in my winter coat, Russian style hat, gloves and climbing boots. I stepped cautiously to prevent tumbling on the icy streets.

I thought back to a similar time and experience years before at Rocky Mountain Gulch. Had I looked back, I would have realized I was leaving a sizeable track. I have not forgotten my prayer then. I spoke out loud, "God if I'm going to remain as I am for one more year, then I'll remain a bachelor."

I would never have believed all that lay ahead and how profound that prayer would prove to be.

Remember how I reported to camp, to be the summer's Director of Sports Field Events, only to find the call had already come at the camp for me to report back to Tacoma, Washington to the Mount Rainier Council. Upon arriving for my interview, I pulled in at the Pony Express, where I tied my reigns for the night. It was there, that I met and found a friend in what I would find later was Sandra's best friend. Suzie proved to be very helpful on that trip. I told her that I would be heading back to camp soon as the interview was completed.

How relieved I was to now have a full time position, not to mention my job for the summer. That trip back was one of reflection by the mile. My mind was traversing the vast space of the hills, forest, and all of the magnificent panoramic view as I enthusiastically looked forward to my assignment ahead of me.

It was years later, after all I am about to share, that a favorite motion picture was captivating for all of us and had attachment to The Empire State Building in, New York City, New York.

The story line that drew us to that pinnacle, with the cast from *Sleepless in Seattle,* and warmed our hearts beyond what we would have hoped for the couple plus one, from two differing coastlines, brought us to hold our breath and wait for him to say, "We better be going…shall we?"

Such a moment is what all wait for their entire lives. When it comes, whether above Central Park or wherever, we are at the precise instant, it undoubtedly refers to our finest moment as well.

Moments like the one I'm about to share are developed unlike any of our beliefs or concerns. When I thought back, I knew a precise time that brought me to coincide with the finest moment yet.

When Sandra and I met, neither of us was aware that such a moment was going to be ours in the future. Our introduction came due to her dear friend, Suzie.

Neither of us was able to keep up with all that occurred, from that moment onward that would become our future together. Our time was spent talking each other's ear off. I met her sons that first night, and came to know them from that time forward as Christopher and Eric. What was evident was how they definitely were all boys! The three of them dearly loved each other and that was so important looking at them. We continued dating after our work each day to learn all we could about each other.

Sandra and I decided to invite the boys over to my place. I was hesitant, for I knew how sparsely my place was furnished, as I had established the policy of purchasing one piece of furniture each month. Neither of us forewarned the boys. Even though I was reluctant we drove them over with us one afternoon.

I have never forgotten that scene, upon opening the door to my place, for them to stop in their tracks after we entered and closed the front door. You see, what they saw was "real world," no bars whatsoever. I took them on a cook's tour of the place. In quick order they knew I had two chairs, which were brown canvas studio chairs; I had made up a bedroll on the floor of the bedroom. I had some utensils, pots, so, to cook and serve others.

They both spoke in unison and said, "This is all he has?" What it did for me and for us right there in that moment, was our equivalent of being at the top of the Empire State Building; when rehearing in the dialogue "Shall we" was hearing both of the boys say, "Mom, we can't leave Gerry here like this anymore." Talk about an answer to a prayer long before, that was it for us, for right there we became a family.

As we prepared and laid our plans to be wed that year, our unity became more and more evident. It was as though when stepping outside and closing the door behind us, we did just that, making way toward our future with each other. I never forgot that moment, for it was the most loving gesture on the boy's part of being welcomed, not only in their family, also in their hearts and spirits.

From there we made all of the wedding plans, to be married during the regular Episcopal Church service in Puyallup, Washington only steps up the walk, from where I was gathering my furniture one piece at a time.

We were married on November 8th, 1981 and had our reception in the foyer afterwards, sharing our love and appreciation for all present, and sharing our wedding cake.

That afternoon we were given the finest present that any couple could have hoped for. Sandra's mother volunteered to take the boys with her for the week enabling us time with each other.

I don't know how many from that time on have said, "What a fine way to spend your honeymoon." We didn't want to be traveling all over the globe. Instead we remained in our new home, which we had to call our "rainbow home". During each day and evening, we enjoyed films, museums, musicals, and art, including *Fiddler On The Roof.*

Later came a moment that needed to be shared. All four of us sat down in the kitchen of our new home in Sumner, Washington and brought the boys to realize that we wanted them to know they could call or refer to me however they chose. But before another word could be uttered, both of them said, "Of course you're our dad." Such times aren't nearly as hard as we adults believe they are going to be. So we were off and today as I write, it has been nearly twenty years, even though we knew the pundits bet against us at first.

Before all occurred there was a thought or vision that we would never forget or disregard, for it was the true source of our being together. How it came about took us back to the strawberry patches together, where we believed we had been together, as two soul mates, Sandi and me, from the start.

In order to grasp the true sense of the moment, I need for you to look carefully and you'll see three children from the neighborhood, stretched out on their bellies, in their blue jeans and bib-overalls, thinking they would play a trick on two of their good friends. They eased up just to the edge of the top of the hillside, very carefully, to not make the other playmates aware of their presence. They had the hardest time to not whisper when they looked at their two friends, the little girl in her purple bib overalls, and freckled light complexion, with her strawberry blond hair in a braided ponytail, to hold it even while romping with all of the kids. Her favorite playmate was that tanned little Indian boy, who lived down the road. He never wore a t-shirt so he was just as red as an Indian from the summer sun.

They could be seen picking strawberries, helping her dad working in the garden, but when he turned away to take care of other tasks, they might be seen reaching into the pail and throwing a few berries at each other. Then the other kids would yell and they would go running down to the creek where they all played.

What nearly broke the silence was hearing how the little boy said to the little girl, "I will always think of you as my, 'Strawberry Girl', forever." All of the kids were playing afterwards and had long ago forgotten what they heard earlier in the day.

Not one of them said a thing to kid either of them after that.

As it turned out, they grew up and away from the strawberry patches, but never forgot their wonderful times of playing and frolicking while the little girl's father worked hoeing and planting in their garden nursery.

What could have been more natural, than for the writer to come to call his Sandi, "Strawberry Girl", from the moment they met?

Much of the upheaval that came has been addressed. What hasn't been stated is the absolute miracle of how we came together and remained that way even to the point of the boys being grown and well on their way. Christopher and Eric are flourishing in their own professional pursuits. We reunite as all families hope to, by both of our sons giving us the biggest hugs and kisses we could ever hope for, when we come together and depart into our own worlds, but never parted from each other in our hearts and spirits.

Thank you God, for that prayer and the words of "shall we".

Chapter 25

It's in Sales

I launched my career in the Cable Market sales industry and later moved to Specialty Advertising. I have always called that my arena of post doctorate work readying me for all that lay ahead.

Afterwards, I was honored as "Stampman of the Year". If ever there was a time when every sign revealed itself of my having to deal with a part of Bi-Polar Swing Disorder that was the time. Months later in the first year of our marriage, I was in a state, neither of us would have ever imagined, due to having left Boy Scouts of America as a professional.

The professional battle within was as though I was in a shock never dealt with until that moment. And I had been affected to the quick of my spirit by being without a key to unlock the office door as before and without a place or common purpose I had all the years before. I found I was worsening daily, weekly, and monthly. Through all of the dealings at this time, not only did Sandra keep us afloat, she called me every day at least once or twice to see how I was, and did all within her power to help by making sure I knew how much she loved me, and believed in me to the end. That time became a total of two years! Toward the end I began to snap back and I continued taking my needed medication and further therapy.

At the same time I learned hurriedly, the very quickest aid was to "do the work", no matter what the work was. Another summed it up by saying: "It doesn't happen just because...only men can do this work." - Robert Bly.

The progress that occurred was as mentioned when hearing, "Victory is won not in miles but in inches." – Louis L'Amour. Another friend said it this way, "Remember to just take a bite out of the elephant at a time." Consequently, healing and professional reentrance began to be revealed more every day. Even more vital were the supporting Birds that surrounded me each and every day, where their guidance was premium, as I engaged in entering and remaining in the arena where true change revealed itself.

Two huge intervening factors were what turned me back on course. First came from much thought and interaction between Sandra and I when we formed what we called, S.T.S., "Sales Training Seminar", which we developed and directed toward small and medium sized businesses. This was the involvement that began to take all of my time and began to heal me psychologically more than all of the therapy together. Piece by piece it came together. I began to find the market for our overall effort and began presentations. Along with this came the option to attend what was referred to as T.I.E., "Tie In With Employment", through the Episcopalian Church. Classes were held in Tacoma, not far from where all had been severed only two years before, dealing with my departure from Boy Scouts Of America and the local Council.

I found I needed to throw my hat in the ring while locating my new position and direction.

Along the way, I heard Sandra and others say: "if ever there was a more perfect person for the field of sales, Gerry was it." It stuck and I took the turn and all the opportunities that came from this decision.

I recalled the moment before leaving Grace Line Inc., while working in San Francisco, California, the one caring Bird, Mr. Eric

Henderson, wearing his beige three-piece suit, leaning back in his big, thick leather chair, smoking on his cigar, made sure I knew "it was in sales". Now all those years later I accepted his advice.

I tied all of my skill, knowledge and experience together and began to work the adds in the newspapers and all sources through networking which were the key to securing my next position.

It came when I applied with a firm called C.M.S., Cable Market Specialty, in the Redmond, Washington area. I can still remember hearing the Vice President share, "Due to your constant effort and not giving up regarding being selected to work with us," You have passed the most important test which is a constant in the profession, of Sales, that of "Keeping on, Keeping on," Here I was in an industry of which I had no background. Through the training received I was able to accept the job description that led to my success step by step.

My work took me on the road being trained by the President himself, who had been in the business all of his days. Together we set up my work plan. I spent three to four days and nights calling on cable dealers from Ellensburg to Yakima to the Tri-Cities; I began my return through Wenatchee homeward, then I spent the evening with my family and left the next day for two days in the Portland basin, where I called on major distributors building a market for outdoor visual cameras and related equipment. This completed my time on the road freeing me from further travel. Consequently, the remainder of each month was spent in the greater Seattle Area working to establish distributor accounts throughout.

That diligence and willingness to glean all possible, to become more and more knowledgeable of the industry brought me to know there were contracts on the table to include thousands of cameras to be placed.

I shared this with our company, but found I was stalled and received word shortly afterwards that the company was going Chapter Eleven and was unable to meet such demands. Before they were to let us go I remember conveying, "I knew one thing for certain, I will be working within two weeks or sooner."

I searched the adds of the newspapers and resumed networking throughout the greater area. What finally clicked was the ad in the paper for the position in the field of Specialty Advertising with a firm known as Brown & Bigelow. I immediately applied and was called afterwards for an interview that was one I still remember. When I went in I met a true Bird, Marshall, of whom I would fly with for years to come. He was surrounded by calendars, playing cards, rulers, lighters, t-shirts, every item imaginable, emblazoned with logos of every description.

What reminded me was my familiarity of these items, thinking back to my working at the Marqueen Garage, at the base of Queen Anne Hill years before. My grandfather had always had various specialty items for his customers so I shared this with Marshall, with my enthusiasm and energy, to find I was assigned to a marvelous area for my territory where there was solid potential.

I worked the corridor from Boeing Field north, to the King Dome in Seattle, Washington and down to the waterfront. The area was saturated with industrial accounts. Unknown to me, even though Marshall trained me, there would be another learning curve ahead.

I know all members of our family saw our evenings as though I was going to hand them another card from the deck. But in truth the cards were catalogues, studied night upon night, as I spread them on the floor and reorganized them, so to make sense of the hundreds of items displayed in them. This may have been considered to be another phase of readying and leading to what would be the finest year for me professionally.

It didn't start that way, as Sandra lovingly and patiently would say, "Honey, you really seem to be enjoying the work." Such refrains were mentioned through the seventh week when I still had not sold one item.

The very next day I had success to the end of the year. I began to develop all of the products into program formats. They were oriented for various industries such as the aviation companies. One of those I served was due to the help of Houston, another true Bird, who was supportive and open to such ideas enhancing their efforts to grow as a company.

I was hooked in the business! Even so, the first year came to a close. Brown and Bigelow provided the staff the shot in the arm we needed through sales meetings and the latest in products more effectively creating ways to gain success.

One night the telephone rang. It was Marshall calling to tell me of an opportunity he wanted me to have. He shared the details and I immediately followed up on them. Due to the volume gained, I was chosen as "Rookie of the Year" for the Seattle District. Who would have ever known, that after that first interview such an honor would come as quickly as it had?

Another year of sales was upon us; The Holiday season passed quickly, with the thrill of sharing such a plaque with my family and loving friends.

It was only a few months afterwards, that I received the first call to become the District Sales Manager for the greater Houston to El Paso, Texas region. Our family did much soul searching and wisely turned this down. In the meantime I continued working in the assigned area.

Later, I was approached to become the District Sales Manager of the Seattle District and I accepted. The assignment was exactly what I had been working for the entire time. However, the company didn't come forth with any training or advising me to better prepare me to be more effective in my new position.

The corporate body was in St. Paul, Minnesota where years ago, I had changed trains to board **The Empire Builder**, bound for my new home in Seattle, Washington. They flew me back for the purpose of the three-day-whirl-wind orientation meeting. It was a wining and dining "Pony Show", including touring the plant from one end to the other, to see the processes in each case.

Earlier that afternoon, I discovered what became quite a joke between my wife and I. I went to the closet in the hotel to select a pair of pants to find none other than the suit I had worn. Truthfully, the only thing I could do was laugh. I called Sandra and asked her to go to the closet and take a look. I heard her gasp on the other end of the line and return to apologize. She said, "I'll immediately go back to the airport and contact the airlines to arrange for your pants to be sent to you on the next flight." She also said, that she would see that they were sent to the hotel. In the meantime we had a loving laugh with each other.

There I sat in my underwear and socks, on the edge of the bed, watching T.V., reading the morning newspapers, waiting for something to wear. Fortunately, the service was speedy; I met my morning schedule. I was off into the second day of training, and related tasks in the suit I had arrived in the day before. This brought chagrin from my boss who didn't see the humor in the occurrence. I thought at the time how nice it must be to never make such a mistake in his world of management.

My position with Brown & Bigelow consisted of having thirty on my staff and recruiting and training additional staff. From the start, there was a lot of flack from various members of the staff as to their having selected me for the position. It didn't matter that I had proved my ability in sales. The way I approached the subject was to provide them the same service I had provided my clients. I set a rigid schedule to be with one and all and purposefully spent time with them to resolve any and all of their problems. These regular contacts both personally and by telephone began to pay off. Keep in mind the staff stretched as far north as Everett, throughout the greater Seattle basin, eastward to Montana. I made every effort to visit them and help in any way possible.

While all of this was going on, my family declared that for seven days a week the only posture they observed was my back bent over and my elbow bent while on the telephone.

A saving force and what became the Bird with the most outstretched wings was our Maestro. He, at the age of eighty-four, still going strong, became my friend and more importantly, mentor, Ed Grimes, who took me under his wings from the moment I asked for his help. He agreed to help me in every way possible. We met many times for lunch at his club, the Washington Athletic Club. He always greeted me with total respect. I fully appreciated him for all of his deep knowledge untouchable by any other in the profession. He was as young in spirit as when he began as I was a new manager of our team.

The first time I met Ed was in Kelso, at one of our quarterly sales promotion meetings. You couldn't mistake him as he stood with a solid stature and his hairline swept back on both sides of his head. He wore a distinguished goatee with a direct point, much the same as the Colonel of the famous chicken house of America. When he spoke he was heard by one and all. His account was one for all of us to follow.

He rapidly made me realize our work in sales was complete only by the attainment of total respect from those we served. I've never forgotten those luncheons and his taking the time to reach out to train and aid me, to conceptualize the job at hand. If that wasn't enough he invited me up to his home on Whidbey Island for in depth training.

The setting could not have been more perfect, as we discussed everything in detail. We had our lunch overlooking the magnificent view across to Port Townsend. When I left him, I never would have imagined at the end of a short, yet furious six months, they never intended for me to be the manager, rather, to bring their choice from St. Louis. Then came their blunt statement, "We'll need the car keys and all of the related materials." They had the audacity to tell me, "You won't be needed." I cut them off by telling them, "I'll go on working my territory as before." This meeting became power verses power, in that I had achieved the record I had during my first year, so we concurred this would be the path I would take. Before launching this, Ed and I met and reviewed everything.

Remember how I wouldn't accept the denial of the first decision, when applying at Seattle Pacific College? The entirety of this action was- I wouldn't take it on the chin; no matter what. I was always defiantly striving to hang on no matter what. Undoubtedly, this had to relate to the condition I had deep within me.

When considering Ed to this day, I respect all he acknowledged, including his effort annually of attaining one hundred and fifty thousand to two hundred thousand in volume, selling only two lines: custom playing cards and calendars. I am sure he is gone now, but I have always remembered him, all of the gifts he gave to me, which I found I could carry forth from thereon. It didn't take me long to realize the stand I took would not work and was cause for me to move on.

In short order, I accepted offers to work with specialty advertising agencies that were more local.

I was never really away from the field even though I heard of another avenue I joined. The firm was Consumer Preferred, out of Green Bay, Wisconsin. I worked on a small team effort within markets including: small and medium sized communities throughout Western Washington. The work entailed my traveling more than fifty per cent of the time. This was a con for our family from the start.

I became more and more versed as to the approach to sell the green and white vinyl telephone book covers and all of the advertising front and backsides. Market by market brought more and more experience.

We were out in all seasons. One day, while working the Issaquah, Washington market, I was sitting drinking a cup of coffee. I looked out the window and couldn't believe my eyes for there was Marshall, who hired me with Brown & Bigelow. I went to meet him and before I could realize it, he was telling me the story about the case he was carrying. As it turned out, he was with Inland Pacific, selling pre-ink stamps, rubber stamps as referred to even then. He opened up his case and began to tell me the story regarding the company's products, and that I would have a position were I to accept.

I told him, "I'm beginning to make headway and believe I'll remain a bit longer."

It wasn't long after, I made the decision to accept the offer with Marshall and the territory that was to be mine. It couldn't have been more perfect as I had been working here back in the days as an Explorer Executive with Boy Scouts of America.

When I began, there wasn't one orange handled stamp in the valley. After planting, cultivating, and nurturing, the garden became full of orange handled stamps! I am now completing a total of twelve years, starting my thirteenth year in the garden.

It wasn't that long afterward that I was having my lunch beside the Green River.

I was praying and looking out in the fields, to see two men working: One was leaning on his hoe taking a break. I knew then this area or territory assigned to me was the same as a garden. All that I did from thereon was become one gardener with the Chief Gardener. That concept was a perfect find; one that remained all of these years.

This took a lot of hoeing! The past years have revealed successful results that have brought *Birds from the Thicket* to guide my path even further.

Chapter 26

Finds in The Garden

I have already brought your attention to the garden; in fact, I mentioned that I came to no longer consider the area of my responsibility as my territory, instead, I picked up my hoe, tiller, even wheel barrow, to till the soil, seed, nurture, and rid each furrow of the weeds throughout every acre. There was so much more to be discovered each and every day, week, month, and year. Those years have become extensive; I hurriedly realized how much merit there was in what Zig Ziglar revealed, "You can get everything in life you want, if you help enough people get what they want." That turned out to be more than enough when launching my career leading me to become, "The Stampman of the Valley," later, "of the Year."

When all of this was assigned to me in 1989, it was virgin ground to be seeded. There had been little or none cultivated, for that matter covered, so the vastness of the opportunity was there for me to care for each aspect throughout.

Before going any further, I had to consider by retrospection our vacation years ago when I was finally able to meet my father in law. I had been told exactly what I would find upon meeting him. Even though he is ninety – seven years old, much of the time each year, he can be seen dressed in his wool plaid shirt, work pants, warm winter coat and rubber boots, bent over his favorite plants, no matter whether vegetables or his hybrid varieties long before planted.

Gerry Bradley

Doing this will ready him to share gifts from his garden with his community. What struck me while with him, were the same parallels from his garden to mine in the profession I have remained in all of these years. How thankful I am that I knew from the start that the last thing I did or would do was sell, I have always stood for the fact that I would serve one and all.

Marshall mentioned to our staff, that what we did didn't take the skill of selling rockets. How right he was, to bring this to our attention so we would simply bend down and grab a good handful of the rich soil beneath us. That was true in my behalf for the ground was rich through and through.

I realized that the very tools and tasks that are used each and every day are exactly the same as the gardener.

Where the gardener begins his day at one end of the garden and works through the day to cover as much of the ground, as possible, was the same way I began. This was especially true then and remains so today.

At the same time my success comes by applying two concepts; first, to absorb all along the path and, even more important, to remain focused. The tools really don't vary that much except I always have extra materials, so when my brief case is depleted I can restock it with brochures, billing records and the like.

Where the gardener can show his quality crop, to looking and deciding whether they want a dozen stalks of corn, I can open my case to reveal the options available.

During my visit with the gardener of gardens, I found my father-in-law has been gardening well over fifty years, seven days a week and

404

he treated all through his garden as his church or chapel throughout his lifetime.

What has been the mere opportunity, to be in the company of so many Birds while being out there has been a gift from God.

I had some special time while on vacation, the fall of 2000 and made sure that my wife had the same quality time with her dad. This was their opportunity to enjoy each other and it became mine to acquaint myself with all within the garden.

A pronounced beckoning call came from the trees covered with gray birds, feeding from the berries of the branches. This was early autumn, and there remained some Robins, Stellar Blue Jays, even a Pileated Woodpecker hard at work, in his perpendicular fashion, sending out his message as he tapped for his lunch. I even heard a wing of Canadian Geese overhead readying for their migratory flight south before the early snow was to fall. English Wrens landed out on the edge of the garden, singing their familiar song, much the same as a rhapsody, for all within hearing distance. I have always enjoyed the birds whether chirping on the edge of a fence before lighting for a short bath, ruffling their feathers, pruning for their afternoon of flight or hopping limb to limb.

You see, all of these mentioned, and so many not are the subject just as I brought to your attention one tiny little bird and all that came from him in my life from thereon.

I have always believed the Birds, are those whom I have been surrounded by all my life. I am sure you will agree none of us could be where we are, had it not been for every Bird along the way. The story reveals so many of them from start to its end.

Before walking away from the garden, it is an opportune time to acquaint you with the Birds that I have encountered along the way.

Those I call on are throughout the garden! They are sitting on the limb waiting with anticipation; furthermore, they have and do all mentioned.

They have held supportive roles, much like how Ward encouraged my writing the story. Doreen and Alford paid such a compliment to me. They knew the overall story would be published in the near future. Such support was so helpful along the way. Further anticipation of the completion came from Mary and William at their antique store, who were vitally interested in the writing and are enthused to see the final book completed. Rachael conveyed her pride in the manner I have approached and attained my goal. Chris and Eric as well as Tiffany and Kristy have revealed they have been eager to read it cover to cover. Andrea has proven to be interested from the start. Andy said, "I found the published newspaper pieces very good indeed and want to read the book as soon as it is published."

Others flew in a formation of support the whole way. Richard and Dee have been there in prayerful support. They remained and have shown interest in the entire project.

Carol and Mickey have been intent from the offset as to my fulfilling the book. Mickey paid me a huge compliment along the way by saying, "I will expect an autographed copy of your book and I will place it next to my other autographed copy by General Colin Powell." Jerome has revealed his enthusiasm from the start. Suzanne has been behind me from day one to the end.

Then there were those that sang a fine song, as the cheerleaders they proved to be. Eric and Kristy took time to listen and sang notes for encouragement. There were countless others that definitely were regarded as *Birds From the Thicket*.

Two new Birds proved to be more than listeners, rather they provided constructive critique each time we convened and shared another portion of the book. I am so thankful for all of the minutes they were willing to avail to me as I closed on the finale of the story. A big thanks for Georgia and Selina, two Birds with keen eyes of needed scrutiny throughout each phrase.

Traits of Birds such as Edward, Rebecca and Faith willing to take time away from the daily flow to listen, critique where necessary and mostly, be supportive the whole way.

What became more and more pronounced has been that of each becoming my friend and I theirs.

There are hidden elements much like the way you look up to see where the singing bird is, but it's somehow hidden behind the leaves and the blowing, clinging, limbs. Comparable finds, came in the same surprising moments of the respect, aid, and assistance I received along the way from one and all.

I'll never forget the numerous times they would notice the tremor was so bad in my hands at the moment, I just couldn't write their order. I was always surprised at each saying, "Let me help you with that order today." They exemplified total compassion. None of this can be forgotten, rather, proudly held and always remembered. Each year the precedence became more and more prominent.

I know all that I gained has to be the same as the gardener or the farmer, when the weather is as hoped for through the entire year. That being so there isn't any less due to a severe frost, entirely too much heat, or downpours that damage the crop.

Over the years, the repertoire has become substantial, as friendships have been bolstered by deeper trust, bringing each Bird to know they can share about their families, even to the extent of conveying the severest accounts they are battling. Likewise, have come equal freedoms to explain to those curious as to my tremor and to be able to share the bereavement due to the passing of my parents.

This taught me the same lesson learned as a teacher who always learns most from his students. What was best was, when I was able to hold them up with a lift of their wings. When these circumstances arise, I immediately respond with cards and support. I always recall, how they did that and more for me throughout the time of standing, listening to their songs and viewing their flight with sheer pleasure.

While I was eating my lunch I saw another friend, rather Bird, who I have known for ten years. Michael was a realtor-land-developer who sat down and we took a moment to catch up with each other. While we sat and talked he said, "I was quite a whistler as a boy, which is how I got through my paper route where I pedaled ten to fifteen miles each day," and continued saying, "I whistled the whole way."

All that he had shared came after I had revealed to him, I was writing my book. At that moment, I had just finished the section pertaining to my experiences delivering newspapers, which brought us to compare our experiences even though mine was within the city of Seattle. The remaining moments of our brief visit flowed as the pages flow one into the other drawing the reader through the complete story.

I'll never be able to thank so many for taking a moment to listen to a short section so I could gain an opinion from them as to my progress. This applied to all Birds in their own right, in order that I could pay the deepest of thanks to all of the Birds throughout the garden all of these years.

Chapter 27

Love for the Birds through the Journey

We had our twentieth anniversary and our twenty-first Christmas together, with Eric, and his soon to be fiancee Kristy, who we love and consider as our daughter.

Christopher and Tiffany are living in Tracy, California and moving to their new home. Both of our sons are doing very well professionally and we kid them, as they are the half of our family working for Home Depot.

Every year, including this year, involves our insuring our Christmas tree is up and ready for the season, not one that needs to be tied to the wall anymore. All within the season is referred to as, *"Canterbury Tales,"* as our home is regal each and every season.

Each is evident, as I know how the fall and winter set in and affect me due to my always realizing I have Bi-Polar Mood Swing Disorder. Much like the seasons, the condition is emphasized and always present. I learned years before it is something that can be lived with.

All that came with us as a family touched on this and more. We as a family would learn to live with this disorder together in a positive way. What came from Sandra and the boys was immediate acceptance. The truth was the boys didn't have any idea, as to what was periodically revealed, by my behaviors witnessed by them and their mother. It was their love and at the same time, their accepting my love toward each of them that won out in the end.

Adjustment and adaptation was necessary on all of our parts. All of us were more than willing to move into the "arena of change" for each other.

There are accounts that stagger the mind, that so many effected by either, Bi-Polar Mood Swing Disorder, Uni-Polar Mood Swing Disorder or explicitly, Manic Depression, have an awful time adapting to such. It can't help but affect all members of any family one way or another. It is for that reason, that many who have such a condition to deal with, finally take their lives. Either they can't deal with having such, and all that occurs because of it, or their behaviors, do have deep effect on their families, loved ones, and friendships.

A saving grace not only from God was definitely true in my case, as was the reading and realizing I followed the same in the case of: "Be what you are and speak from your guts and heart-it's all a man has." – Hubert Humphrey.

The saving grace for me was my diagnosis and my willingness to accept that I would take the Lithium and recently changed to Lamictal, as prescribed. I thoroughly recall saying to Sandra, "My having my medications, far surpasses my having food." The statement itself depicts how vital it became to me years before we met.

It wasn't something that was shared with the boys, although they knew I had to take my meds regularly. What stood out years later, was realizing in Eric's case, he had no idea that I had such a condition. All that came for us wasn't always perfect, but rather, workable for us as a family.

We as a couple, had to arrive at some guidelines that would prove best for all of us. Where this became evident was in how to deal with two

411

growing boys regarding any discipline administered. At first I was too rigid, but soon realized the most effective way to reach out for the boys was to hug both of them and love them. Fortunately, this policy overruled.

Even though we had come from such differing places, it was that loving touch that helped us along the way. We faced the same pressures and trials that all families endure, making a living and dealing with tensions while progressing forward each day and each year.

When I revealed my lack of patience, or willingness to endure and go through phases of our lives together, they were always there for me. I was blessed from the beginning in finding them as I did. A profound finding and admonition I came to realize was, we fixed each other through and through. What a gift this was for all of us from start to the present day.

Years later, I can significantly hear the boys say, "Dad, you don't need to continue repeating the same thing over and over. We got what you said the first time!" Honestly, I wasn't aware I was so redundant to confirm what I was sharing with them.

Hearing this, I couldn't help remembering all the times I heard the repetitive messages from mother, during my junior year, relating to my making up my mind. She used to drive me crazy over her agendas, which she seemingly had, regarding her every move. What was overbearing, was to hear her instruct that such and such "must be done by..." The end result was for me to follow the same.

The key of having this behavior is to gain stability and assurance regarding living daily life. And that doesn't just come; it takes discipline to follow the guidelines provided by the doctors and therapists in our lives no matter what. It requires a sensible and right way to first accept that diagnosis and act upon it. Fortunately, I did just that and had time to practice all of this and more, before making my way across the wide divide, known as the Cascades back into the region of Seattle and beyond.

During that time, I read everything I could get my hands on to better understand all related; to discover a better path to take in the future. That helped me more than I can describe. Truthfully, it was the first time I faced the reality of all related and became the winner into the future. I confronted the absolute truth of learning to live effectively and the following: not to be lonely, but rather to live alone with myself, to attend a movie without another present, to shop for groceries, cook, bake, take runs, enjoy all about me, to walk and pray, to read and enjoy the arts; yet how to better share with another at the same time. Consequently, after being introduced to who came to be called, "My Strawberry Girl" and her boys, it worked for us from the very beginning.

Another occurrence or behavior that comes for those who have the same plight is the lack of assurance of themselves and to always keep filling the cup, not realizing that their cup is full or can be. This was true in my case and came under the heading of dealing with my self-concept. I know this was very hard on my wife; however, she kept pursuing what was best throughout our marriage. In fact, her caring spirit was always present, in that she understood and helped me to gain this turnabout. I can say now after all of these years, the cup is full all the time! This is a phenomenal piece of growth and well deserved. Finding all of these elements has taken a long time and an immense amount of experiences or, "necessary hoops", as referred to by Dr. Wayne Dyer.

I have strived to be forthright throughout the entire story as to what occurred. Erratic behavior was one of those thoroughly mentioned.

However, there was much more that occurred, such as: finding how rattled I can be from time to time, or nervous, unable to focus on daily tasks or works; unable to deal with distortion of facts, understood by others, even when called to my attention.

The reason was I found the overall imbalance was due to having a shortage of sodium carbonate in my system; periodically flaring with anger or vehemence toward others or circumstances that occurred; inability to deal with frustrations present in daily life; emphatically making far too many choices of friends, loved ones I would unite with, where all mentioned affected my inability to reason regarding decisions needed to be made. They were what I termed as "cut-offs", where I would accept just so much from others and I would cut them off, many times to no longer return; making irrational decisions brought way too much upheaval during everyday life with those about me.

All mentioned couldn't help but have effect on Sandra and others throughout the years.

Now consider each of these aspects and examples. There are days when it seems near impossible for me to keep the bearing and remain with it.

Those in my profession of sales, are known to duck their work; by taking longer lunches or quit well before the end of a workaday. In my case, there were times that I met myself going around the same blocks, but not producing or making the needed calls to serve those of my territory or garden mentioned.

A perfect example was gaining the respect of new or present clients, by resuming all that equaled total service, holding tight and working into the latter hours of the evening, even to hear more than one say, "My word man, are you still out here working; let's see what you have"…followed by, "I'll take…because I really do need them."

What has greatly improved has been my being able to discern and break the behavior for a focused productive one. I can still recall, when working for other companies, there was the fact of not being able to approach the maze of buildings and uncertain areas where I was working. Understandably, the element of fear from that of rejection, which is more than apparent in the profession of sales, was a part of this. The overriding fact was due to such a rattled state this would bring on me and how it would be all encompassing to the point of not being able to move. This took a long period of time to overcome. Such isn't something that is present only sporadically and when it occurs, I realize it and make the needed change. What usually happens is I determine I haven't taken my medication due to tending other tasks and plain forgetting, but that doesn't last, as I stop and take the needed dosage and on goes the day of work.

I was finally able to admit that this overall effect was due to the lack of both a chemical imbalance and definitely psychological as well. This wasn't easy to admit, but revealed a deeper understanding of what I had been dealing with, interrelated to the feminine lines of my heritage. The truth is it is definitely evident this is passed via our heredity; this is becoming more and more evident due to all of the research throughout the years and the findings related to the overall condition shared.

All to often the heated anger came when dealing with a principle or other's behaviors. In fact, my dealings with such, brought anger to the top! This isn't that different to that of others, as all of us arrive at such times in our daily lives.

Admittedly, there were far too many spontaneous decisions made regarding my selection of friends, acquaintances, even the women I chose and married. This brought far too much discord for them and me in the long run.

I have always been one to continue to rise to the occasion no matter what happened. My hope is that in every case you have gathered that this in itself is something that has taken a lot of faith. At the same time, I have realized that the Birds have always been present along the pathway, to reach out in their wonderful ways to help uplift me in all accomplished.

The miracle of having found Sandra and the boys was just that, **A TRUE MIRACLE**.

Many never gain such a gift, so they drift as mentioned, as so many others throughout this world.

Ironically, when cruising through the garden, I saw a spectacular sight of two blue herons flying low over the wetlands in unison flight. I realized I was gazing at two magnificent species unified in pursuit of the last catch for the day to feed their young. I was profoundly aware of their mutual togetherness, which is equally true of us as a married couple and family.

Later that afternoon, I got out of my car and was walking across a parking lot; I realized I was beneath an immense flock of black crows that just kept coming. They seemed to crown the fact of that announced to my spirit, how far we had come and I equally had progressed, while sharing our lives together, in our own kind of flight into our future years.

Yes, they too were *Birds from the Thicket*, revealing they were always present. All that was needed, was to look up and about, and know they were there each and every day of our lives, to aid us in miraculous ways to be sure.

Chapter 28

Our Years Together

There are so many of us who have taken such a long time to find our way following the tracks taking us to our destinations. As for me, the place and time occurred after riding those tracks and derailing more times than I would have imagined.

Sandra's position was solid, as she had worked long and hard as an outside sales representative. And, as mentioned, I was a District Executive for the Mount Rainier Council of Boy Scouts of America when meeting who I soon came to realize was my "Strawberry Girl".

After our wedding, we had made arrangements to meet my Best man and his wife in Seattle for our first toast where both our drinks and our spirits were brimming to the top. We bid farewell to them and began our honeymoon, by our seeing *Fiddler on the Roof* at the Fifth Avenue Theatre.

All the way home we thought back to how we discovered our home, the Rainbow House.

One, Sunday afternoon, while we were out for a ride, the clouds were looming in the background, where the rain had been pouring down before. There was a break in the sky and a perfect rainbow was arcing over this one house with real heritage.

I blurted out, "This has to be it, much like an omen and a Rainbow to boot." We realized our place was to be in the rear of the main house with all that was palatial. Our home may as well have been the servant's quarters.

What was memorable for me, about the owners, was the way they helped to place bouquets of roses in each and every room, before we returned from the wedding as I had requested. And Sandra's surprise was there when we returned on our first night.

The "Rainbow House," had a meager living room with an oil, stove center stage next to the stairwell and a sun porch was enclosed from the kitchen and dining room. The stairs took us to the two bedrooms at the top floor and one bathroom. We found that the oil stove was the heat element for the entire place. You can imagine the laugh we had, over the blinders we had on, going in there and accepting it in the first place.

Memories and more became ours, trying to stay warm during the cold winter months ahead, bringing us to bundle up in our sweaters, sweats and blankets.

I was determined that the sun porch would be my study area. You should have seen me in the warmest coat available, stocking hat and gloves trying to do my work. I finally opted for heat in the kitchen on the dining room table.

Our bathroom wasn't too bad, except the lid on the toilet froze over; which proved to be rather slippery for all of us.

If that wasn't enough, Eric became petrified of the place, concerned that there had to be ghosts throughout.

We enjoyed the snow coming down, which left us with memories of being out front with the boys, pulling them on their sled down the lane. Chris and Eric had a delightful time and didn't fall off their sled once. These were the kind of moments we needed most. All of us were having the best time, but of course dad and mom got the worst of it when the snowballs started to fly. This was our first winter together, one, we would mention many times in the future.

The Christmas tree was one, we tied to the wall, as it wasn't straight, nor did it remain upright to keep all of our decorations on the limbs.

Without a doubt, we enjoyed that clunker of a tree more than any in the future, as it brought many a laugh that season.

The boys were making the change from their schools.

We knew there wasn't a couple that wouldn't go through the tests we were facing. All that came was like the teetering decorations on the Christmas tree I described.

The boys had been with their mother alone all of this time; my coming into their lives was a total switch for them. One sign that was shown was, Chris' bolting in on us in our bedroom.

Christopher was hearing impaired; I soon found such behavior was due to this. Furthermore, that little guy had gone through his own kind of havoc earlier, due to having a Nevus mole removed from one side of his nose and cheek. In fact, this required multiple procedures, so it was no wonder he was behaving as he was. I didn't grasp all of this at first. However, I came around. They were anything but used to me. We soon came to realize, the levels that needed to be looked at, were aggravation and sheer annoyance buttons being pushed too many times.

Retrospection brought me, to discern, how my behavior came from facing the loss of my position as a full time teacher and my discharge from the Air Force. That definitely set me back, but prepared me to begin taking my classes at Allan Hancock College. .

I was on my way full speed after becoming acclimated to the new schedule. It was those breaks in the flow toward progress and goals which I had before me where similar ways of behaviors rose hastily.

When all was said and done, a view back to the beginning of the story made me know when such breaks occurred, became the time I buried myself doing any of the following: the cut-offs, closing myself from everything, people and places frequented; finding how I could and still can peer out through a veil or curtain for minutes, even hours, all with the purpose to dodge and accept others help of any kind; locking away in total silence, as if in a grimace of kinds, all for the purpose of not allowing another to touch that part of my soul touched so badly in the past, yet always rising as from a two legged landing position to a lilt at first, then gaining enough height so to soar once again.

How fortunate I was to have my Strawberry Girl, who deeply revealed her grasp of how my having Bi-Polar Mood Swing Disorder played in that occurring each day. Yet, she remained compassionate and seemingly understood all that I was going through. The daily phone calls were filled with sunshine in her voice, with intent to help me to regain the posture to reenter the daily work of the past. No one could have hoped for more. Toward the conclusion of the two-year period, I attended T.I.E. (Tie In with Employment) offered through the Episcopalian Church, which brought me to understand the power of networking.

Consequently, I finally began practicing the skills found each day more and more. My contacts went back to when I was in Professional Scouting and extended to everywhere I was able to get an appointment, which I say with complete gratitude to every person that gave me their time and willingness by giving me ideas and contacts continue along the way. That in the long run put me back in contact with the work-a-day world and all therein.

Due to this, I began to enter the working world again, drawing on my contacts of the past. It was the process that was the awakener for me, bringing me back from those awful hours, days, months, into a much longer period than I would have ever imagined.

From there, I began to regain strength in the process of interviewing, including other forms of networking with one and all. My despondency lessened each day.

Furthermore, I gathered all of my materials and formed our own company called S.T.S. (Sales Training Seminars), to be directed toward small and medium sized businesses. This brought me back and afterwards, I was reemployed again back in the real work-a-day world. George F. Will said, "It is extraordinary how extraordinary the ordinary person is."

The entire experience was perfect in drawing us closer than before. I have never forgotten that terrible time.

Sandra's real fiber and strength was tested during that period, as she continued working, but always made sure I knew she was there every day. How many times during and afterwards have I shown her gratitude for all she did then.

Before we faced this juncture, we took the boys and headed up to Mount Rainier National Park. It was one of those times, we weren't able to convey to the boys that the back seat wasn't the playground for them to fight with each other. As all parents do, we kept trying to get them to stop. It became apparent, they were not about to, so before arriving at Longmire Lodge, I pulled over at an elementary school, and I took both of them back to the rear of the school. I was fair, using the paddle on both of their butts.

Before we left I asked if they understood they were not going to ruin this perfectly planned day. Believe me, they recognized all!

You know what. We had the best time. We shared the time on the mountain picnicking, hiking, taking in the exhibits and enjoying each other's company. We could never think of or find ourselves at Paradise National Park, Mount Rainier, turning our eyes on the summit of Mount Rainier, without remembering that just walking from the lodge, was the very spot that we peered down into the spray of Myrtle Falls, where moments afterwards I stopped, kind of clumsily, and surprised Sandra by asking if she would be my wife.

The boys were ahead sauntering down the trail from us and must have sensed something was happening, as they came running back to us just before Sandra said, as softly as the water falling below, "Yes, I will marry you." There was no way I could have been happier, as I took her in my arms, then to feel the boys experiencing the moment by wrapping their arms about us. They were so curious and wanted to know what had happened. When Sandra told them, they were really pleased and that made for such a heightened mountain top experience for all of us.

As we made our descent from the marvelous crescendo like moment just before, we knew we were becoming a unified family.

Over the years we have talked about that day so many times. It isn't the events or the placement of such that are standouts in our lives.

We found, as all couples and families do, it takes more than one move to finally make the biggest one. At long last we located our first home, which we didn't take due to another rainbow, rather to what seemed right for us as a family. It was there, I perceived as all homeowners do that feeling of pulling in the driveway and the deep pride of knowing this was ours. We thoroughly enjoyed our home. We both were working to, the hilt including my traveling, as I was with my work assignment. Consequently, the only time I was there was on the weekends. My family always treated my time home as though it was a homecoming. Only hours away I would be off for another market and away from them.

Before leaving Auburn, Washington, I found Christopher had real interest in the neighborhood football league. Both of the boys became involved in one form of sports or another. Their interest swung from football practice and games, and later Eric merged into his true game, basketball. While in Junior and Senior High, they were on the wrestling team. Their size and strength brought them to excel wherever they turned out season by season.

It was then that Sandra accepted a marketing position with a firm in the Tacoma area, which involved her having to travel much more than any distance I had before. They had to attend the big shows in New York, Chicago, New Orleans, San Francisco and other points of destination.

I was working locally, so it became my job to hold down the fort, while she was away. The business trips proved to be the test of all for the boys and me. When it came to a head on, it was at the dinner hour. I cooked for us; they would turn their noses up. Consequently, the finale came to cooking eating alone. They chose to get by with McDonalds; I was far past arguing with them. The glory statement made by so many others, of the success of their marriages of living on two different coastlines was anything but true in our case. I finally made it clear, that it would be much better if Sandra would accept a position that was more local and we could once again be together.

Chris and Eric were graduates from their Junior High scene and were now attending high school. They were entrenched in their studies and athletic pursuits.

Where we as a couple really came through for them, was being at every game, match, contest or event scheduled.

They have said so many times, that was the finest they could have ever hoped from us. Even though those football games proved to be the coldest evenings remembered, sitting in those stadiums on our blankets or anything we could haul to keep warm while there, rooting for our boys and their teams turned out to be our greatest gift in the end.

The most jarring event of all, far beyond our having to sell our home, came later. It wasn't long after and we found Sandra had incurred Rheumatoid Arthritis; that turned out to be the severest event that hit us during our years together. I knew as she did we had to keep her going no matter what. All the times previously, where Sandra proved to be the angel, now it was my turn. I wouldn't let her quit. Instead, I made sure she was up each morning, which took my having to prop her up in bed and prepare her for another day of work. From there I helped her out to the car. There she was tested every morning, as she had to crook her trail leg to get inside of the car. This brought her to tears every morning. The triumph was hers by ten a.m. and beyond, as she would have limbered up and would be well into her day. This went on for months before the disease took a positive swing which all of us appreciated, especially Sandra.

We have never felt we had more trials and tribulations than any others, but are glad we have had our share, for it bettered us as individuals and certainly as a family. Our years together were being added up by now and the pundits were falling away, as our marriage was proof of its own, a lasting one to be sure.

It has been many years that have passed and, not only are we still together we are looking toward our twenty-fifth anniversary.

As mentioned earlier, life is glimpses or photographic sequences of one setting of the scene after another. All that I am conveying are those photographic moments.

Thinking back, our home life wasn't all that easy. As the boys completed junior high and were on their way to high school, we realized immediately what was stated by all of our friends who were doing the same: living or feeling as if we were taxi cab drivers. Scheduling events around our work schedule was at times the same as a "three ring circus". How many times we found ourselves saying, "Won't it be wonderful when they have their own wheels."

But you know something, it seems the moment they get those wheels, is the specific time they're no longer kids anymore, rather, soon to be grown adults preparing for their own futures. Not to be solemn, but I know both of us would give anything for more of those days of hauling them and their friends a bit longer.

When this hit us was when we no longer had to set our schedules to attend each of their games any longer, particularly after Chris' year where he was to play football at Central Western University, and shortly after to go and see Eric play while on the Junior College team, though that was short lived as he soon graduated and was working full time.

My recall was one morning Chris and I had the ride we wouldn't forget. He was in the midst of his special school, with the hearing impaired, where we were readying him to mainstream in the near future. And ahead of us was, facing the overnight snow and the grade of which we were able to make, holding our breath the whole way and finally exhaling in relief, as we made the crest of the hill, then to head directly to his school to prevent him being late.

It wasn't the climb, it was our antics of trying once, no twice, turning around one more time to hear, "Come on dad. I know you'll make it this time," and at the same time our laughing and seeing Chris pounding his foot on the floorboard to do his part as we trudged up that grade. Such a moment is one he and I have to this day when reflecting back to those days.

Prior to the entire family adjoining each other again, my loving Aunt Adeline, in 1988, suggested that I make one more call and try to contact my mother and Jesse. I explained to her that we had done all of that before for naught. We found that miscommunication played into the turn of events described.

We had seen each other several times. Arrangements were made so they would have a day ferrying across from Bremerton to Seattle and able to take in the waterfront and Public Market, then come and join us for dinner at our home in Federal Way. We never heard anything! Neither did we see them or hear from them. This left us wondering for sometime.

Later, we found that there was an emergency with mother's parents in California, bringing them to turn and tend them toward the end of their lives.

Long ago, I learned when Jesse and I had moments alone with each other, he knew he was secure and would have safekeeping with his sharing at the time. He always prefaced by saying, "Now don't tell your mother," which always seemed like a young boy dealing with the shame

427

of his actions before completing his thought. I asked him, "What's going on?" So he shared how he walked over to the Senior Center to visit, taking them cookies and snacks.

He continued by saying, "The other night your mother nearly lost me, I was walking down that alley and passed out and fell down." I asked him, "Has this happened more than once. He told me that he had fallen once, but he had been having fainting spells before this occurred. Then I asked, "Have you seen a doctor regarding this?" He replied, "No, I don't need a doctor."

After he shared all the facts I told him, "Either you get in and see a doctor or I'm going to carry you in myself." In no time he pursued the inquiry that brought him relief by having open-heart surgery at Providence Hospital in Portland, Oregon.

We drove down and picked up mother, then went to be at his side upon his being out of surgery. Neither of us has ever forgotten the look in his eyes, wet with tears by seeing that we cared so much. In no time he was up and going slowly, but like all too many, he didn't hit the road for his walks as he should have. Undoubtedly, that came back in the end to haunt him more than he would have imagined, as he just couldn't keep the water off his heart. So the original symptoms of being dizzy came back to the point he couldn't stand, which was more than all of the drinking over the years.

We found my mother chic in her designer jeans and tops, with her hair in the cutest perky cut, just as she had kept herself all of the years before. At this time she had taken the advice to quit smoking and had complete hope she had done this soon enough. It seemed that sooner than any of us would have imagined, she began to decline visit by visit. Before and after, Sandra and I made sure to go down and visit them every month or two! Both of them looked forward to every one of our visits.

I was sure in the beginning to set precedence on two crucial points. The first was, it would do no good for us to dip back into the past, rather, to begin from where we were and go forward. The other was my insisting we hug each other, especially he and I. I made sure of this in every case. This was more than he could stand, particularly at first. However, as time went on, he began to realize we would be there, as stated, therefore, he began to soften somewhat.

I entered another arena of change that was in the end too much for him. That was my stating that he was in truth the only dad I had ever had, even though he wasn't my father, I grew up with him and had long before come to love him. So I went on and said, "I'm going to call you dad, not Jesse from now on." He responded gruffly and scoffed at the whole thing; nevertheless, I kept it up. It became evident this was far too much for him, so I reverted to the former, Jesse. At the same time the hugs became more and more between the two of us, and he always hugged Sandra and gave her a big kiss before we departed after our visits.

One night we decided to stay over with them and mother and I were typically visiting up until eleven-thirty p.m. He couldn't take anymore of this, and came out, revealing his ugly behavior, I had seen all too many times in the past, raising his voice and being abrupt to the point, "When are you to going to go to sleep, so others can do the same?"

I immediately thought of all the nights of scurrying to pick him up from those____ ships and bringing him home. Each time he would insist the whole family remain up to visit with him until four a.m., and later until he unwound. That is what we did!

This time I told both of them "We won't be underfoot, as we will be leaving early in the morning." Mother was all broken up knowing that would be our last visit for sure. I told her, "The same old thing just never will come to an end, and we didn't have to remain and put up with such anymore as life is too short for all of us."

Our return trip was that of silence. As the time passed, Thanksgiving was coming and we had been delving into whether or not we would be going down and finally decided to go. We did much more than go down, carrying the wretched pain that was Sandra's, as every previous visit was for her. It didn't do a great deal of good to stop so she could get out of the car and stretch or walk, she would just tough it through each time. I never heard her complain once.

On this visit, we had the turkey and all of the trimmings all wrapped so to take Thanksgiving to them, which sure turned out to be a total surprise for them. They never quit mentioning that gift from that moment into the future. We also decided to never stay over anymore. We drove down and visited and returned home the same day. This was taxing, but far better than penetrating his little world as before. We saw from that time into the future, a soft little man who just loved the hugs from both of us, who couldn't get enough of them each visit. If this was ministry, then we must have done something right. That Thanksgiving was when we saw how the disease mother was battling was tearing on her daily.

Where it had only been a short time before, while visiting Jesse after his surgery that she looked so great. Now she came to the table dressed only in her pajamas and her robe. She hardly ever put on any of her clothes anymore. Mother had always taken such pride in her appearance. Her hair always looked so sharp and glistening clean. Pregnasone, destroyed her skin and left bruises up and down her arms. Past visits, she came to the window and waved welcoming us, or stepped out to give us a big hug. As the years passed, she no longer had strength and spent days sitting on their sofa.

Where neighbors believed she was waving, the truth of it was she was making way to die. We were sure she would do just that on that sofa. Before that, we enjoyed taking them out for drives, stopping in Milwaukie, Oregon for hamburgers and strawberry shortcake. Another dining favorite was the Bomber for family style, where we sat and enjoyed each other's company and afterwards returned home.

While all of this was reassuring, mother was hooked to her oxygen at home. There wasn't a time when we were there, I didn't ache to see how her life had become, being tied to that umbilical tube.

Seemingly, on the same visit mother called me over to her side to say, "Jesse has his pistol in his holster back in his top dresser drawer, bring it to me." This, made me, hesitate, not knowing what was to come next. I was able to find his gun and brought it in where she could see it. Then she continued saying, "Son, I know you know about these things. I want you to show me how to use it," and at that I took his gun, shoved it back into the holster and went and hid it away from both of them. Then I turned and went back to mother and told her I wouldn't show her any such thing. Here, I was pleading with her as I had way back, when she was screaming, "I'm going to just hang myself!"

So much time, tracks, crossings, switches on those tracks had passed us. Yet as is true for any suffering from this behavioral condition, all of this is a matter of fact and won't ever be suppressed or otherwise until the individual or another loving, caring person is able to reason with the other, to reach out and grasp the hand of hope that has been there for so many of us. The hardest thing is thinking of so many that, never reach out and realize the blessing was there all the time!

And to think afterwards, on one of those visits toward the end, I was reminded of the scene in *The Godfather*, after the Godfather was nearly left to retire to his garden, where he and his son Michel, sat together having a glass of wine. Michael's father said, "I'm drinking too much wine" and Michael replied, "It's good for you Papa."

This became the resolve from all of those years with Jesse being an alcoholic, the worst kind never to admit it. He always had his stash out back or in his shed.

The worst was finding remnants in the back seat of his car. I still remember cleaning his car out to find sacks of beer bottles. I couldn't help but be thankful to God that he hadn't hit some child while out driving, or injured others, not to mention kill another, due to his absurdity of disregarding the help he could have received only for the asking long before. It sure is something how all of this flashes in your face, heart and soul, as those flashcubes used by the photographer mentioned throughout. It does much more than make you wince to be sure.

What hurt me most was that the potential had always been there. He had been the finest salesman I had ever known. However, he couldn't persevere long enough to make it work, as it was meant to. Consequently, he continually corresponded for catalogues for quick rich ideas ranging from selling signs, balloons and displays for auto dealers. You name it, he, sold it over the years.

I helped him to become "the Stampman of the Milwaukie-Clakamas region" which he tried, but finally this slipped away as in the past.

He never remained long enough to see how it could work!

Years before, I had read *Death of a Salesman*. I came to realize how the death was in our home; I carried this is in my heart as I truly came to love Jesse over the years and saw his inability to complete the course as a professional.

All the time Sandra and I continued our professional pursuits.

In retrospect, our boys had graduated from high school. Chris continued on to Central Washington University, where he intended to play football. Nonetheless, it was short lived, and he severely injured his collarbone requiring orthoscopic surgery. I went over to help him as best as I could. I was to meet him at the first practice game. As he approached I saw, what took me back to an earlier event, to hear this terrible thump of his body thrown to the mat while he was wrestling in junior high. I sprang to his side and looked into his eyes and thought we had lost him, and after the quickest prayer ever, he began to come back. For that fleeting moment, I thought what am I going to tell his mother.

The season was beginning and he was teetering up the stairs and I said, "Son, let's get you back to your dorm." All he remembered was my getting him out of his clothes and getting him into his bed. Fortunately, he had pain pills so he could get through the night. This was the end of football for him! He completed his year at C.W.U. and made us very proud of his work.

Eric, in the meantime, attended and fulfilled his A.A. Degree at Highline Community College. Later, he was considered for the University of Washington football team but this passed due to his grades not being approved. Therefore, he returned to his first love, that of hoops and playing for the colleges' team.

The complement that every parent hopes for was hearing them say, "Both of you were always at every event of ours through the years!"

We finally decided to move to Tacoma, Washington making the trip south to the folks considerably shorter. Our daily commute to and from our work was so much better at the same time.

I had a hernia operation, which laid me up during recovery, and my parents were "cheerleaders", for us.

Unknown to me, mother had discussed with Sandra toward the end sharing, "Gerry has known how we have been just that, his 'cheerleaders' the whole way and I want him to have something to remind him of our presence."

We received the call regarding Jesse's passing on March 12th, 1998. We made our way to be with him to arrive a bit late, which had real impact on me. When we gathered to see him at the hospital, relatives were gently rubbing his forehead and his hair. I looked at him and crumbled. All I could do was pat his chest for the last time and say how much I loved him.

Afterwards, Sandra and I went to see mother and share the news; however, she had realized the truth before we arrived.

We did all possible to be there for her. Sandra convened with County, State and Hospice personnel to gain a "go" to transfer her to our home in Tacoma. Even though we knew it wasn't to be long for this little woman who had deteriorated to the sameness of those found coming from Auschwitz, we made sure she knew we would do the very best for her.

I called ahead and arranged to have her hospital bed placed in our apartment, to make it comfortable for her, so she could look out on the grounds below. Sandra was wonderful by being able to take leave while we got mother settled. We knew we couldn't keep her at our home indefinitely, so we arranged to have her taken to the neighboring Nursing Hospital. That was one move too many for her and she began to take a turn shortly afterwards. She left us on March 26th, 1998 at 1:30 a.m. They called us and we went over immediately to find her gone, no longer gasping for breath as we had seen her the days before.

We saw the most dreadful death, all for the sake of having smoked far too long. We finally made our way out into the morning air from all we had just seen and we were completely relieved. I'll never forget, how we got into the car and together we let out one primal scream or cry of sheer relief, from all we had witnessed these last fourteen days. I write now, going on the second year of their being gone. I have more than mist in my eyes and a heavy heart of their not being with us anymore.

It has been one-and-a-half months since being aboard the thirty-five foot craft and I couldn't hold up anymore. I fell to my knees in a sea of tears and grief for all experienced.

What stood out was the realization that during these last ten years, they revealed how proud they were of me and us as a married couple. Their actions and words revealed this and more, as they became aware as to all I had achieved. What was so wonderful was the interest they took in my wife and me.

Now, what I want most in life is to continue to earn growing respect from those I have contact with each day. Along with that has to be love and respect. I am convinced that the more I am able to give away every day will prove the better.

Riches and wealth are not only there to care for our loved ones and self, but to give freely to others. A mainstay is to live comfortably in the latter years. Our prayer is that our investment will enable us to attain that and avail us opportunities to travel much more than in the preparatory years. I hope to remain in good health, especially, with my professional plan of standing in the garden, until either seventy or eighty- years young. Doing this, I will have spent twenty-to thirty-five years serving, hoeing, seeding, cultivating and nurturing with the "Chief Gardener".

Remember the gift mother wanted me to have, that she had arranged that Sandra would see I would have? Afterwards, I heard Sandra return from her shopping trip. She asked me to stay in my office and not come out until she told me it was OK. Before I could believe it, she had unwrapped the gift which has been in place ever since, making my daily work so much more comfortable and putting me in touch with my "cheerleaders". The gift was the most handsome leather office chair for me to sit and write the story. Even as I am now concluding, I want to remind you of that song that, stayed in my heart far longer than I would have imagined, as I continued to believe throughout all of these years.

Fairy Tales Can Come True

Don't forget between the stances, that God gives us moments to look up and remember there will always be *Birds from the Thicket* there to help us in our lives daily, no matter where we are on the tracks.

The End

Addendum

Remember how I wanted you to know the truest weak link for me was through my tears, which have been like rivers throughout my life. Not everyone that I have been in contact with has understood where or why such happened at the most unusual times. And I'm not only talking about touching stories in the movies.

What we have is tough for us and even much harder for others. What I'm about to share is paramount, that will bring you on course, as to the reason for this book being written in the first place.

Granted, it came as you might imagine in the night of January 7th, 2003 when the fog had intensified revealing it was still winter. The nights have become so cold that it's necessary to get up during the early morning, put an extra blanket on the bed to burrow into to get warm and be able to go back to sleep. The answer was there the whole time, but didn't hit me as answers to prayer, finally became complete as all of this has for me. I now know what was missing and now I'll make an attempt to hit on the very reason this book was written.

I wrote this not only to share my story; no, I wrote it to reach out to all that have the same condition I have had to live with from the very beginning of my life, but not to surface until I was ten years old, which you're more than aware of after reading regarding my childhood to the current date. As mentioned those about knew something was amiss. The doctors didn't have a clue of all that surfaced, knowledge that has become a huge break for all of us, either having the same Bi-Polar Mood Swing Disorder, Manic Depression, or Uni-Polar Mood Swing Disorder. It isn't only for all of us it's for all with whom we have lived with, or have shared our lives with throughout and the very friends, neighbors and foremost, our families, that have equally been aware there was something not quite right with us. I can bet you, like me, wouldn't have any idea we affected them as we did. Furthermore, I couldn't understand why others seemed to treat me differently at times in daily life. Well, the truth was they were right in most cases. And why not, as they perceived and were shown by our behaviors, we were different from the norm, whatever that meant. Sure we believed we were "normal"; however, if you were much the same as me you couldn't see or understand the real reason for the following happening in your lives.

I know it took a long time for me to realize I was different. I don't mean extremely sensitive, which I am, but more so than others. It's tougher for all about us. They see us in quite another prism of light that we can't even begin to view. I believe that we believe we can see it and grasp what is going on. The real truth is we are unable because what we deal with is not only an imbalance chemically it also is psychological and anything but easy to admit to ourselves. So we either live daily life single or married, and then come the children, relatives, friends that love us, also the acquaintances and our business associates that work with us who can see that something we have, that we are not possible to put our thumb on, undoubtedly bring a series of traits and behavior that are plain different than others. It is different!

How fortunate we are that thirty some years ago so much more became evident to the research scientists. It would have brought so many with comparable conditions up out of the "Snake Pits", they found themselves caught in, to surface as we have been able, to by the current findings where we can identify what we have and further to realize it can be treated. Our lives can be more improved by our complying with the diagnosis from day one.

I know it mystified me when in group therapy there were those who either didn't take the prescribed medications provided, all too many times because "they didn't want to come down from their highs" or would treat the whole thing with the attitude. "Well why should I have to keep taking those lithium pills? I'm much improved". Then they rapidly found themselves in a worsening state afterwards. Where in my case, when the real reason was shared with me, I began first following the diagnosis and prescription that was given to me and kept coming back for additional blood tests to get the level where it should be, making the quarterly checks to insure all was as it should have been, marveling at the fact that the finding was a "true miracle". Consequently, as I shared, I have been on lithium, recently changed to lamictal, proving to work even better removing the long- term concern that my kidneys would go in time and further finding Amantadine greatly helps with the tremor in my hands.

When one would not follow, or worse, chose to not take their prescribed medication, then went out and deliberately drove their car in such a manner to literally push six cars in a row up on the curb, or "accidentally" hitting mailboxes or trashcans on the side of the road, it did make me wonder why. Others would sit there session after session and moan about how tough it was for them and those they related with in their daily lives. To think all was because they chose to allay taking the medications prescribed.

I knew groups were not for me! Consequently, I requested individual sessions that brought me to the level of an outpatient who could check in even during the night, to unwind and return to my regular lifestyle.

I didn't just want to know what the reason for having such thoughts of wanting to take my life was. I wanted to know whether or not it could be treated. Once I realized I had something so different than others, there was the hope I needed and worked to sustain. I found what I hope just one of you have found, "There is light at the end of the tunnel."

This story is for you that are so tired of dealing with all that is a part of this awful condition and the way it effects others, that you give up and each day one of either shooting ourselves or takes some other measure to rid ourselves and others as well. It is for you I write to with hope, that you can see you can rise to the occasion as depicted and say to yourself, if he is able to do it then so can I. You see the true goal has always been and remains, that if one life can be saved through what I have written then the true goal has been met.

Believe me; I know a great deal about what we all have because I have lived it. I know you are up in the early morning hours prowling through your homes as I still find I do regularly; I (we), are only restless so we peek outside, sleep lightly to hear everything outside that is going on, even when our loved ones snore on through the night and are far beyond where we really want to be fast asleep. That prowling usually will bring us to have a bowl of cereal or something to drink, or even to read or write as I'm doing.

Activity is a must for us, to the point we have to call a friend at an unreasonable time, because we want to get out and do something exciting such as the night I did years ago. I phoned my friend and asked whether she would like to take a drive with me. She said yes, which was the answer I wanted. So what did I do? I went over to pick her up and we began to cruise and several hours later I had driven all the way to the Canadian border into Vancouver, B.C. Then I turned around, not even getting out of the car for coffee or to stretch, rather return to our homes on Queen Anne Hill in Seattle. That was the ride! You say you've been there.

Another example was the day I wanted to go shopping so I asked one girl friend if she would come along with me. Downtown we went and I entered the men's department and immediately selected a new three- piece suit off the rack, tried it on and, you're right, I bought it. She said, "How could you do that?" My reply was equally glib as not taking into thought I might need that money for more important items such as tuition or books for the coming quarters of work in my pursuit to gain my degree.

Those about us have no idea until they live with us as to the harshness of our condition. The results for you, as me with medication, are something others come to abhor due to their not totally understanding. They don't know what it is like to either soar to the top of the peaks, perhaps remain until we're to worn to stay there or to plummet to the bottom. I do mean bottom, and find we're there for days and nights, even weeks, months and, in one case, I remained there for nearly two years unable to even get out of the house. It's devastating for others to deal with; so many times they go by the wayside. And that is more than understandable. It would be for everyone of us, **as** we put them through a kind of hell that we aren't aware of when we do. That should bring us to seek counseling or therapy and accept the diagnosis prescribed. By doing this we become healed and whole and all about us will see and accept us. Our lives will greatly improve as theirs will with us. Our coping with the tensions, daily stresses and pressures that bring on added stress can be where the "light at the end of the tunnel is and can be yours or mine."

441

I know the outbursts that we regret afterwards. I know the falls from the pinnacle of soaring through life, the excelling above that of others, whether in the totals of sales or activities, and not being able to focus and absorb all about us in our daily lives. At the same time I know how all of us plunge into the most disdainful conditions so that we can do is barely move or function. Having been there as in both cases, I can agree with what Patty Duke said, "Thank goodness it's only a disease." You say, well you don't know what it is like for me. That may be true, but the overall has been the same suffering all of us have. Only in the recent past has all of this behavior and conditions been so evident that there is hope for us, and others via our listening and accepting that administered. Your life and mine can reveal there is hope for each of us! Furthermore, you can see through the story you've just read that you too can become healed and whole as well.

Ponder, if you will, that your research has revealed that this illness we have is due to a slight amount of salt or sodium. Can you imagine, by our merely remembering to "take the pill", all definitely will improve. This may not occur when you or I forget to take the daily dose, well it does for me. The real sign of this is when I begin to become agitated and annoyed by others, even short or find myself letting go of adjectives that shouldn't be spoken. Then I take a deep breath and reach for the daily dose and all immediately subsides and you know as I that we're back on course. So, consider if this is the case, then why not do it in the first place. How fortunate we are when we adhere to the basics, for then we can "Keep On, Keep On" and proceed with the best of them.

Don't wait; care for yourself, because such care will insure that you live a happy and long life!

Gerry Bradley

BIOGRAPHY

GERRY BRADLEY

Places are important to Gerry Bradley. Like postcards from the edge of highs and lows unknown to many, his perspective is unique. Bradley's experiences from Oklahoma to Seattle to Marin County and down the central California coast are documented not only in his memory, but now in his memoirs. His debut narrative, *BIRDS FROM THE THICKET* is available on the World Wide Web; and subsequent books, *CHIT-CHAT* each of short stories and written in his Paul Harvey-commentary style will be available in the near future.

Born in Enid, Oklahoma, 1941, Bradley was raised in Middle America in the post war era. Until age ten Bradley grew up with the red clay of Oklahoma on his hands, a memory he holds to this day perhaps a metaphor to a man molding his life using the gifts he's been given.

In his fifth grade year, Bradley moved with his mother and brother to Seattle's, Queen Anne Hill. From sixth grade through his junior year in high school Bradley remained with his family in Seattle. John Doty an English teacher at Queen Anne High asked Bradley to read his work to the sophomore class. At the conclusion, Doty mused "You have just heard the work of a future American writer."

Just before his senior year, the family was uprooted again moving to Marin County's San Rafael, California. Tumultuous in any era, the move lent angst to an alchemy of emotion Bradley had yet to recognize.

Reporting for duty in 1961, Bradley enlisted in the United States Air Force, stationed at Vandenberg Air Force Base. Bradley was honorably discharged as an Air Police Officer in 1965. From there, he earned a bachelor's degree in education and speech communication at Seattle Pacific College, for several years he taught English, developmental reading and coached junior high sports in Washington State. In 1987 Bradley became a manufacture's rep for Inland Pacific. Bradley is the host of "Chit-Chat" featured each Tuesday morning on talk radio, KLAY-AM from Tacoma, Washington. He has written as a guest columnist for weekly newspapers in Washington and Oregon.

By all accounts Bradley's life looks like a pattern of the American dream. But within the folds are glimpses into a nightmare that was unlocked within minutes when Bradley was diagnosed with bi-polar disorder, a chemical imbalance that plagues 2.3 million Americans. The malaise is characterized by alternating mania and depression and the frenzy eclipsing the swings from euphoric, creative spurts of sleeplessness to rock bottom depressions.

BIRDS FROM THE THICKET chronicles Bradley's life illustration how the disorder tips the scales from normal behavior to a realization that things aren't quite right. More importantly, the narrative shows how the disorder isolates those afflicted and the affect it has on family, friends, employers and co-workers. In other words, if 2.3 million are directly afflicted, the disease conservatively affects ten to twenty times that many by association.

Mr. Bradley lives with his wife, Sandra in Tacoma where they raised two sons.

Printed in the United States
31920LVS00002B/61-141

9 781418 403645